HOW TO HAVE A PERFECT MARRIAGE
—WITH YOUR PRESENT MATE

Jess Lair, Ph.D., in collaboration with Jacqueline Carey Lair
HOW TO HAVE A PERFECT MARRIAGE—WITH YOUR
  PRESENT MATE
I DON'T KNOW WHERE I'M GOING—BUT I SURE AIN'T LOST

By Jess Lair, Ph.D.
SEX: IF I DIDN'T LAUGH, I'D CRY
AIN'T I A WONDER . . . AND AIN'T YOU A WONDER TOO!
I AIN'T WELL—BUT I SURE AM BETTER
I AIN'T MUCH, BABY—BUT I'M ALL I'VE GOT

By Jess Lair, Ph.D., and Jacqueline Carey Lair
HEY, GOD, WHAT SHOULD I DO NOW?

How
to Have
a Perfect Marriage
-with Your Present Mate

A different understanding of marriage
that suggests that you,
your marriage and your mate
might be far more perfect
than you had ever dared hope

JESS LAIR, Ph. D.

in collaboration with
JACQUELINE CAREY LAIR

DOUBLEDAY & COMPANY, INC.
GARDEN CITY, NEW YORK
1985

Library of Congress Cataloging in Publication Data
Lair, Jess.
How to have a perfect marriage
—with your present mate.
"A different understanding of marriage
that suggests that you, your marriage
and your mate might be far more perfect
than you had ever dared hope."
1. Marriage. 2. Marriage—Religious aspects—Christianity.
3. Commitment (Psychology)
I. Lair, Jacqueline Carey. II. Title.
HQ734.L19 1985   646.7'8   82-45571
ISBN 0-385-18191-4

*This book is dedicated
to my spiritual partner,
my soul mate,
my wife, Jackie,
whose beauty and love
I am so grateful for having in my life
for thirty-six years*

Contents

1.

What Is Marriage All About?

FROM THE EARLIEST DAYS OF MY MARRIAGE I had questions about marriage running through my head. What is this marriage of ours supposed to be like? How come it goes so good at some times and so bad at others? Why can't the joy and beauty and peace of our togetherness stay with us for longer periods of time? Why do some people seem to be doing so good at marriage and I so poorly? Why don't I just throw this marriage over and start again? Why does Jackie stay with me when I hurt her so deeply? When I first had the idea for this book, about five years ago, I was still wondering some. Why was I drawn back into this marriage when it seemed only a fool or someone who loved to suffer would want to come back? Why did I persist in this marriage when we had so many problems with it? Was it just because I was such a creature of habit that I didn't get out? Or, was it because I'm so full of fear?

From the earliest days of our marriage, Jackie and I have been laboring under one of the heaviest loads of personal difficulties and family difficulties I've heard of. In a way it's a miracle our marriage survived. But it did survive some terrible tests of fire. In the process, Jackie and I have had a chance to go to depths in marriage and life that many don't seem to have to go to. But as life tested our marriage, we learned some things that I've found other people find helpful to them in their marriage difficulties.

In the first twenty-odd years of our marriage, we had a number of unusual difficulties that were very hard for each of us to handle. But then, about eight years ago, I had the catastrophe of all catastrophes. It brought me to a dark night of the soul where I came to see what a big part I had played in our troubles. My dark night of the soul helped me see some deep truths about myself and our marriage. The most principal of those truths was that I was a dependent baby. Another central truth I saw was that Jackie was the one person in this world I most wanted to be with. Well then, if that was true, why didn't I act like it? Any time there was trouble between Jackie and me, why did I put my tail between my legs and run away like a scared dog?

From that day on I began to dedicate myself to finding the help I needed to be a more responsible person in our marriage. And I started doing some things that were very obviously needing to be done.

I'm the kind of person who needs to have an understanding of what I'm trying to do to help guide me. A friend of mine is a great improviser and works largely from day to day. I can work from day to day too, but I need some kind of an understanding to fit things into to help me find my way. When I had my big catastrophe, I found that my understanding of marriage wasn't able to help me make sense of the terrible problems I was facing in that marriage. And I didn't know what being born a man and being born a woman meant. So as I was working at doing the obvious things that needed doing, I was also trying to find an understanding of marriage that would help give me answers to my questions and could help guide me.

This book is about the understanding of marriage I have come to during these last ten years when I was working at getting rid of my dependency and some of my other defects and seeking a guiding principle for marriage. I have finally found that guiding principle for me. The understanding of marriage I now have gives me peace at the most troubled times. It gives me ideas when I need help. And, it gives me a way to get out of confusion and chaos when nothing that is happening seems to make sense. It lets me appreciate the good times for what they are. And it has brought me to the place where I have a deep and abiding peace in all my life.

In the old days there was a big part of me that, in times of trouble, so desperately wanted happiness and peace that I didn't see how we could keep on being married. Yet, another part of me would hear words of the marriage vows ringing in my head, "for better for worse . . . in sickness and in health . . . till death do us part," and the words of the minister, "Those whom God hath joined together let no man put asunder." I knew deep inside me that there was something to those vows.

The answers for me didn't come from studying religion or going to church. They came out in the battlefield of life where I would try out an idea under real conditions and see if it would work for me. If it worked, I kept it. If an idea didn't work, I discarded it. From that constant testing and retesting, I have finally found this understanding of marriage that works so well for me. This understanding gives me answers that satisfy me on any of the questions I ask myself, or that people around me bring up.

The understanding of marriage I have is that the purpose of marriage is to help each of us make our spiritual quest, to find God as each of us understands him. I believe each of us was born separate and alone and that our lives here on earth are spent in finding our way to God. For most of us, our marriages are the best things we have to help us make our spiritual quests. A spiritual quest means finding out the truth about ourselves. And marriages do a great job of helping to shine the light of truth on ourselves.

But we tend to forget that, if it wasn't our marriage that is shining the light of truth on ourselves, something else would be. So it isn't marriage that's the problem, we're the problem. Lots of the time, the truth hurts, and that's the pain of marriage. But the great hope for all of us is in the very simple idea that we need to find the truth of ourselves. Once we see that the pain in the marriage isn't coming from the other person but is coming from the marriage and its interaction, causing us to see ourselves too clearly, then we can start working on the real problem. I have met the enemy and it is me, the big "I".

Let me give you a simple example. Say you look in the mirror and see a smudge on your face. You figure something is wrong with the mirror so you try to wipe the smudge off the mirror. Yet, each time you look in the mirror, the smudge is still on your face. It's hopeless, you think, you're never going to get rid of the smudge! But then suppose someone tells you that the mirror is accurate. The smudge is really on your face. You might think that's awful news, but it isn't. It's very hopeful news because you can now do something about the smudge. You can wipe the smudge off *your* face. Now, when you go back and look in the mirror, the smudge is gone.

In our marriages, it is only our own spiritual quests and our own lives that we are responsible for. We don't have responsibility for anyone else's spiritual quest. Our only responsibility is to admit to the smudges on our own face and proceed to start wiping them off. We do have a responsibility to be of help to the marriage partner by providing leadership and a good example by doing our own work to the best of our ability. But we fulfill that responsibility best when we focus our attention on the mirror and admit humbly that it is a true and valid mirror and so look only for our own smudges to remove.

I have found that by applying this understanding to our marriage it has revolutionized our marriage for me. In recent years I have been able to concentrate more and more on just doing my work and looking for my smudges and doing something about them. Many people who hear me talk like this scream in their anger, "But what about the partner and all that's wrong with them?" I know how they are feeling. I still feel that way myself fairly often. But most of the time, now, I don't do anything about that feeling. I just let it be there but don't act on it. I tell people that when I get all the work done on me that I need to do, then I can consider starting to work on Jackie. Some people fail to laugh when I say that. They are so caught up in what they see as their problems with all the people around them, most notably their husbands and wives, that they miss the humor.

As I have achieved more and more concentration on doing my own work, an interesting response has occurred from Jackie. She now often tells me how much help I am in her spiritual quest. Hopefully, that's always only a side effect of my doing my own work.

I have had a great advantage during these hard times. I have had the advantage of Jackie's working on her own program, too. This has been a huge help to me because I have been able to benefit from her help, her example, and her spiritual leadership. These ideas I'm talking about will still work even if the partner doesn't have a program, but it does make it a lot harder. In our case, there are many times when I'm heading down a harmful path and Jackie refuses to go along with me. Her clarity in that case helps me look quicker at what I'm doing. There are many times when Jackie gives me important help with problems I'm facing or supports me emotionally as I'm going through a tough time. And, by being clear, she stays out of my problems and doesn't further confuse my situation, so it is easier for me to see what I have to learn from the problem.

Another good thing I have seen is that I'm so much more peaceful now when Jackie is doing her own work. It's easy to be peaceful when Jackie is happily doing her own work. But I am also able to be peaceful when Jackie is upset. I can now be peaceful enough to check out what she's saying to see if there's some part I played in what she's angry about. If I don't see that there is, I can just sit there and listen and not confuse the issue by throwing in my reactions. When the storm is over I haven't confused things with my reactions and it is simple for Jackie to see what went on. Jackie does the same for me.

What happens if the partner we have or are considering doesn't have this understanding of making their own spiritual quest? As near as I can see, that's not really a problem. It seems to me all of us come to this understanding I'm speaking of in one way or another. So my thought is to work on my own spiritual quest and let God as I understand him deal with the other person. I find that for each situation I'm in, there is a good reason for being there. I see that this is especially true of marriage. I believe my marriage and most other people's marriages are working just fine, it's just that people shy away from too much self-knowledge too quickly.

I think that's why most people leave their marriages. I know that most people who get divorces would have a hard time understanding this idea. But I've had an insider's view of a lot of divorces. The people in those divorces have come to see me, as students of mine or friends. They are more honest with me than they are with most people. What impresses me about the divorces I've seen close-up is that the marriages were working very well for them from this special perspective we're talking about here. We're talking about marriages giving us happiness through facing us with ourselves so we can see the parts of ourselves we have to give up to move on with our spiritual quests.

My students understood the idea of making their own spiritual quests. Many of them would finally agree that there was a lot of truth in what the troubles in their marriages were offering them about themselves. But, even though they could see this, they usually still weren't willing to face any more of the pain these marriages were bringing them. My students were even able to admit that their divorces would just postpone the work they would eventually have to do on themselves. But they were tired and angry about being asked to do so much work with what they felt were uncooperative spouses and just wanted out. I could understand their feelings. But the experiences I had with couples who were divorcing made it very clear to me that the marriages were offering them too much truth about themselves rather than too little. And so, in the special sense we're talking about marriage here, their marriages were working too well rather than not well enough.

No one came to me and said, "My marriage is not working well enough to help me on my spiritual quest. I'm not learning enough about the parts of me that I need to get rid of in order to move closer to God, as I understand him. My marriage isn't showing me enough of my own selfishness and self-centeredness reflected in my mate for me to benefit from it." I didn't hear stories like that. I just heard from people who knew they were faced with truths about themselves in their marriages but couldn't stand what they were facing. Now, I must repeat again that these were exceptional people in that they were students or friends. They had had some understanding of these spiritual principles in marriage and they had had some special experiences in being honest with themselves in this special way or they wouldn't have come to talk to me.

So the people I talked to had marriages that were working too well. They just didn't like what they saw about themselves reflected in the marriage. Also, as I see it, we might as well stay in the present marriage because we never get away from the person anyway. A divorce paper doesn't do it. We're hooked up with them in our head the rest of our lives, so the quicker we get at solving our problems with the relationship, the better.

The title for this book was originally *Marriage: A Spiritual Affair.* I later found I didn't care for the title. It was in the right area but it was heavy and pretentious. One evening in a class on Alpha Awareness* a couple of years ago Wally Minto had us doing a meditation exercise. I thought about needing a new title for the marriage book and used that as the problem I took to his meditation exercise. In meditation I asked for a new title. It came clearly and quickly, and I felt completely comfortable with it and have

* Alpha Awareness, Drawer G, Susanville, CA 96130.

ever since. The title that came to me is the one on this book: *How to Have a Perfect Marriage—with Your Present Mate.* I thought the title was great, even though I didn't know just where it came from and just what it meant.

After a while, I had the idea that maybe having a "perfect" marriage meant that the two people had an adequate system for working out problems. When I would explain that to people, they would nod and figure that made sense. I now see the "perfect" part more clearly and the new understanding helps me make sense of the "present mate" part.

I see now that Jackie and I have a perfect marriage not because we have an adequate system of working out problems but because this marriage has been perfect in giving me the chance to learn just exactly the things I needed to learn about myself, about the other half of the world—woman—and about life and God. So the "perfect marriage" part means it's perfect for teaching me what I need to learn. The "present mate" part is about Jackie, the one who is to teach me the surrender and other things I need to learn.

It doesn't matter if tomorrow Jackie told me she couldn't stand to live with me. I now see that this marriage would still be perfect because it would still be doing what I most needed to have done for me and what nothing else could do. That may sound crazy. I know Jackie, at times, thinks that's just a crazy rationalization on my part, and it might be, but that's okay. I know what's going on inside me and I like what's happening.

This new and sharper understanding of perfection in marriage clears up the last stumbling block I had about marriage and so about this book. When our marriage was in a precarious time, I had the thought, "Where does that put the marriage book?" What I can see now is that nothing that can happen affects this book and this understanding of marriage. Marriage is like a river. It is a process. It is neither good nor bad. It just flows. Even a divorce can't end the process because the relationship still goes on and I still learn about myself in how I handle what offers itself in the moment.

When Jackie and I were married, I took a vow to care for her till death do us part. If she couldn't live with me anymore, it would be my responsibility to continue to care for her emotionally and materially in whatever ways she needed. If her need was to be independent of me, then she could have half of our assets or an income paid by me equal to half of those assets, if that was her choice.

Even if Jackie chose to take half the assets and, through some unfortunate circumstances, later lost her money or something worked to substantially reduce her income, then I would still have a responsibility to help her as much as I could. The fact that I had made some reasonable settlement wouldn't matter. How I would act in that situation would be me handling the relationship in the most responsible way I was capable of. I would be continuing to have a perfect relationship with Jackie even though technically divorced, as I continued to learn and continued to watch myself doing things I needed to do, and seeing myself failing to do things I needed to do.

It's just like my golf game today. I saw myself making five or six very fine golf shots. They weren't accidents. I played golf for thirty years and never got over the tension and fear of failure that hurt my shots. Now I've been taking lessons and practicing a new way for three years. The other eighty-four shots I hit today tell me what I need to practice and about the tension and fear of failure that's still in me. Golf is a little dance that happens in less than a second. Golf is just a short form of the lifelong dance that all of life was meant to be. As I learn the dance of life, my golf shows it to me clearly.

There have been many periods in our marriage where there has been a lot of peace and joy and contentment. But when I have been off the spiritual path or Jackie has been off the path, there are times when there is a lot of pain in our marriage. Now, most of the things I need to do are done without much, if any, pain. I just go about my business as well as I can with the light God shines on my path. But when I or Jackie put off doing the work on ourselves we need to do, there will be pain to help us pay attention to something we've been trying to avoid. I was a very childish, dependent, selfish, self-centered, blind, callous person when I came into this marriage. I've had a lot of pain because there were lots of things I had to learn that I didn't want to face and only pain could make me face. But not all the pain in my life came from that. In some cases there was pain for me because someone around me had a destiny, a gift from God, that I had as much trouble accepting as they did.

I see that I had a lot of pain in this marriage because that's what I needed to learn from, but that doesn't mean the pain needs to go on forever. I can learn my lessons, and I can learn to greet with great gratitude and more acceptance and serenity the gifts of my destiny that God brings to me and the people around me.

Also, the fact there has been a lot of pain for me in my marriage doesn't mean that pain is good or that the more pain in a person's marriage, the better the marriage it is. Each of us has certain things we need to learn. Some of us have a lot and some maybe not so much, and each of us can learn our lessons quickly and easily or slowly and painfully. The choice is ours. I see no special merit in suffering. It seems to me that I need to learn my lessons as quickly and easily as I can. But I do know that if I don't pay attention to the first clues that tell me I have something to learn, I'll keep getting pounded harder and harder until I do learn. That knowledge has helped me pay better attention and learn lessons more easily now. So, as I look back on our marriage, I don't see that there was any virtue in the slow and painful way I often chose to learn things.

The way I see it now, this has been the perfect marriage for me. And my present mate has been perfect for me. I have received riches beyond imagining from this marriage. I was separated and isolated from the whole world, lost inside myself. I was a stranger to everyone as well as to myself. I was unable to be a man; I felt like a childish adolescent. I was unable to be a husband to my wife, a father to my children, a brother to my brother, and I was not even able to be a close friend to my friends. During the thirty-six years of our marriage, all this has changed for me and I have made substantial progress in all of the areas just mentioned. I can't conceive how any other partner could have been more helpful or any other marriage more fruitful in leading me to the work I have had to do for myself.

As I've been faster to see the work I needed to do on myself, there has been so much daily joy and peace in marriage for me and for Jackie. We've just finished working our way through the hardest years of our marriage. Even in these hard years there has been joy and content mixed in with the pain. But, an even more important quality than joy has been operating, and that's the strength of our marriage, which I believe comes out of this spiritual approach. I believe that we are soul mates.

While I have made a good start at recognizing and accepting what a dependent baby I was in this marriage relationship for so long, I see that all I can say is that I've just made a good start. There's so much for me to learn about being a human being and being happy and content with the way God made me instead of hiding out in some cobbled-up concoction I dream up for myself and then trying to live in that foolish fantasy. For me, coming out of fantasy is a long, slow process. My marriage has helped give me a start. I'm happy with that start and happy with the help I've gotten from writing this book for you. It's very clear to me that I know only a little and that I will continually be learning more. But that's no reason not to write this book. Twenty years from now, when I know more about marriage, I will write a new book on the subject, if I'm still around and it seems like a good thing to do.

My writing this book has been hard for Jackie. Her nature is to be a private person and be in the background. Writing a book as personal as this one is very hard on her. There was so much pain years back that Jackie couldn't even read a couple of the books I wrote, like *"Ain't I a Wonder . . ."* and *Sex: If I Didn't Laugh, I'd Cry*. Things had gotten enough better between us by the time of the writing of the last book, *I Don't Know Where I'm Going—But I Sure Ain't Lost*, that Jackie could collaborate with me on that book and the writing process went pretty smoothly. I had spoken to a group in Phoenix for about ten hours and Jackie wrote a first draft of the book from those tapes. I had been quite low on energy when I "said" the book so there was a lot that Jackie had to fill in from her knowledge of what I believed and what I would have said. Also, Jackie put in stuff of her own for me. And she put in some stuff of her own as her viewpoint.

When she finished with the first draft, she handed it to me and said, "Here, now you take it. I don't want to see it anymore. Change or throw out anything you don't want." So I went ahead and edited it a couple of times and plugged in material at the beginning and end of chapters and other places. Much of what Jackie had written for me from the tapes or from her understanding of what I meant to say, or wanted to say but didn't, was beautifully expressed. I left it as it was because it was so accurate and so clearly written it needed little editing. Where Jackie had expressed her viewpoints for both of us, I let that stand too. And, where Jackie had expressed views that were uniquely hers, like the long statement on her as a woman in relationship to me, I urged her to include that in the book. So that was how the last book happened between us.

But this book is very different. It's personal for both of us. There is a lot more involved here than just my ideas. Even the sex book wasn't as personal and didn't involve both of us as much as this one did. As a result, the early parts of the collaboration on this book were sprinkled with moments of fire and storms and loud discussions. But part of a marriage is, hopefully, an adequate system of working out differences between the partners, and we have that, so our marriage has weathered these storms.

The last stage of this book has been a very peaceful one. Jackie has made peace with what I've written and really likes the book. That has made the final revision of the book a quiet time for me where I could concentrate all my energies on making sure the book expressed as clearly as possible the understanding of marriage I presently have, and that the sharing of life I am doing is as clear and fair as I could make it.

In the course of writing this book, we have been faced with the problems we needed to work on. Some of those problems came out of writing this book. Other problems were the ones life has been handing us as Jackie and I both work our spiritual programs, which are partly involved with clearing away the wreckage of the past. As I have gone through this past year, I have come up with a much clearer understanding of our marriage than I had before. So writing this book together has been just what I needed.

In the early stages of writing this book, Jackie had a question as to whether this whole book wasn't one long rationalization of mine —an attempt to put a pretty face on a bunch of troubles. I surely hope it isn't. One of my weaknesses is denial. A part of my illness is denial. As Jackie has said to me, "You can sit on a pile of horse manure and call it roses longer than any human being I know." Jackie also thinks, at times, that if I had married someone else, someone less determined, I might not have had all these troubles. It's hard for Jackie to remember that I brought these troubles of mine with me into the marriage. She had nothing to do with creating them or making them worse. I keep telling her that I feel I married the right person for me and that most of the time, even in my deepest pain, I'm happy I'm with her. So far, I guess I haven't been very convincing because there are times she doesn't believe me. But even if Jackie still isn't always deeply convinced that we belong in this marriage, I know I'm sure convinced.

My first real love was with Margaret when I was seventeen. I went in the army a few months later. After a series of letters, she broke off the relationship. She said, "I can't have a relationship with you. It's like trying to have a relationship with a dependent puppy dog." She was a very perceptive seventeen-year-old. She spoke such truth. I was a dependent puppy then, and forty years later I'm finally giving up that childish dependency of mine.

A year and a half ago, I had another spiritual awakening with a jet assist from Jackie that helped me see I needed to clean out my head. There was a lot of sexual fantasy and sexual thinking that I was using in my head that was really hurting me. It had been with me all my life, so I just took it for granted. All of a sudden, in just about five minutes, I saw that all that sexual thinking of mine was very destructive to me and I hadn't even known it. I realized to my horror that that sexual thinking, my lust, was what had been causing so much trouble in my life and had been the reason why I couldn't get as much out of the spiritual programs I was in as the people around me. So it was such a relief to finally find an answer to something that I didn't even realize was a problem. (I'll go into detail on my sexual compulsion later.)

Since a year and a half ago, then, I've kept my head clear of sexual stuff. My resulting clarity and steadiness and integrity has enabled me finally to feel like a man instead of a perennial baby-adolescent. I feel like I'm rooted in the earth so strongly that when I walk it's like a tree walking around with its roots sinking into the ground at each step. The integrity that I finally feel is the most important gift I've received. So even the small beginning I've made in this area has produced big results for me.

The troubles I have had being married for the last thirty-five years have had very little to do with Jackie and a great deal to do with me, as you can see. But it's part of Jackie's nature to take things personally and I need to be understanding about that.

What I love about this marriage is the way it has persevered and constantly shown me what I needed to learn. I don't know if I could have learned those things some easier, softer way. I doubt it. But no matter. There's no place in my life for spending time on speculative questions. What it takes for me to learn something is what it takes. I'm glad I had the chance to learn those things. I'm glad I learned them. The results in my life are a priceless asset to me. I wouldn't want to live life without the learning that's come to me through this marriage. These learnings are the pearl beyond price.

I'm deeply grateful to Jackie for sticking with me, and I'm glad I didn't leave and go and marry some other sex-nut, or a woman who needed me so badly that she closed her eyes to my behavior.

If I had left this marriage, it might have meant a detour of some years before I was again faced with the reality of myself.

I've seen that there are two things that are great at creating oneness. One is romantic love. The other is a spiritual awakening coming out of an immediate understanding of truth or, more usually, a gradual awakening to the truth. Early in our marriages, most of us experienced the oneness of romance that made us take down all the walls. All of a sudden, we saw and felt the true inner nature and beauty of the other person. We say love is blind. But maybe it isn't blind at all. Maybe in romantic love we truly see each other as the gods we truly are. What is really blind is our crazy mind. All it can see is division and separation and it calls that reality. Worst of all, it convinces a big part of ourselves of that division and separation.

Have you noticed how boring it is to talk to someone deep in the throes of romantic love? All they can talk about is how great that other person is. The person in love is overwhelmed with their oneness with the other and they see we don't share their vision and that makes them try all the harder to show us how blind we are to the other's God-likeness.

I was so aware of that feeling when I was a college professor. My students would come in and want to talk to me about being in love. It was so hard for me to listen to them because the student who came in just before and after that person would probably be telling me how awful the person they used to love was treating them now. I wanted to tell the person in love that we should make a tape recording of what they were saying so we could keep it and play it back later when they had fallen out of love. In fact, I even told some of them who had told me of their love and later were complaining, "Tell me the good things about that person you told me about when you were so in love with them." That would make people mad. They didn't want me to remind them of the oneness they earlier felt. By now their minds had them convinced of their separateness from the other person. And, willful child that the mind is, it didn't want to hear anything that would interfere with the self-pity and separation trip it was now on.

Those early romances brought us closer together and we each took down the walls we hid behind as we felt the warmth, but we usually wouldn't share completely. We hid the darkest, most secret stuff that we felt no one could know about us and still love us. But still it's a fact that romance makes us open up to someone around us in a way we've never done before.

Besides romance, the other thing that creates oneness is a spiritual awakening. A spiritual awakening is when, all of a sudden, you see some deep truth about life you had never seen before. Spiritual awakenings are something that the person who is all caught up in the rational mind can't understand because they are so out of touch with the spiritual part of themselves. But for most people, when they have a spiritual awakening, it is confirmed from deep inside themselves by the voice of their spirit as a truth about life. The process isn't perfectly accurate. There are times when we think we've had a spiritual awakening and later find we were going down a blind alley. But that doesn't happen often. Most of our spiritual awakenings are solid as a rock and stay with us the rest of our lives. They bring into our lives the true fruits of the spirit, which are peace and joy and serenity.

I have had my share of spiritual awakenings where I felt a deep oneness with everyone. Most of those awakenings left me changed, but they also left me. They left me to wrestle with the gradual awakening that seems to be my destiny rather than the once and forever awakenings some people tell me about. This is especially the case with my relationship with my wife. I was able to see I was one with everybody a long time ago. The only problem was that "everybody" didn't include my wife. It was "everybody except my wife." My sense of being separate and alone was so strong with her I couldn't or wouldn't put it down.

After all these years, I finally came to see that this woman, this Jackie, is the one woman I must make my peace with. I have come to see that she symbolizes all women for me, and as such I have reacted to her more from my own attitudes toward women, which I brought into my marriage, than from any terrible things that she is or does. And I came to see that any woman I had married would have presented me with this same dilemma. She is the woman in the center of the tapestry of my life, just as I am the man in the center of the tapestry of her life. When I accept this woman, everything else will fall in place. I was going to say she was the final piece of work I had to do, but I know that isn't so. There is always another piece of work to do. Also, there is the Irish superstitious side of me that is afraid of getting all my work done because then I will die. It's like the story old Lame Deer, the Sioux medicine man, tells on himself in *Lame Deer—Seeker of Visions*. As a young man he had his vision. He saw that he was to be a medicine man and that he would teach twelve medicine men. At the time he was telling his story to the Hungarian who wrote the book, old Lame Deer said, "I've trained eleven of those twelve men already and I'm in no hurry to get the twelfth."

My writing this has made me aware of at least one big piece of work I have to do past marriage, and that is death. I can see in my head the oneness there, too, but on this journey, head trips don't count. At best, they're a start. I know that until death becomes like a close friend, the job isn't done.

All day long, everyday, I need to see my oneness with Jackie. There are still some times when the arrows seem to be coming at me so thick and so fast it is a struggle to even keep my balance, to say nothing of my sense of oneness. That's okay. But as soon as I possibly can, I need to get back to remembering who I am—that's God. God lives within me as me. And remembering who Jackie is —that's God. God lives within her as her. And God is indivisible. So we are both one again. That's such a big job and it's why I so needed to write this book. In the writing of it, I could work out these things in my mind and get them down on paper. That way these ideas are subjected to that special scrutiny of being out of my head and then out of my mouth so my ears can hear them first, then my eyes can see them. And being fixed in writing, I can reflect on them.

Some of the things I have written in earlier books, I don't believe in anymore. I believed in those ideas at the time, but some things I see differently now. In some of the earlier books, for example, I talked about how you have to have love before you can give it away. I now see that quite differently. I see now that we *are* love, deep and inexhaustible love, because God lives within us as us. Since God is love, we are love. To get all the love we need, all we need to do is turn within. The deeper within we go, the more love there is. And, since it is love's nature to spill out, the more we get in touch with the source of love that is God within us, the more that love expresses itself through us.

Another idea I had but don't have anymore is that I need to love myself before I can love others. I still believe I have to learn to accept myself. I have to learn to like myself. But I don't need to love myself because I am love. And I don't need to do anything to love others. Because my nature is love, I can love others no matter how screwed up I am by just putting all my craziness down and letting the love out. In fact, I see now that a way to realizing that I am love is to put myself into the best kind of relationships I can and I learn that I am love by loving others and being loved in return.

So Jackie and I are one. When you hear one of us, you hear a lot of the other one of us. When I presented the marriage seminar for this book, one of the women at the seminar wanted to know when Jackie was going to come and talk to them. She didn't understand that when I was talking, she was hearing from Jackie too. How could it be any different than that? Or, when Jackie was talking, she was hearing from me too. Sometimes Jackie will go by herself and talk, and sometimes she will come along with me and say something, but mostly she likes to stay home. So the lady who asked the question wasn't quite hearing what was there to be heard. Her mind was still too full of ideas and speculations for there to be much room for Zen.

Again, let me repeat, Jackie and I are one. That's an idea that has pretty well moved on down into my guts now, so most of the time, even in the times that used to be hard, I can be calm and not forget who I really am and not forget who Jackie really is. At those times, I deeply appreciate what I see myself doing. A lot of times I'm filled with wonder as I see myself be so steady doing something that used to be so impossible and so foreign for me to do. I see myself having a strength or a gentleness I never dreamed I had in those early days when I was watching my mother and dad fight and hating what was happening so much. I'm so grateful, too, that that old part of me is gone and I don't need to be afraid like that anymore. And I can look at a woman who knows all about me and be fairly comfortable with her and not try to fix her or make her feel different and not be so afraid of her that I want to run like a dog. That's nice.

One of the major sources of catastrophe in our family's life has been addiction. Some of those encounters with addiction have been very painful for me. One day in January a few years ago, I was looking out our trailer window and I saw that my next-door neighbor's young son-in-law and his wife had come to visit her parents and have a vacation in the sun away from the ice and snow of the North. He was a golfer and loved to swim, but he was spending one of his precious days sitting at a little table trying to be a part of a little game with his two children.

I called Jackie over to the window to watch what was going on. I said to her, "Look at him playing with those two little kids. He's spending time with those kids when maybe he'd rather be out on the golf course. Do you know, Jackie, the way things are going, there's a good chance that fifteen to twenty-five years from now he'll be sitting in a treatment center with one of those kids and they'll be screaming at him, 'You never did anything with us.' He'll remember the times he spent playing with them when he could have been out playing golf instead, and he'll be wondering what went wrong."

As you can probably tell from that story, I was kind of raw about addiction. One of the big things that has happened in our family that we have all had to face is that we are a fully addicted family. Of the seven members of our family, only one isn't addicted. It was quite late in the process of writing this book that Jackie and I saw that the addiction throughout the family needed to be mentioned for the book to make sense. We can't give any detail of another person's story, but you have to know there's a story, otherwise what I'm talking about is confusing.

The young father could have been me. I spent quite a bit of time with my kids when they were young. And the idea that dad might someday be sitting in a drug treatment center opposite his children came from my own experience. I've sat in a pile of those places and had more than one kid yelling at me, and I've done my share of yelling back.

I know now that I am not alone. I've found out that the way things are going in the world right now, our addicted family isn't even much of a minority. Alcohol and drugs and other assorted compulsions have become an epidemic in America. In writing this book I stress heavily the power of the twelve-step program as begun and typified by Alcoholics Anonymous. There's a reason for this. I'm not an alcoholic. But in all of my study and work as a psychologist, in all of my work as a human being and as a husband and a father, it is the only tool that I have seen that has the power and the depth and the understanding to offer a lifelong recovery program for addicted people.

In our family, my wife was the first one to realize that she had to have help. She had been seeing psychiatrists and taking tranquilizers and antidepressants for years. Then the day came when she realized that she was drinking too much. She stopped drinking and found out that it was easy to quit alcohol. What she didn't realize for nine more years was that she had to stop taking those prescriptions from the doctors, too. This realization finally came when the pills took her to a place where she didn't want to live anymore. She made a suicide attempt and to this day she knows of no logical reason why she walked into our house, shut the door, took the phone off the hook, and overdosed. She didn't think about writing a note to me and the kids. She didn't feel depressed or anything. She just did it.

Looking back now, she knows that those pills were working in her in a way that had taken the power of decision from her and she was making what seemed to her a logical decision according to her deluded mind. Since that time she has talked to countless others who were addicted to tranquilizers and antidepressants who have experienced the same weird, zombie-like reaction to years of an accumulation of using pills. Needless to say, she didn't die, and help arrived in the person of a good friend of ours named Walther H. Lechler, a psychiatrist who has a clinic in West Germany.

Walther came to Bozeman to teach in the first School of Life* in 1977. He walked into our house on the day before the school was to start, took one look at Jackie, and said, "You are going to die." Jackie said, "I know." She traveled to Germany, entered his clinic, and went into recovery from her addictions. This had a powerful effect on the rest of the family. Most of us were also addicted to things. Four of the five kids were addicted to alcohol and drugs, one of them was also a compulsive gambler, and I had my own sexual compulsion.

In America today we have all been affected by the use of alcohol and drugs. It used to be that the experts figured ten percent of families were directly affected by addiction. Now you can see or hear statistics quoting over thirty percent. We have all been affected, however, if we look at the billions of dollars lost to the work force, the entertainment personalities who have died of alcohol and drugs, and the use of drugs among athletes. All these things have made us aware that we are in the middle of a plague in America.

This book is about marriage as I understand it, and the way I understand it has to do with commitment and work and walking through a lot of pain and a lot of joy in a mutual journey toward God. For me and for my wife, a lot of the pain in our marriage has come from addiction and from being a whole family who has

* School of Life and Jess Lair tapes, Bozeman and Phoenix, P.O. Box 249, Bozeman, MT 59715.

addiction problems and I want you to know that right up front so that you can see more clearly why I came to the beliefs that I came to.

For most people, the idea of alcoholic and drug addicts is pretty stereotyped. They imagine that those are people who are on skid row or who sleep under bridges or rob liquor stores and old ladies at gun point to get enough money for their habit. This is not true for most of the alcoholics and drug addicts I know. Most of them are very ordinary people who are law-abiding and who are very quiet about their addictions. They do a lot of their drinking at home or with other drunks in the same bars, night after night. Most of the young people I know are quiet, gentle men and women who use all the money they earn to support their habit, and if they steal, it is from their mother's purse or their father's billfold. Granted, there are many sensational types of addicts who make the newspapers and whose horror stories are incredible to listen to, but for the most part, addiction is a quiet, deadly killer that sucks all the energy and ability and outgoingness from a human being before it kills them.

In my family there was a lot of confusion for many years trying to find out what had happened to the delightful young children we had known. When we first began to realize that they were addicted to alcohol and drugs, we wanted to blame something or someone. My wife still thinks of the first time one of our sons told her that a student teacher from Montana State University, who was practice-teaching at the middle school in our town, sold marijuana to the fifth and sixth graders. Her reaction was to go out and find this young man and kill him. She wanted to blame him for starting our two youngest boys on the road to addiction. She now knows that if it hadn't been him, it would have been someone else.

The tragedy of addiction, that is so hard for people to understand, is that the addict or alcoholic is powerless. Once they have taken their first mood-altering chemical, they will always go back to it whenever they feel stress or simply want to have fun. This is because it does something to them and for them that it does not do to or for "normal" people. We have one son who had three of his friends die before they were grown from three separate drug-related accidents. This did not stop him. He knew what caused his friends to die, and he was frightened about it. But he sees now that he never made the connection that he was doing the same things that his friends were doing. Another son had a friend who killed himself while drunk. The friend was only sixteen. This tore our son apart. But again, he did not make the connection to his own life. This is the tragedy of alcoholism and drug addiction, and of all the compulsions, really. Denial is part of the disease, both for the addict and the people around the addict.

My wife smiles when she reads newspaper articles about the football players who are on drugs and how they don't recognize that they are role models for the younger generation and are letting the younger generation down. It seems to be impossible for people to recognize that these young men literally do not know what they are doing, and are powerless to stop until someone in their lives can have the strength to show them that they will lose everything if they do not get help. And then they must realize that they can't stop *on their own* and stay off alcohol or drugs successfully for any length of time because of the nature of their disease. For most of them it takes treatment and a lifelong follow-up program like Alcoholics Anonymous or Narcotics Anonymous. The reason my wife smiles is because she used to think just like the baseball and football team managers and the newspaper people. She thought that our children just needed to be told or shown or listened to or loved enough and they would stop what they were doing. She learned! We both learned.

So this is where I'm coming from. These issues have to be faced. We all need to see that there is hope and that whole families can be restored to sanity. We need to see that life can not only go on, it can be better than it has ever been. For our family, my wife and I did the very best job we knew how to do in being a husband and wife to each other and parents to our children. No one sets out to be an addicted person or a part of an addicted family. I guess the best answer I have come up with as a way to live with addiction and the problems it brings is Baba Muktananda's statement: "It's destiny— accept it."

In the case of our family, we all had our God-given free will, up until the time we took our first mood-altering chemical. When our children made the choice to "try it," they became different people, and lost the power of choice. They became slaves, just as surely as the football players and baseball players we read about, and, indeed, all addicted persons, become slaves. And one of the key areas of the brain that is affected by mood-altering chemicals is recall. Hence, thousands of parents are sitting in treatment centers all over the world wondering why their children only remember the bad and have no memory of the good. They don't remember because they have lost their power of choice in that, too. They don't remember Dad spending all those times playing with them and teaching them, and they don't choose to remember just the bad. The chemicals, like alcohol and marijuana and cocaine, distort reality in a very negative way and drive the users down into a private hell of depression and bad memories until that is all there is.

The powerful thing about recovery through abstinence and living a new way of life through the twelve-step program is that the good memories do come back. When recovery progresses, a real miracle occurs and oftentimes the bad memories fade to just a whisper, while the good memories come powerfully alive again.

Most families do the best they can in raising their children, which maybe wasn't enough. But each of us makes his or her own choices. As a family, we must be sure we don't interfere with the just consequences each of us faces from his own choices. Learning that is a big part of marriage. So no one can run from their marriage and all it entails. That's what this book is about: "In the acceptance lies the solution."

2.

Let's Get Married
So We Can Be Somebody!

WHEN WE WROTE THIS BOOK, we used four more chapters to prepare you for the marriage chapter. We felt we needed to go into my story, tell about the crazy mind, go into my core addiction, and talk about our compulsions with other people's problems. By doing this, we felt you could really see much more clearly how this understanding of marriage had come about and why we believed in it so strongly. But at the last minute we thought the better of it and decided to jump right into our understanding of marriage without all the preparation and windup. When we go into those other topics later, a lot of your questions will be cleared up as you see what led up to all this. After all, that's the way most of us got into marriage. We got into it with lots of excitement, some or much fear, and almost no preparation. I've never heard anyone say, "I was well prepared for marriage." I've heard plenty of people say they were well prepared for their careers by their schooling or apprenticeship, but never that they were well prepared for marriage. I don't see much that can be done about that. This book is what I would teach in a marriage preparation class so students in their teens would be able to understand and apply what I'm saying without the hard experiences most of us needed. There would be some young students who could understand and apply these things, but they would be the ones who least needed the course. The students who really needed these ideas couldn't hear them. They would have to make the same mistakes most of us made.

When I got married, I didn't have much of an understanding of marriage. My understanding didn't get much better until about eight years ago, when I heard an understanding of marriage that expressed what a deep part of me had always longed for in marriage. And it expressed a guide to marriage that has been of constant help to me through the past eight years, which have been the toughest years by far of the thirty-five. This understanding is at the core of the joy and peace that Jackie and I experience each day now as we greet the good things and some of the tough things that still come to us.

In marriage, I see a principle that seems to me to be vital for a marriage to move into its spiritual reality. I see marriage as a triangle with God at the apex and the husband on one side and the wife on the other side of the base. They are both journeying up the sides concentrating on their own spiritual quest and joying in the companionship of the other as a helpmate. In this, there is a back-and-forth leadership. Say that the wife sees a piece of truth in a clear, clean way and moves upward on her side of the triangle. The husband can't help but be pulled upward by the example and spiritual leadership of his wife. Then the situation is reversed where now it is the other, the husband, taking leadership and example and moving upward. That movement tends to pull his wife up. If either of them gets their ego involved and refuses to be open to the clear, clean leadership and example from the other, they will stay stuck where they are until the pain gets so intense they will finally be willing to get unstuck.

Jackie started this process in our marriage when she went to the psychiatrist at the age of twenty-four. I had the spiritual awakening with my heart attack at thirty-five. As this book shows, spiritual leadership has been a back-and-forth process that has gone on in our marriage with increasing rapidity.

To give such an understanding of marriage to most of us as young people would be almost pathetic. How can two people with the crazy minds we have discussed see such an idea in the late teens and early twenties when most people get married? How can two people who are already firmly fixed in the early stages of their compulsions have the spiritual clarity to make such a commitment? How can two people living in our society where there is so little recognition and support for each person making their own spiritual quest, possibly have the counsel from their families and the clear example of their families to help them see this understanding of marriage I have given?

Sure, there are young people in our society who do have the deep understanding of marriage as I have described it. There are millions of deeply spiritual families in our society. But the members of those families aren't the ones who read books like this. Many of us were brought up in spiritual families but refused to pay attention to the example and principle that was all around us. Others of us were brought up in families with little sense of the spiritual in example or in expression. No family I've ever seen was as completely lacking in the spiritual as some of its sons and daughters have come to me and claimed that they were.

How can we make such a refined spiritual decision as marriage is when we are coming out of such chaos? It's very simple. God lives within each of us, as us, no matter how blind we are to the fact. So no matter what recognition for the spiritual there was in our families, there was no *escaping* the spiritual. When God lives within each of us, as us, how can God be absent from any family? God doesn't move and we can't move away from God. How can we move away from God when God is always within us, waiting for us? We can shut ourselves off from God. We can refuse to heed the voice of God speaking within us, but we can't get away from God and neither can anyone else in our family.

There's an old expression of a family being a God-less family. Following my line of thinking about God, such a thing is an impossibility. To me, the best expression of the God within us working in our lives without our knowledge is in the process by which we select a spiritual partner. We marry someone because we think their hair is beautiful and we end up with the perfect person to make our spiritual quest with. We marry someone because they are rich and we want the security and prestige their money brings us and we end up with the perfect mate. We marry someone because they can make funny faces that make us laugh, and we end up with the perfect mate.

In all my experience of working with husbands and wives who have come to me for help, I haven't yet seen a marriage that wasn't working perfectly. That's why they came to me for help. The marriage was working too perfectly and it was bringing each of them more self-knowledge than they could understand and stand. They wanted me to tell them they needed a divorce and that they needed to be out of the marriage.

What do I mean by that? I mean that I never found a husband or wife that was wrong for the person they were married to. Sure they thought they had the wrong mate and had all kinds of complaints about that mate. What they couldn't see from their perspective and I could see from mine was that they were blaming the other person for their own problems. And the personal qualities they were blaming the other person for, they had, themselves, in great abundance. I didn't see sweet, kind, sensitive, caring, responsible men and women married to spouses who were the exact opposite.

Instead, I heard a bunch of angry babies criticizing and blaming the other. I saw them taking no responsibility for choosing the person they were with and for contributing to their problems. I didn't see many people wanting to know how they could work on their own spiritual program so they could be happier with themselves. Always the focus was on why they were unhappy because of what the other person was doing. No one wanted to talk about how they could work on themselves and so be happier with themselves. Someone else wasn't making them happy and they wanted out. Right now.

What those people couldn't and wouldn't see is that they were married to someone who was doing a beautiful job of bringing out the worst in them so they could see that and work on it. But they didn't want a spiritual quest. Or, if they did, they didn't want one that hard. They were looking for romance and didn't find it and they wanted out, and I wouldn't sympathize with them, so they usually didn't come back very many times. Only a few were interested in finding out the truth from their spiritual partner, their perfect mate, their soul mate.

I never operated as a psychologist. I never took money from anyone who came to see me. I don't believe in that for me. But that also did give me the advantage of being free to say anything I wanted to say to people. As near as I can remember, I don't think I ever supported anyone's arguments as to why they should get a divorce. I supported some people who wanted to separate for a while, but not divorce. And that position never came from a religious position. I was born a Baptist and they allow divorce. In the situations people brought me, I could see this idea of marriage being a spiritual affair long before I had that idea in clearly expressed form.

In my earlier years, I had spent a fair amount of time feeling sorry for myself and blaming other people. But I don't think I ever got so deep in that that I got away from the idea that I had a major responsibility for the things that were happening to me. At first I carried that into the idea of being powerful, and I tried to change everything. I believe I've been able to give up a fair amount of that now and can see that it is God who makes the potatoes grow. I just hoe away the weeds in the potato patch.

I believe that there is a deep spiritual force working in us in the selection of a marriage partner and in most cases we are pretty blind to it. In Sicily they call it the "thunderbolt." That's what happens when we see the person we must marry. I felt the thunderbolt with Jackie despite all the fear I had of getting married. She felt that with me. She tells how the first day we talked, she reached out and touched my hand. She said it was like touching her own skin. When I came in the door of her house to get her for our first date, her mother had a strong feeling that this was the man Jackie would marry.

Someone says, "Baloney. I got drunk with a guy and woke up married to him." Sure, but she very likely got drunk with some other guys and didn't wake up married to them. I'm convinced by what I've seen. You don't have to agree with me that there is a spiritual principle operating and that we have selected our soul mates. There is another principle I see that I've never heard an effective argument against.

When someone is having trouble with the person they are married to, I'm always amazed at how much opportunity there is for the partners in the trouble facing them. The troubles I see go right to the heart of the person. The problems are fundamental and desperately need to be solved. To walk away from problems like that could be a great harm because the person involved might never have the chance to solve that problem again. No one might ever love them enough to face them with this part of themselves. If they told me they had trouble believing the mate loved them, then I found myself telling the person, "Well, all right, but how will you ever again find someone so good at bringing out the worst in you as this person?" No one ever had a good answer for that, they just wanted to get away from the other person. They couldn't admit or they couldn't see that all their problem was just an aspect of themselves. No one else can ever be a problem to us unless we carry some of that quality they are criticizing us for within ourselves.

When someone tells me I'm a lousy writer, I just yawn. I know my writing isn't perfect, but it's sure adequate to get my point across and to give people the feeling I'm right there talking to them. But if someone tells me I'm a domineering, aggressive steamroller, that makes my stomach do a little flip, I can tell you. I'm coming to some peace about that aspect of myself but I don't yet yawn at that statement. When you say that, you've got my attention. It's from experiences like these with myself that I learn how helpful marriage and the so-called troubles of marriage are.

I still can't believe how effective marriage is at causing us pain where we most need it. If Jackie died or was killed, I can't imagine how I would find anyone who could do so well at finding the sore, sick places in me that need to be worked on if I'm to get closer to God. And I don't know how I could find anyone who could love me so deeply knowing so intimately all the weaknesses I have.

Many people who know us say, "Well, you can talk the way you do about marriage, because you've got such a good marriage." I think it's the opposite of that. I think, because we have the understanding of marriage we have, we've got a marriage that works so well to give us plenty of pain and plenty of love. What this book is offering you is a new understanding of marriage that can give you what we have by changing your understanding. Perhaps I shouldn't say that you need to change your understanding. I should say that you need to uncover within yourself this understanding I'm talking about because I believe this is the understanding that was hidden deep within everyone when they married, otherwise they wouldn't have been able to find such perfectly suited spiritual partners. So it is an "uncovering" of something within yourself that I'm talking about rather than taking in some foreign understanding and trying to be comfortable with it.

The title on the book says "perfect marriage with your *present* mate." There's a little humor there. Many people are sure they could have a perfect marriage with someone else's mate but not their present mate, not that unfeeling person. Also, many people are on their second to tenth mate by this time. That's fine. You can have a perfect marriage with this mate if you're ready to face the lessons that this mate and all your previous mates were lovingly offering to teach you about you. Or, you can try to run away from the lesson again, for a while. I've never seen anyone succeed at running away for long because we're always going to end up being faced with ourselves. It might be that our moment of truth doesn't come until the last few moments of our lives, but I believe it comes for everyone.

In this book you will hear a number of voices speaking. What you have just heard for the last few pages is my voice speaking for me and in some places for Jackie, too. Some other voices you will hear will be Jackie speaking about what I said on the tapes, Jackie saying what I didn't put on the tapes but what she knows I believe, Jackie saying what we both believe, and Jackie saying what she believes. In most cases, I let what Jackie said for me and what Jackie believes just for her, stand as they are. In a few cases I will identify Jackie's voice or she will identify her voice because she needs to be credited with the idea to make it clear or proper.

A funny thing happened as the writing of this chapter began. My wife Jackie decided she wanted a definition of marriage. The first thing she thought of was the old definition of marriage she remembered from her childhood. It began: "Marriage is a sacrament instituted by God . . ." and she couldn't remember any more. She started looking for Catholic churches in the phone book. She called a few and no one could remember the official definition. She found the name of an organization listed in the phone book and felt that they, of all people in the Catholic church, would have the old definition.

A Catholic priest came on the line and, when Jackie put her question to him, said, "I don't remember exactly, but I do know that prior to Vatican II in the 1960s the primary purpose of marriage was for the procreation of children and the control of concupiscence, whatever that means." The priest chuckled in an embarrassed way at his use of the old-fashioned word for the control of sexual desire. He went on to say, "After Vatican II the definition that has been generally used goes something like, 'Marriage was instituted by Christ for the joining of two people, in love, and to open them to new life.' "

Jackie smiled as she put down the phone. "Well, that was nice and vague. I'll bet I know a religion that won't be vague. The Jews will have a clear, strong definition if anyone will." She turned to Synagogue in the phone book and started dialing. The woman who answered the phone laughed out loud. "An official definition of marriage? Boy, you'd have to ask a rabbi." Okay, my wife answered, who would you suggest? "Well, that depends," said the woman. "Do you want a conservative, orthodox, or reformed to give you the definition?" Jackie just smiled again.

Those two incidents aren't much, but they make you think. The words of the Catholic priest showed the extreme swing of the pendulum. The Jewish religion has three different factions to call for a definition, then there are the Lutherans, the Baptists, the Episcopalians, the Methodists, etc., etc. Jackie's reaction was: Let's chuck the chapter, or write our own definition on which to base it. Here's what Jackie wrote—and I share her views:

> Marriage is a sacrament instituted by God to join a man and a woman in a lifelong commitment of physical, mental, and spiritual union in their journey to God. Its purpose is twofold:
>
> First, for their spiritual progress as individuals and as a couple, and for the spiritual progress of however many children they may choose to have.
>
> Second, for the preservation of the family unit as the stabilizing force required for the physical, mental, and spiritual health of the human race.

The definition is as complete as we could make it. To view marriage as the joining of two people together, in love, is too nebulous. To view it as anything less than a spiritual union just does not make sense. And if it is a spiritual union of two people who are journeying toward God, then their understanding of God had better be mutually compatible. At first, the other partner doesn't need to have the same understanding of God or any understanding of God for these ideas to work. But after a person has lived out these ideas in marriage more and more clearly, I have seen that there comes a growing respect from that other person for what they have seen happen in the true spiritual growth of the partner.

At the same time, each individual in the marriage must act only for himself or herself. "I am the one who is interested in going to God, and if I am interested only in going to God, I can use whatever happens in this marriage as stepping-stones to God. I can take whatever difficulties, whatever problems occur, whatever joys and pleasures I have, to transcend the human ego. Transcending the human ego is what Christ did on the cross. It is the willingness to surrender totally our selfishness and self-centeredness. This is hard for most of us. We like to carry our crosses.

The ultimate case of transcending in the alcoholism world happened in 1935 when two guys sat down together in Akron, Ohio. In the grip of the iron hand of humility these two men sat down with each other because they needed each other. They recognized a mutual need to admit that they were powerless over alcohol, that they needed to surrender to a God of their understanding, that they needed to live a life of honesty, purity, and love. And that they needed to work with one another and with other drunks if they were to stay sober. This meeting started Alcoholics Anonymous and changed the history of this country. We'll see the contribution of AA even more as this country goes deeper into its continuing need for substances and compulsions to get relief from pain in this drug and alcohol plague we are now dealing with.

This concept that AA discovered intrigues me so much because of its success with a hopeless disease. Until 1935 no one, no religion, no medical group, nothing had saved these people. Today there are over a million people sober in Alcoholics Anonymous, plus hundreds of thousands of people living healthy lives using the same concept on other afflictions. I saw personally how I could use this concept in marriage to give me the tools to a rewarding, fulfilling, stable life for me, for each other, and for our children because it takes us out of meddling in each other's lives and centers us upon ourselves and our own spiritual journey, and shows us how to be honest and open and kind.

Two of the biggest problems we have as human beings is first admitting our powerlessness and the unmanageability of our lives. And secondly admitting that there is a God who has the power to restore us to sanity. "Who, me? God helps those who help themselves. There's nothing wrong with me that I can't fix myself."

There's a big problem that is just coming to the fore that I think is a good example of a problem we can't fix ourselves. Our divorce rate is climbing. The number of children being raised in single-parent homes is soaring, and recent studies seem to show that children are being hurt far more by divorce than we thought. Some figures seem to show that children whose parents stayed together in a traumatic marriage for the sake of the children fare better than children whose parents divorced.

In most marriages, when trouble comes, almost all of us try to figure out how to get the other person to change. Or, we try to figure out how to change our work, our home, our town, change anything outside of ourselves so that we can feel well, for a time. It doesn't work permanently. This spiritual program I believe in so much shows me how to get my eye off of other people, places, and things and on to what I can do to change myself. In my marriage I've learned to keep my focus where it always belongs, on myself. Then whatever happens, I can use this principle of marriage as a crucial part of my spiritual quest to keep me from constantly blaming that other person, and constantly criticizing and having expectations of that other person. It keeps me from constantly seeking things I think I need in order to feel better about myself.

One thing that helped me a great deal in understanding marriage in this new way was when I experienced that I was love. This happened to me in Baba Muktananda's ashram in Florida some years ago. I had always believed that love was something outside myself that someone gave me and something I had to get to have.

From my earliest memories, I guess, I was always seeking love. I imagine everyone is, because we are all born separate and alone. And what we are seeking in our limited, finite way is an identification with someone from whom we are aware of unconditional regard. From this experience, we decide whether we are lovable and loved. My wife always attributed her sanity to having had this feeling from her grandfather Carey. She never could explain it, but she always felt that she was perfection in his eyes. And from it, no matter how bad things got for her, there at the bottom was that love, inside of her, a free gift from her grandfather. He died when she was sixteen and she feels that love as strongly today as she did as a small child. Now she sees that her grandfather showed her that she was love because, to her, that is what *he* was.

I, on the other hand, never made that deep a connection with anyone in my family. I knew I was loved by a lot of people, but I never felt a lot of it. It was more an intellectual idea than anything else.

Now, remember, I wrote earlier that the one way in which we are all born equal is in our loneliness. We are all born feeling separate and alone. Our journey then is to put down our separation and aloneness and become the love that is within us, which is God as I understand him. The hook in this is that the tool that God gives us to realize and experience love is each other. That's the hard part. If there's a little bit of God in me and a little bit of God in you and God is love, then we need to make that human connection in order to awaken our spirits to life and to love. And a good number of us can't seem to believe that it's to be done—one human being to another. We seem to want a more esoteric deal. We want to do it on a different level that won't involve those other people in our lives. We want to go up on the mountaintop to meet God, or, we want to watch Billy Graham on TV with the door locked so that none of God's noisy children will come barging in on us.

Separation, separation—that's the name of the game for so many of us. We need love so badly, in order to find God, but it is so hard for us to accept that love from his messengers, God's creatures, our fellow men and women. So we either reject them or we use them, when what we are meant to do is simply embrace them.

I, like every other human being, needed that connection, and through a series of incidents in my life, which were all a part of my spiritual journey, decided that love was out there somewhere, and my job was to keep on looking until I found it. By the time I was about ten or twelve I had made the connection that so many people make, that love is somehow connected with sexual arousal.

I set out on a journey that led me to loneliness. But everything we do is part of our journey to God. Our need to become that love that is God is so great that we invest all of our life's energy into it whether we are aware of it or not. God is whatever or whoever we bow our knee to. An alcoholic is a person, born separate and alone, feeling the pain that all of that implies, who finds that alcohol stills that pain. Alcohol does for them what it doesn't do for me. It metabolizes differently in their body and for months and years it brings the illusion of peace and joy and love as long as they are drinking. But like all false gods it soon throws the alcoholic on the rocks of despair.

Money, sex, food, work, all of the compulsions do the same thing. They give the illusion of love from without and lead the person down the path that any false god does, and we are all worse off when we hit bottom than we were when we first began to bend our knee to this false god.

Getting back to the ashram: I was there, all by myself, and I suddenly was aware of overwhelming love. It was so strong it took me over and I understood that I *was* love. From this experience I began to understand so many of the reasons for my loneliness and fear. I began to understand the burden I had placed on other people in my life.

If you believe that love is something from outside yourself and put the burden of proof that you are loved on other people, then nothing is ever enough. Love becomes like a brief rain shower in the desert for a dying, thirst-starved person instead of a flowing cool river that you float in all of your life.

In marriage, this is where ninety-nine percent of the problems come from. If my feeling of love must come from you and your feeling of love must come from me, then we are in bondage to each other. This never works. We each have married our respective myths and when troubles come we look at each other and say, "What the hell! You've got problems! I don't want problems, I need love." So we split.

Another myth many of us bring into marriage is the belief that the love we need is like breakfast food: it's something we buy. My wife calls this the "gold star on the chart" syndrome. When we are children we learn that "being good" is what will give us what we call love. We've already substituted approval of others for the love we really need, and most of us learn to be people-pleasing little phonies which, by the way, isn't very pleasing to other people. It's simply our selfish, childish attempt to control the people around us so they will do what we want them to do.

We become "public perfect" and do all the outward things that we think will bring us approval. It usually doesn't take too many years of this until we see that approval isn't love; it doesn't do anything for us. Then about half of us become rebellious and nasty and stop seeking love in approval, and the other half go underground and stay people-pleasers on the outside while inside we become critical, selfish, self-centered, and full of resentment. But all of us are still simply seeking that nebulous thing we call love.

So we marry, children come, and Mom and Dad are two babies themselves who believe that love is out there. Typically, Dad is finding his substitute in work, Mom finds her substitute in what she feels she gets from those tiny, dependent children. In a few years, Dad can't get enough promotions to make him feel love, the children go into the terrible twos and some start school, and Mom isn't feeling what she calls love either. Dad is working harder and Mom doesn't feel enough from him. Mom is busy with home and family so Dad doesn't feel enough from her, so Dad works harder or turns to sports or television or women. Mom decides to go to work or involve herself outside the home with volunteer work or hobbies or church or men, the kids get noisier and more demanding, and the full catastrophe descends.

This, typically is what happens as each person involved in the catastrophe continues on his or her separate journey toward false gods. A few of us can stay separate and alone and continue to live in the same house, presenting the illusion of a happy family to the world for the rest of our lives. Most of the people who do this are dead already; they just go on silent and alone for many years until they keel over from heart or cancer or die in a one-car wreck on a lonely road. They do this because it is too painful to do the work it would take to come alive to themselves and the rest of the world. They are too afraid.

Other couples want to stay separate and alone and continue to live in the same house, but their children do their work for them. The children, being strong souls, start getting into trouble. This crisis will awaken Mom and Dad. If it doesn't, more crises will come. Then the whole family has to make a choice. Do we work it out, or do we split? For many of them a divorce is easier than doing the painful work, so divorce it is and the kids either get help or go down the tube.

For some others, one of them will feel a lot of pain and start seeking answers. The other one doesn't want any part of it. This soon presents terrible pressures on them as a couple, and the decision to work it out or split becomes an issue, and all too often divorce is the answer.

In all of these cases everyone involved is seeking the same thing, that thing called love. I believe that the only answer is to finally come to see that what we call love is not another person, sex, money, job, power, prestige, family, or any of its thousands of other disguises. It is found within us, the last place we think to look, and it is what I believe is God, that one who has all power to bring about a change of personality.

It's at this point that we see the ultimate craziness of our mind. Our mind is constantly sweeping the whole earth for problems or stimulation to think about. We can sit in a chair and our mind will take us anywhere and we can think of anything. But there is one place our mind stubbornly refuses to take us and that is deep inside ourselves where the God within waits. Our mind balks at that like a Missouri mule. It insists that there is no God or, if there is, inside us would be the last place he would be. But finally the desperation becomes so desperate that even our stubborn mind isn't able to resist anymore and we finally go in search of God and find the God who is with us at all times and can guide us in every way.

Once this idea is understood and accepted, it has been my experience that love becomes limitless and we can finally begin to give it away instead of seeking it. In fact, the more we give love away, the more we keep it. Once we know the secret, and the secret is that love is what we are, not what we do, then it becomes like a fountain that just flows out of us. There is no longer any choice. The more we realize we are love, the more the selfishness and self-centeredness go away. The more love comes out of us, the more we become aware of our own inner perfection. The more we become aware of our own inner perfection the more we are able to see that other people are love, and the more we begin to experience their inner perfection.

In order to achieve this goal for ourselves and for our marriage, we have found nothing clearer or more satisfactory than the twelve-step programs. These steps, when they are worked, will give us the tools we have been seeking all of our lives to overcome our sense of being separate and alone. These steps brought us serenity and peace in times of sorrow that would have surely killed us before. Here they are, as I have adapted them to my use by simply removing the word alcohol, since I am not an alcoholic.

THE TWELVE STEPS

1.   We admitted that we were powerless; that our lives had become unmanageable.

2.   Came to believe that a power greater than ourselves could restore us to sanity.

3.   Made a decision to turn our will and our lives over to the care of God as we understood him.

4.   Made a searching and fearless moral inventory of ourselves.

5.   Admitted to God, to ourselves, and to another human being the exact nature of our wrongs.

6.   Were entirely ready to have God remove all these defects of character.

7.   Humbly asked him to remove our shortcomings.

8.   Made a list of all persons we had harmed, and became willing to make amends to them all.

9.   Made direct amends to such people wherever possible except when to do so would injure them or others.

10.   Continued to take personal inventory and when we were wrong promptly admitted it.

11.   Sought through prayer and meditation to improve our conscious contact with God as we understood him, praying only for knowledge of his will for us and the power to carry that out.

12.   Having had a spiritual awakening as the result of these steps, we tried to carry this message to others and to practice these principles in all our affairs.

When I made a decision to live by what these twelve steps represent, I began a journey. I went in search of my being in order to be transformed as much as I could. I figured that what I turn out to be finally is what I was meant to be. That may sound like rather circular reasoning, but that is the path I am on. It's like the description of Michelangelo creating the statue of David. He took a block of stone and chipped away all of the stone that was not David. The God of my understanding is a better artist than Michelangelo, so what will eventually emerge out of this block of granite is Jess. As my wife continues her spiritual quest, what will eventually emerge will be Jackie.

In marriage we get assistance in emerging from our block of granite. All too often the assistance is improper and painful. I will pick up my hammer and chisel and start chipping away at my wife. Or she will pick up her tools and start chipping away at me. This usually forces the other person to flee in one way or another. Through the spiritual discipline of this new way of life we can learn to stop chipping on each other's stone. We learn to lovingly detach from our emotions about the other person and this makes us calmer and less reactive. When we become more calm we become a loving mirror to that other person by which they can see themselves more clearly if they've a mind to, and the pieces of stone which are not them can just fall away.

It has been my experience that most of the parts of each of us that are not us are simply reactions which we have to people, places, and things. These reactions are habits we have developed in order to keep us from experiencing the fear we have of being separate and alone. The place where these reactions are the strongest is in marriage. This is where the oppositeness of the other sex is the most threatening to us.

Okay, now what is divorce? Divorce is when there is too much oppositeness. For all practical purposes, I was divorced in my marriage a number of times. From the beginning of our marriage, my own sense of being separate and alone would set me off and I would flee compulsively into recreations like hunting and fishing and golf. Later I divorced Jackie for business because a man has to get ahead, you know. Most recently, of course, there were the years where I chose sexualizing relationships with women as my way of divorcing my wife. Some of these things are more painful for the other person than others, as you can well imagine. It was easier for my wife when I was catching fish and bagging elk than doing the same with the opposite sex. There were times when I hurt my wife so horribly I thought that I had lost her forever. And this would be devastating for me, because all the time I knew inside myself that she was the woman I wanted and needed and loved.

In most cases like ours the couple actually gets a divorce through the courts. In talking to literally hundreds of divorced people the majority of them realize that it is themselves they are running from. "Wherever I go, there I am." Though they've tried marriage two or three or four times, many realize that they could have faced this the first time around and that the first marriage would have been all right.

My wife laughs when we talk about this and says our marriage was saved because she so paralyzed herself with tranquilizers and alcohol that she couldn't possibly have planned a course of action. She recognizes that this was one of the ways she divorced me while still married to me. Sometimes she says to me, "Jess you wouldn't be anything today if you hadn't married this alcoholic broad." And there's a lot of truth to that. If Jackie divorced me, I would have gone on doing exactly the same things to any other woman I might have married. And, furthermore, I see that I would probably have found another woman exactly like Jackie, if I could have found her. We need our mate's strengths but we also need their weaknesses.

Typically, the strengths and weaknesses we find appealing in the person we marry are appealing to us because they are familiar. They fit a pattern we grew up with in the majority of cases. This is why children of alcoholics will marry alcoholics. They don't want to marry alcoholics. They may not consciously see that the person they are marrying is alcoholic, but five or ten years down the road, the mate turns out to be an alcoholic, and the person is asking, "How did this happen?"

In all the divorced people I've talked to I haven't found very many of them who tell me that, in their next marriage, they found that slick guy or gal who solved all their problems for them. In one or two cases this might be so, but there are mighty few marriages where the problems are completely the other person's fault. We'd like to think that is the case, but it isn't. Many of the people I've talked to admit that it probably would have been better to work it out the first time, because there was no place to hide from themselves.

I see this so clearly in some of the problems that come up in discussing marriage with others. If there's one thing I've learned about, it is that whatever makes me angry, whatever pushes my buttons, that is where my work is. It is my observation that the angry button for many men is to tell them that they must be responsible. All men want to think that they *are* "responsible, thank you, and don't you dare to think that I'm not." For women, the angry button gets pushed when they are told that women's basic nature is to be nurturing and receptive. It's observable from that that men accept that they should be responsible and outgoing and want to deny that they do not live up to this. For women, it seems that they do not want to accept the basic premise that this is their nature. They feel put down and controlled by the very idea that there is any difference between themselves and men except anatomically.

In the last couple of books, Jackie and I have been talking some about men being responsible and women being receptive and nurturing. Many readers have written telling how helpful the ideas are, but they have had a lot of questions. One reader recently wrote and asked what he could read on the subject where we had gone into more detail than we did in our last book, *I Don't Know Where I'm Going . . .* I told him I was sorry but Jackie and I couldn't go into much more detail because we didn't know that much more that could be said or needs to be said. I guess the best I can think of is: you do too know what we mean. I find that there are a few simple ideas in this area that we have been working on and having our hands full for the last ten years. So I don't need to know more on the subject, I just need to work on the basics I already know.

The way I see it, men and women have very different natures, and that's not an accident. In fact, I think it's the exact opposite of an accident. I think it was meant to be that way for our spiritual quest. For some reason which I don't understand, I needed to learn what being a man meant and what going to God as a man meant. I know God lives in me as me and you as you and I know separation is not of God. So no matter whether I am male or female, black or white, rich or poor, I am not different from another. Everything is equal. The pile of gold and the pile of manure are both equal. They are both manifestations of God and both are simply aspects of the one God. But each of these aspects has a different nature and that, I think, is part of the point of this trip. We need to come to see that we are one, but with different natures.

I'm finally learning to look at a woman and see God instead of a sex object. When I forget who she is and see a sex object, I get my mind back on the fact she is God. Muhammad X, as I understand it, preached hatred against the whites to the blacks. Then he went to India and heard their spiritual teaching that all are one and became so persuaded himself he changed his teaching. I feel the same way. To me the point of spiritual teaching is that we are all one. So there's no question of the oneness of men and women.

The Chinese spent about five thousand years of civilization thinking about the subject and they felt that men and women each have both male and female energy. They saw the male energy as responsible, creative, and outgoing. They saw the female energy as receptive and nurturing. They saw men as being primarily male energy and secondarily female energy. They saw women as being primarily female energy and secondarily male energy. This understanding led to seeing the two sexes as opposites in their primary energy but both having both energies.

That is a big and controversial idea. But I'm not interested in controversy. I'm just interested in what works for me. So I don't want to argue that idea with anyone, I just want to explain how it works for me. I'm sure some of you have different opinions on the subject. That's fine. If you want to express those opinions in a book like I'm doing, find someone like my editor, Ferris Mack, who is willing to publish your ideas and experiences. Meanwhile, Ferris has asked me to put down my ideas and experiences as clearly and as honestly as I can.

The understanding of men and women as opposites leads to two very fruitful ideas in marriage. First, it gives me an idea of what my nature is and so guides me into certain areas of work I might do. Second, it says that because women are so opposite from me, I can use that oppositeness to help me bring out the worst in myself so it can be given up and the best in myself so I can see it and accept it as me.

Let me talk about the first idea, responsibility. When I had the spiritual awakening some years back, when I finally began to see my sexual behavior as my being a baby, I saw my need to be responsible. I went back home and began to be responsible in every way I knew how. I hadn't got the word "responsible" out of some book. The idea came to me out of my life, out of my experience. So that wasn't theory.

As I attempted to deal responsibly with my wife and my children and my other duties, I was sometimes very responsible and other times very harsh and manipulative. But none of us can do anything for the first time and not make some mistakes. A few years after I started to act more responsibly, I came across the idea of the man being responsible and the woman being receptive. The idea hit me because the responsibility part was what I was working on and the idea of the woman being receptive and nurturing appealed to me. I soon proceeded to abuse the idea by telling Jackie how receptive and nurturing she should be. I see now that some of that abuse came out of the twisted thinking that was a part of my sexual compulsion, and the rest of it came out of the same beginner's mistakes I made with the responsibility idea.

Jackie agrees with the idea that a woman's nature is to be nurturing and receptive, particularly now that I've stopped my abuses of the idea. She has gently hinted to me that I would have found her receptive and nurturing thirty-five years ago if I hadn't been too dumb to see it and too neurotic to accept it. Jackie finds the idea useful to her just as I find the responsibility idea useful to me. She also gently states that she was too dumb to see some of my attempts to be responsible, and too neurotic to accept them, thirty-five years ago.

There's an interesting corollary of the above idea. That is that the way each of us gets at the secondary part of our nature is to first make sure we have adequately developed the primary part of our nature. That means that the only way I can get to the female characteristics of myself, the receptive, nurturing parts, is by being more responsible. And, I have seen this happen. As I've worked for some years on developing my responsibility, it's Jackie's opinion that I am becoming more receptive to her and our sons and daughters and more nurturing. The same would apply to the woman. To be more responsible, she would have to make sure she had adequately developed her nurturing, receptive side. I have suggested this idea as possibly worthy of a trial to some women who have come to me for help with problems with men. Many of them have found the idea useful.

A woman recently came to me for help who was having a lot of trouble in a group she was in, particularly with one of the men. I told her about this idea and she was receptive to it. I suggested she start bringing some food she had prepared or purchased to the meeting and serve it and coffee to the people there. She had a little trouble with the idea but was spiritually developed enough to see her resistance. She tried what I suggested and liked the results she experienced inside herself.

So many of the guys who come to me for help have been so irresponsible. I tell them what an irresponsible baby I was and they can really identify. It has taken me eight years to finally feel that I have all my responsibilities caught up and current. All my financial affairs are in good order. I have good budgets and controls set up so we know just where we're at financially. The two places, Phoenix and Bozeman, have both been made very livable for Jackie and me. There are no jobs lying around undone. I had a screen door to replace when I got back to Bozeman, but that was one of the first things I did. It is a good feeling to know that I'm meeting my responsibilities as well as possible.

I see that I'm now much more able to be receptive and nurturing than I used to be. There are many occasions now when I see where I need to nurture people and be receptive to them. So this is the use I'm making in my life of this male-female idea. I'm not pushing it on anyone, just saying it as I see it. If you have trouble with the idea, that's fine. I need again to make the distinction between the usefulness of an idea and its truth. I don't know if this idea is true or not. It might be I'm just kidding myself in a little word game, but the ideas I've mentioned have been useful to me. They run counter to much of what is written today, but that doesn't bother me because I don't see many women or men making a very fruitful use of a lot of the stuff that's being written today.

Even if I later threw out all the ideas I have about the characteristics of a man and of a woman, I think I would still hang on to the idea of how opposite they are. The fact men and women are so opposite is, to me, one of the big arguments for marriage. The old, fat, gentle Pope John we loved so could go to God without a woman, but it seems to me that about ninety-five-plus percent of us guys need a relationship with a woman to bring out the worst and the best in us so we can get the help we need in our spiritual quest. I've been in plenty of bachelor apartments and there's no life in them. No love and no fury to speak of. But put a woman in that apartment with one of those guys and usually all hell breaks loose. Lots of love and lots of hell and usually not dull. Beautiful. Perfect for a spiritual quest.

I have some close men friends who have loved me for as many as forty years. If I were to go live with one of them, I wouldn't learn in a year about myself what I learn in one day with Jackie. So I need that oppositeness in a marriage. If Jackie and I sort of blur what we are and go away from our nature, I think we lose oppositeness. I don't want that. I want all the woman Jackie is. Sure, I have lots more woman than I can stand at times, but that's my problem. Sometimes, when the going gets tough, Jackie will say, "If you wanted a woman who was quiet and didn't get into things much, why didn't you marry someone like your mother?" I say back at her, "I don't want someone like my mother." To which she sometimes will reply, "Well, you sure don't act like it." To that I would have to concede, "You're right."

So I'm glad there are men and women and I'm glad they're so opposite. I don't think our problems come from the oppositeness, really, as much as the fact that oppositeness isn't recognized and appreciated but is blurred and confused as men and women are frightened at what they see and run away from who they are into alcohol, drugs, sex, work, and the other compulsions with self or with others.

What about homosexuality? That's a topic I've thought a lot about because many homosexuals have sought my counsel and others have challenged me. Maybe it's as they say and that homosexuals are born different. There is some evidence of hormonal and other differences that put some of them someplace between men and women. Since there is evidence of some homosexuals being born into American Indian society, maybe some homosexuals are born that way and others make a choice. It is my personal belief that, through the power of a spiritual program, there is a new power of choice open to us that we never had available to us before. So the issue of choice is a very important one to me. And, as a theoretical person, I'm interested in understanding something as well as I can. I have to watch out for myself and not carry that too far because there are many aspects of the spiritual that I can never understand. All I can do is use them and watch out that my attempts at understanding don't get in the way.

I'm not in the debating society. My ideas are just for me and the friends I have who want to read my books. I think that, for some I've met, homosexuality is a way of running away from too much oppositeness in the opposite sex. I can understand that fear. Lots of times, I saw so much oppositeness I could hardly bear it. It's usually okay now, but not too long ago there was so much fear of the opposite in me. What I see about homosexuality that most fails to convince me of its arguments is the fact that so few choose permanent relationships with each other. If most homosexuals were living in reasonably committed long-term relationships I might find it easier to believe in it as an alternative.

My recently discovered sexual compulsion has thrown new light on the subject for me. (I go into that in the next chapter on my story.) Sexual compulsion looks to be a preoccupation with sexual thinking, lust. Lust isn't sex, it's thinking about sex. Even in sex, lust is thinking about sex with someone else. Now lust may be fine for some people, but I can't handle it. I don't like what it does to me. I don't like the way lust isolated me. Lust kept me from ever having a wife, my children, even my men friends. I lost everything to lust. So I don't want any of it in my life anymore. If there are people who can handle lust, fine, let them handle it. I don't want it.

So being free from lust, having sexual sobriety, means giving up pornography, masturbation, sex fantasy, sexual conquests, one-night stands, and any kind of destructive sexual thinking, and any of the other ways that a person might use for sexual stimulation, for those who really want this freedom. The only thing that isn't lust is the feelings of sexual desire that come at the sight or thought of something sexual that occurs in the normal circumstances of things and the act of intercourse. The only way I see that there can be intercourse without the planning and anticipating of lust is in a committed relationship which we call marriage, because it's impossible to have a committed relationship without its being at least a common-law marriage. I say impossible in the sense it is impossible for someone with a sex compulsion, because the point of the compulsion is the sexual preoccupation and sexual conquest.

If Jackie were to die, I know there's no way I could have sex with a woman before marriage without lust. If I remarried again, it would only be with the understanding that if lust came into the sex, we would stop having sex until the lust was gone. And I think that could easily take some time. I say that to make the point that lust is the problem. It has very little to do with marriage. When a person is married, they have some protection from lusting in that relationship because the newness and conquest wears off. In a new marriage, that wouldn't be the case and it could take awhile. I used to think a lusty, new marriage was a great idea. Now I see it's something I wouldn't seek, and if I experienced it, I would have to get rid of the lust part. Those views sound very strange in today's society, but I have seen the good results of staying out of lust in my life and in some of my friends' faces that now shine where they used to be dark.

Another big part of the sexual compulsion is conquest. For a sexual compulsive, it's chasing the rabbit around the track that's the sport. Once the rabbit is caught, it's no fun. The chase is more fun than the catching, oddly enough. That's why the sexual compulsive eventually realizes he or she is sick. After they catch and don't want too many times, they have to switch compulsions, or add a new compulsion like drugs, or face themselves.

This is another reason that a committed relationship is the only one where it is possible to be free from lust. Without the commitment, the next conquest (and that always involves lust) is always lurking in the back of the mind. It is so easy to fall into the trap of right or wrong on this issue. We don't need that idea here. We can look at this problem just from the standpoint of the harm to the individual. So here, it isn't a question of the morality of marriage. That's a different issue. The issue here is where the mind is. That issue is lust.

There are two Zen stories that make that clear to me. One story is about the new Zen master who went to visit the famous old Zen master Hakim. It was raining and so the new Zen master put his sandals and umbrella outside Hakim's door. Later, as Hakim was pouring tea, he asked the young Zen master, "Outside by the door, on which side of your sandals is your umbrella sitting?" The young Zen master realized he did not remember—he had been too eager to meet the great Hakim and talk to him—so he renounced his Zen mastership and went back to study for two more years so he could learn to practice "every minute Zen."

This story tells how we must always be where we are. It tells of Zen as the direct experience of reality. Lust is thinking ahead or thinking back, it is never being where we are. The whole concern is the preoccupation. I did a lot of fantasy on elk hunting, too, as well as sexual stuff. One time, as I was driving to the place where I was going to hunt with a friend and my son. I suddenly realized this hunt wasn't going to live up to my fantasy and I started planning the next hunt in my fantasy. That's what fantasy is all about and the direct experience of reality is the opposite of that.

The other Zen story is about a pretty woman in a beautiful kimono who is standing on one side of a very muddy street looking to the other side. Two monks come along. One monk goes over to her, picks her up, and carries her across the street and puts her down on the other side. They walked on and the other monk was silent for hours. Finally he said, "About that beautiful woman you picked up and carried across the street today—we aren't supposed to go near beautiful women, to say nothing of picking them up." To this the first monk said, "Are you still carrying her? I put her down in the marketplace this afternoon." Lust, as I am talking about it, is carrying the pretty woman around in your head like the second monk. Again, only in marriage, it seems, can someone with a sexual compulsion avoid carrying the pretty woman (or man) around in his or her head.

All this bears on homosexuality because it seems to me that most of the homosexuals I know are preoccupied with sex and constant sexual conquest, which I think of as lust. Our God is whatever we bend our knee to. We can't have both God and sex at the centerpoint. Lust is when we carry sexual memories around and play with them, as did the monk in the Zen story. Lust is when we spend time ahead of sex thinking about it and planning it. Lust is when we spend time thinking sexually about the people we meet in our lives. Lust is when sex is power, greed, and control. Lust is harmful for anyone, married or not. That is my experience, and that of a few of my friends, married and single.

When I talk this way to homosexuals, some can see it. I'm in touch with a few homosexuals who have spiritual programs who have seen that they had put sex before God. Once they put their own understanding of God first, the secret, full-of-shame sex they had been having didn't fit in their lives anymore and they went to celibacy.

So that's how I see homosexuality. And that's how it looks to me like it might fit in the scheme of things. I have told you about men and women and marriage and lust. But I'm not a homosexual so I don't need to decide for me. All I've told you is what a few close friends and I have come to see for ourselves.

I believe that a great many of us are finding that what we are doing isn't producing the results we thought it would. I think that great changes in our society's attitudes and beliefs are going to be happening in the near future as we see more clearly the consequences on the family structures that are so important to each of our survivals. Social change isn't planned. Social change is simply the product of a whole bunch of individual choices. As we find things that we thought were good not working for us, we change them so they work better for our long-term interest. As each of us makes a change like that, society changes. Gandhi sat in his ashram spinning cotton leading his reformed life. Out of his change came a change in all of India and England that affected all the rest of us. Yet many argue that one person is meaningless.

As Einstein said about Gandhi: ". . . a man who has confronted the brutality of Europe with the dignity of the simple human being, and thus at all times risen superior. *Generations to come, it may be, will scarcely believe that such a one as this ever in flesh and blood walked upon earth"* (italics, mine). The point isn't that each of us have the fame of a Gandhi. The point is the spiritual principle his life came from, the point made by Einstein. Each of us simple human beings, when guided by the spirit, are people of immense consequence. I'm so aware of this because I have spent a lot of time being guided by my own crazy mind in search of the object of my different compulsions as an escape from what my crazy mind was so afraid of, seeing me as the imperfect human being I am. I am now seeking the spiritual path for me. With that seeking is coming a dignity and an integrity that is so precious to me partly because I had been so long without it.

Now, more and more, I see how perfectly imperfect I am. I see that I was broken on the rocks as I received true justice for the way I lived. So for a time, I was broken, transparent, and vulnerable. That's good. But the real problem is to stay broken, transparent, and vulnerable. My constant temptation is to believe, "Well, I've been changed by that experience and now I'm well. Now I can be normal and forget what I've been through and *tell* other people how to change their lives." Instead, I need to be constantly in fellowship with my fellow human beings and *sharing* with them my brokenness and staying transparent and vulnerable. I haven't found anything harder than that to do. I see that it is truly a man's work and a woman's work. It is not the kind of work that could be done by the dependent baby I often was in my past.

I heard a beautiful story about ten years ago that illustrates this point to me. A woman told a story about her father. He had noticed how once an apple went bad in the barrel, it spoiled the whole barrel. He took some rotten apples and fastened them to apples that were still on the tree. He found those apples weren't rotted by contact with the rotten apple. I see this same point. I can't go run to the mountaintop and sit alone with God. Maybe some can. But for me I need to be like the apple on the tree and stay in fellowship with my fellow human beings in honest, simple communication with them.

This means we have to be willing to open ourselves to whatever pain that comes to us as a consequence of our lives. And we are going to have to find powerful tools that can help bring about the changes that are needed. I believe that we have run out the string of blame. For most of us, the tool of having scapegoats no longer works and we are looking for a more valid way. The way I see for me is that at the center we are love and we are God. Nothing in the past or the present changed that. All we need to do with the past is put it down.

So there you have it. You see now, I hope, why I think it is necessary for us to rethink our position on marriage and to allow back into our consciousness the awareness that marriage is a life-long spiritual trip. This nation of pleasure-seekers that we have become is finding out very fast that there's no money, pleasure, job, or power that can help us get rid of grief. We have to accept God—or be God.

3.

My Story
to Nail Up
on the Courthouse Door

I'M GOING TO TELL YOU MY STORY as honestly as I can. Later on in my story there are some parts that are hard to tell you because I'm afraid of what you will think. But I need to tell you my story as honestly as possible because I see now that I'm as sick as my secrets. Another way of saying that is, I'm as separate as my secrets and I now know that I'm not separate from you even if I do feel that way fairly often. So I want to give up my secrets. As an old friend of mine said, "We aren't well until we can write out on a piece of paper everything we ever did and nail it up on the court-house door." This book is the paper I'm nailing up on the court-house door, written as honestly as I can manage. Some years from now, I may have the courage to be more honest. If so, I'll nail up a new piece of paper.

This is my story as I see it today. I think you need to have a chance to know some parts or all of my story to make sense out of what I'm saying about marriage. The ideas I have now about marriage didn't just happen. They came from my experiences and my understandings. The ideas I talk about in the two chapters on marriage and the way I may seem to throw the word "God" around might make you think I'm some deeply religious person, and always have been. Not so. I've had lots of problems with religion, as my story will show.

As I've said before and will need to say again, lots of times, the program I follow is a spiritual program, not a religious program. It doesn't matter what religious ideas a person has or doesn't have, all of us have a spiritual program of some kind, even if it's something as seemingly not spiritual as: "I don't believe there's any kind of power greater than myself and I don't want to discuss the subject." A person making such a statement doesn't realize it, but that is a very spiritual statement, because it has to do with what I have come to believe is the fundamental issue facing us all. That issue is how we see God and what our relation is to God. So each of us has a theory of some kind about God and that theory is our personal theology—the basis for our spiritual program.

What we usually don't realize is the consequences of our theory about God. We don't realize that our theory about God can have a big consequence in our lives. That's an idea I will go into detail on later. The point here is that my story tells of the background I had and the experiences I had that led to a gradually changing set of ideas about marriage and about God as I understand him. If the word "God" gives you any problem, insert your own word, like "higher power" or "supreme intelligence" or "nature" or "order in the universe" or "the old Indian on the hill"—whatever works for you. It's God as you understand him or her that I'm talking about.

Some parts of this story have been told in earlier books, but each of the books has to stand alone and can't depend on a reader having read any earlier book. Even though there is some repetition in the details of my story, it's still a different story because I see those experiences through different eyes than I saw them before. So the story is changed. There is another reason for telling my story. When I have told my story in the past, I have tended to make it sound like I had a great big spiritual awakening at the time of my heart attack and then there was a complete change in my life. There is some truth in that. But I had some earlier spiritual awakenings that didn't take too well or seem to last too long. They were a part of my spiritual growth in some way that I cannot ever completely understand. For all these reasons, here is the story of the little guy who grew up to be a hustling young guy who had some ideas about marriage and about God and what happened to change those ideas about marriage and about God.

I was born in a southern Minnesota farming community under some difficult circumstances. My life is a beautiful example of how, in a so-called ideal time, you can have somewhat less than ideal circumstances.

My dad had left Minnesota to work in Montana and met my mother, who was the daughter of pioneers in Montana. My dad married my mother but he was homesick, and a combination of that and a chance at a good job took him away from Montana and the land my mother had been born on and loved very, very much. Times were tough, but they were for everyone, so no one felt too horrible about being poor. If they had a roof over their head and enough to eat they were reasonably satisfied.

I was born about a year after my folks moved back to Minnesota. I was one and a half years old when the little house we were living in caught fire. My mother was sitting beside a wood stove, and my dad had thrown on some gasoline to get the wood going better when the stove blew up right on my mother and set her on fire. My dad had to get me out and get my mother out. My mother was pregnant with my younger brother at the time, and she was horribly burned. Her hair was burned off, her face was deeply burned, and one shoulder and one arm were burned. At first, the doctors didn't see how she could live.

She was taken to the Mayo Clinic in Rochester, Minnesota. In 1927 they had skin grafts, but it was the bare beginnings of this. Because of her crude grafts, she was horribly disfigured. She had been a beautiful woman, but she was now a woman you would stare at in shock and horror. She had to suffer under this burden through the years that it took to rebuild her face, and all the rest of her life.

She came home long enough to have my brother, and then went back to the hospital for more skin grafts. It must have been an incredible strain for both of my parents. I'm sure they survived it only through a deep dedication on both their parts and a deep love for each other.

A lot of people today are strong on the use of terminology like, "I was programmed. I was raised this way. I've got these tapes and that's why I'm this way." I don't find this psychological approach to life useful to me at all anymore. I'm a psychologist and I'm fairly familiar with most of the psychological ideas. But I'm not impressed by the results of them that I see in the lives of the psychologists and their followers. I don't see the world as an enemy doing all kinds of perverse things to me. I don't see myself as a victim. I don't believe there are any victims, only volunteers. I'm not sure just how this principle works in other people's lives, but I sure see how it has worked in mine.

What I am so aware of is choices that I made at a very young age. I literally made the choice to feel down on myself, and I remember that there was something delicious about that for me. It's hard to understand how you could decide to look down on yourself and find it enjoyable, but that is the perversity of the neurotic, and I am neurotic. I was raised in a little town with folks and friends and relatives who loved me, but I didn't pay much attention to that. I made a neurotic response to my feeling of being separate and alone.

Now I grant that I may have made these choices because I was born neurotic, just as some are born alcoholic and some are born sexaholic. "But, but," you cry, "what about the fact that alcoholics come from families with alcoholics in them?" That's fine. If in some mysterious way that I don't understand I chose the destiny of being neurotic or it was a destiny chosen for me by a loving God, then what better family to be born into to get a good grasp of that than a neurotic family? It is not very good science to say that because two things occur together, that proves that one caused the other.

It is very difficult to understand neurotics. A neurotic is someone who can screw up a free lunch. They are people who can walk into a bar to eat the free lunch, get in a fight with the bartender, get thrown out and get their nose busted in the process, instead of just shutting up and eating the free lunch. A neurotic can screw up a one-car funeral. A neurotic enjoys screwing things up to get noticed. They need to feel they are somebody special, so they'll create havoc, get fat, get drunk, do anything to get noticed. Any dumb thing will do. A neurotic wants to be the bride at every wedding and the corpse at every funeral. Anything to get attention.

I very clearly see where I made some neurotic choices. I'd sit in sixth grade and plan birthday parties for myself that never came off. I didn't ask my mother for a party. I only remember planning parties. I don't think I really wanted a party. If I had had a real party, I would have been very uncomfortable and not known what to do. My fantasy parties were always perfect. If I'd had a real party, invited people, and they'd come, I would have had to deal with reality and my lack of power to control it.

I was a very successful neurotic from my early days. I tried to be an athlete even though I had absolutely no athletic ability. No matter how hard I practiced, I remained what I was, a very crummy athlete. I knew I had no muscular development. I knew I had lousy eye-hand coordination. That didn't stop me. I needed to be noticed. The coach finally made me the water boy because he liked me. I broke his heart because he saw how hard I was trying. It was a delicious feeling.

I finally realized I couldn't compete on the football field, so I turned my grim, competitive drive to the classroom. It was another delicious experience to be able to go and take a physics test so that afterward I could ask my friends, "How many did you get wrong on the test?" They would have to answer, "One, two, three or four." And then they would have to ask me back, "How many did you get wrong?" and I could say, "None!"

I was the kind of person it was easy to hate. I was doing a very good job of screwing myself up at a very early age without any help from society. Any help society gave me in being neurotic was of small consequence.

My wife, when we were writing this part of the book, said, "You know, Jess, I had a friend who acted like this when she was young, too. She was always putting the screws to me about what she did versus what I did. I instinctively knew that she loved to draw me into a comparison so that she could feel superior to me in some weird way. She really gave me the creeps. It seemed like she defined herself by other people's failures. I had a hard time with her. Funny thing about my friend, she married an alcoholic and had a bunch of alcoholic children. I suppose by comparison to those members of her family she can still feel superior."

I know that I did not consciously know that Jackie was going to have problems with addiction, and I certainly wasn't omniscient enough to know that my kids were, but I knew that there were some ways that I felt superior to Jackie when I was going with her. And I know that I needed that feeling to sustain a relationship. I was afraid of strong women and didn't dare ask them for dates for fear of being refused. I think that many of us are this way. We seek relationships where we are either dependent or superior. We can't stand the responsibility and intimacy of equality relationships. And it's necessary to look at this in a marriage.

My junior year in high school I moved to Minneapolis. My senior year I fell in love. It was not my girlfriend's plan to fall in love with me. It was her plan to go to the University of California in Berkeley because she was advanced beyond her years. She was an egghead, and she wanted to talk to and be with other eggheads like herself. Berkeley had that reputation even then. She talked about philosophy and psychology and stuff like that. Well, she fell in love with me six months before we were to graduate. So we had this beautiful love deal going.

I went into the Army carrying Freud's *The Interpretation of Dreams,* Münsterberg's *The Eternal Life* (which says science can be in harmony with the spiritual), and a copy of Emerson's *Essays.* These books were ones my girlfriend and I shared a common interest in. I see now how much those books foretold a lifelong interest of mine. My girlfriend and I wrote long love letters. After a while I got a letter from her telling me that she didn't want a relationship anymore. She said I was just like a dependent puppy dog. She was so perceptive! She was wise beyond her years. That puppy dog dependency was another characteristic of mine that was to rear its ugly head constantly in my life and in my marriage.

In the Army, I was stationed at Coe College in Cedar Rapids, Iowa, and I was soon in love again. But I was a real loser. This gal had a boyfriend who was a pilot in the Air Force. When you're a real loser you don't go for the real clean deals, you date engaged gals or married ones. I was going with two other girls at that time, and both were banker's daughters with freezers full of steaks and warm welcomes for me. One I went with on Saturday night and one on Sunday night. Those two girls were my age, they were pretty, it could have been a clean deal. But that wouldn't have satisfied a neurotic. As soon as this other gal came into the picture I think that I saw deep inside that if I went with her I could get a messy relationship going, so I switched and left the nice, clean deals I had.

She was old—she was nineteen. I was seventeen. She was wise beyond her years, too, and she was in love with another man and I had to have her. She began by wondering if she could love two. She found she could love two if one was far enough away. So I set up a love affair that was doomed to disaster.

I was soon transferred to Scott Field, just outside of St. Louis, Missouri. I'd get a weekend pass and hitchhike to Cedar Rapids, Iowa. I'd arrive exhausted, go out on a date, sleep for four or five hours at the YMCA, then hitchhike back to Scott Field. One week-end I hit town at the same time as my true love's other friend, the pilot. She found she couldn't love two if they were both in town at the same time. So I was number two in that deal and my heart was broken. And I loved it, just loved it.

That's weird, you say? That's right. That was the way I was then. In the old days, in my defense, I would rush to point out that everyone has their weirdnesses. My wife, Jackie, laughed at this point and said that her weirdness in that area was that she could never have stood the pain of breaking up with someone she loved. So she would put up with any kind of nonsense rather than experience the pain of loss. She has a real fear of abandonment. It has made her "hang in there" beyond all measure. She has come to see that this fear is the root of what she used to call her "male dependence." I am just the opposite, as you can see. As I see it, the issue of dependency on another is something both men and women have to face.

I'd also had a spiritual awakening in a Methodist church when I was seventeen. An evangelist came to town and I made a decision to accept Christ as my personal saviour. I had a powerful, moving experience. I'll never forget that night. Afterward, I went down-town to the old Marigold Ballroom and told my friends, "I'm not going to be coming down here anymore dancing and holding these gals so close." I'm surprised now my friends didn't throw me out. One week later, though, guess where I was? I was right back at the Marigold Ballroom dancing and holding the girls close.

That spiritual awakening lasted a few days less than a week. You know that story in the Bible about the seed? Well, that seed of my spiritual awakening fell on solid rock, or at least it seemed to. But that was me at that time. Life was just starting to soften me up.

Once again, my wife had to get her two cents' worth in. She just winces whenever I tell the story I just told, coming from where she was as a teenager. She would never have been caught dead in the Marigold Ballroom in the first place. And in the second place, anyone so "uncool" as to announce to his friends that he had been "saved" could never, never have been considered for a friend of hers, let alone a husband and the father of her children. She would have considered that sort of person a jerk! "I never saw any of those traits in you when we were going together," she protested. "I just saw a big man on campus, who seemed to have it all to-gether." "Immaturity, my dear, immaturity," was her answer to herself. "It was partly because I was a dependent person which led to my own addiction. I was just as sick as you were," she said.

But I don't think it's that simple. A psychological analysis is never enough to explain why two people marry. To me, there's always a lot more at work than logic. They say love is blind. I don't think so. I think that, no matter how sick we are or seem to be, underneath the surface of the seeming chaos of our dating and courting behavior, we are searching for and finding our soul mate.

I was discharged from the Air Force early because they didn't have room for any more pilot trainees. I enrolled at the University of Minnesota. Earlier, at Coe College during my Air Force cadet days, I'd been a straight A student because the regimented routine kept a neurotic like me from screwing up too much. At the University of Minnesota, the Phi Beta Kappas came to me and said they were interested in me. But I was all alone with twenty-five thousand students and lost inside.

I jumped into the campus activities rat race so I could be president of something and be somebody. I didn't want to do the work of the president, I just wanted to be president so I'd get noticed and get attention. It wasn't enough to be president of just one organization. I tried to run two or three things at a time. By my neglect, I managed to kill off a couple of campus organizations, enjoying the prerogatives of being the president without doing any of the work. And I was careless about going to class. So my grades started down and I never heard from the Phi Beta Kappas again.

A couple memories of that time stand out especially clearly. Saul Bellow was my teacher for advanced composition, but I was too busy being a conspicuous success to go to his classes much. Also, because of missing so many classes, I had nightmares for the next twenty years about having to take tests in classes where I didn't even know where the class met.

During my junior year a gal who was involved in the same campus activity scene started to hustle me. I reciprocated because it was the easiest thing to do. We started going together the spring of my junior year. She loved me—unfortunately for her—and she was a lot like me, so we got along in a rather dull fashion.

Wince from Jackie again. "God—to be called dull. I guess I'd rather be called anything in the world besides dull. I hope that girl doesn't read this." And that is one of the main reasons Jackie attracted me in the first place. She is at the opposite end from being dull. Remember, I'm not saying the other gal was dull. She wasn't. No one is. That was just our relationship to each other.

In January of my senior year I was a chaperon on the University's ski train to Duluth, Minnesota. A friend and I were chaperons because we were big men on campus and veterans and over twenty-one—just barely. Saturday night there was a dance at the Duluth hotel for all of us on the ski train. My buddy and I spotted two girls sitting there. One is now my wife, Jackie, and the other was her friend. I, with my unerring eye, went for Jackie's friend. She was really stacked, and I noticed that right away. My friend took Jackie and we all danced. Jackie dumped my friend, but I spent the evening dancing with her friend and talking very seriously at great length.

The next day at the ski hill Jackie came up to me and my friend and started talking to us. I saw right away that this girl was different and I was fascinated. She was laughing all the time and she looked at the world lightly. She made me laugh. Jackie was younger by almost four years and she was at the opposite end of the world from an egghead like me. We started going together right away. But I put off telling my other girlfriend the truth until she finally confronted me. I hated scenes, so I would go to any length to avoid them. It took me nearly forty more years to find I had to be honest when I found myself in a pickle. But even more to the point, as I got over needing messes in my life, I stopped getting in so many messes.

At the time, I was somewhat embarrassed by what I saw as Jackie's lack of intellectualism. I'd take her into my group of intellectual friends and feel kind of funny that I had this young noncerebral girl with me. At the time, I didn't know that Jackie thought that my friends and I didn't have sense enough to pound sand in a rathole, for all of our brains.

Another thing I found out later was that Jackie's I.Q. was comfortably higher than mine and most of my friends. She seemed somewhat dumb to me because she refused to take the world as seriously as we did. I noticed, though, that all of my male egghead friends were pretty fascinated by her. Because she was so pretty and warmhearted, they were able to adjust to her lack of interest in the political problems of the world. She was a breath of fresh air in our fairly dull crowd. So, I felt embarrassed, but at the same time I felt a lot of fascination, too. Something deep inside told me that here was the balance I needed, here was someone who was deeply moved by some of the same things I was. Here was a soul mate who would stick with me no matter how tough the going got.

Now you might wonder how some mixed-up twenty-three-year-old guy like me could have figured all that out. I didn't figure it out logically, so there had to be something lots bigger than logic operating.

Jackie was aware of some of these feelings of mine about her lack of interest in the cosmic issues, but she just felt they came from my being a jerk. But she saw that I was a balance to her, also. She knew that she needed more of my plodding ways to offset her twittering around and never sticking to anything. One of the first things she knew that she would have to teach me, though, was how to laugh so I could lighten up.

We shared many common beliefs and dreams from the beginning. We both loved books and music. Some of our first dates were listening to a program called "Let's Listen to the Classics" on the car radio, and reading and discussing Kahlil Gibran's *The Prophet*. We agreed with what was written in that book and in many ways the agreement found there gave us the deep understanding of our deeply shared interests, a feeling that has never left us no matter what we have gone through with each other.

At the University I was in ROTC because I was determined that if I had to go back in the Army again, it wouldn't be as an enlisted man. I got money each month from ROTC. I had myself vaccinated with whooping cough germs so I could sell my blood back to the University once every six weeks or so for a healthy sum. I had a half-time job with a real crazy neurotic where I didn't show up much except to get my paycheck. That was good for a hundred dollars a month. And I had my monthly check from the GI Bill. So I had about two hundred and fifty dollars a month for spending money. Today that would be like seven hundred and fifty dollars or more a month to throw away.

I remember one time my mother suggested that maybe I should pay a little money each month for board and room. I thought that might be all right later on when I got things together better but not for right now, so I just ignored her suggestion. Like an alcoholic or a drug addict, I needed my money for my escapes, so all the other things in life had to be provided by someone else. None of my money was used up on nonessentials like food and shelter. I didn't even have a car to keep up, since I borrowed the old man's car. So I had a lot of money to throw around. My wife thought I was rich.

How we came to get married is interesting, and typical of the way I was. We'd gone together about fifteen or sixteen months and things were progressing. Jackie was doing her best to be a good Catholic girl. She finally came to see, "Hey, either we get married or we quit seeing each other. This has gone as far as it can go. I can't take any more of this." She was pretty clear and direct even then. I had come to see the same thing, and it was clear to me, too, that Jackie was the one for me, but I was afraid of marriage and commitment. I didn't want to decide anything, I just wanted to stumble along the way we were without any regard for the next day and the progression of the courtship we were in.

The only marriage I knew much about was the one my folks had. They had fights that really scared me. My mother would stand there and torment my father. And he would keep on doing the things that made her angry. She would torment him so that I would want to crawl through a crack in the floor and disappear. What was the problem? Was the problem marriage, or their marriage, or me? Well, now I can see the problem was how I reacted to what was going on. If they had had a nice, quiet marriage, I would have been bored and complained about that and used that to justify my problems. How could a person with my neurotic nature see the truth of my parents' marriage? Their marriage lasted nearly thirty years, until my father's death at fifty-four. Their marriage weathered many severe traumas that would have broken other marriages, even back then when divorce was uncommon. So the big point, as I see it now, wasn't my folks' marriage but how I reacted to it.

Sure, fighting scares me. But I think fighting would have scared me and I would have been scared of marriage even if my folks had had a perfect marriage. I'm just not comfortable anymore blaming my problems on situations in the past. And I'm not comfortable with the constant, self-serving analysis that a psychological approach to my life keeps me into. How often does a psychological approach to life lead a person to the idea that the person using it was bad and all the other people were good? You never hear that result of a psychological approach, do you? It's always that "I was a nice little guy and the bad people and bad situations nearly destroyed me." So the psychological approach is almost always used to blame other people and circumstances for problems and never the sick mind that is using the psychological approach.

But look what would happen if the psychological approach put the blame on you and me. "Your troubles are all your fault. Stop causing your own troubles and stop blaming the people around you and in your past. What's happening to you is all your own fault. All you need to do to have a happy life is to put it all down and live at peace with the loving God who made you and all his people. Get out of your selfishness and self-centeredness. Stop blaming people and start forgiving people for what you thought they did to you. Just put it all down and turn to the loving God within you and you'll have peace and happiness instantly."

If the psychological approach took that tack with us, how long would we keep coming back to pay the psychologist? That approach doesn't fall sweetly on the ear. It hurts our puny little ego and makes us feel bad, maybe even makes us mad. We wouldn't come back for more of that story. But that's the story the spiritual approach offers us. That's why we won't take the spiritual approach until we're really at the bottom and suffering from what the psychological approach to life has produced. Then we're ready.

So that's why my analysis of my folks' marriage was so self-serving at the time. I was afraid of marriage and it must be somebody's fault, so I blamed them. I came out of a little town in southern Minnesota where I saw lots of good marriages among my aunts and uncles and other people in the town. Why didn't I say, "I'm afraid of marraige. That's my problem. Sure I suffered at what I saw my folks doing, but they are the exception. Most marriages I know work beautifully and I can hardly wait to get married to this lovely gal." You won't hear a statement like that out of a neurotic, and that's what I was.

So for all kinds of reasons, I had a ton of fears and emotions about women and marriage. So I was not real interested in the idea of getting married. When Jackie put it to me that we were either going to get married or quit going together, I was forced to make a decision. This was the first of many times in our marriage when my wife would speak the truth and I'd be sitting there avoiding reality with my head in the sand hoping I wouldn't have to do anything. So I said, "Okay, we will get married." Real romantic! Each of us likes to think that we are unique, that our problems come from some unique circumstances in our lives. I don't believe that. We've all had problems of one kind or another, and that's not unique. So Jackie and I got married.

I was so irresponsible I made no provision for money for the little weekend honeymoon we were taking. My dad was real irresponsible too, so I was put in the position of having to pay for the rent of his tuxedo and some other things that stripped me down even further, so I think I had about twenty dollars for our honeymoon. Thank God, one of Jackie's relatives gave her another twenty dollars, so we were able to stay the night at the Lowell Inn in Stillwater, Minnesota, have breakfast, and then go to Brainerd, where we would live.

That whole blind thoughtless mess on my part was a complete mystery to me for a long time. But recently, I have come to an understanding that helps me realize what was going on at the time. Because of my own compulsion, I was in a preoccupied daze. I didn't know what was going on.

Ours was a typical neurotic marriage: you take one neurotic and you lean them up against another neurotic and hope they will stand up. It doesn't work because if either one of them moves, the whole thing just falls down. I call our marriage "neurotic" when I want to avoid going into detail, but I see now, for the purposes of this book, a little more explanation is needed. A neurotic, as I am using it, is a person whose drug is helplessness, hopelessness, and chaos. A preoccupation with hopelessness and the chaos of their melodrama is the way they escape from facing life. How can they be a part of a relationship with anyone when they are in the midst of overwhelming problems? If you want to test this idea, just try taking one of their problems away from the neurotic. They hold on to that problem with a grip of steel. And that's why neurotics are so good at creating problems. Problems are their alcohol and they need a good supply to help them avoid looking at themselves. The more pressure they face to look at themselves, the more problems they will list for you. If they ever run the risk of running low on problems, they run out and create new ones.

About the only thing more pathetic than the neurotic is the person trying to help the neurotic solve their problem, or trying to help them see their problem isn't so bad. What the helper doesn't know is that the neurotic needs that problem and only wants to pretend not to need it. And of course the person helping the neurotic is usually only doing the helping to run away from facing their own life. So the mellow-drama goes round and round like the dog chasing its own tail.

The thing that Jackie and I have had going for us ever since we first met is that we have good hearts toward each other. There was an earnestness in me and an earnestness in Jackie. There was in both of us a deep desire to really try to make the very best of things. We laughed a lot and enjoyed each other.

Both Jackie and I laughingly say we made a terrible mistake early in our lives. From our earliest times, even before we met, we each had a hunger for God. We wanted to be God's man and God's woman. One of my wife's earliest childhood memories was of wanting to be a saint. That's very dangerous to do, because when you pray for wisdom, do you know what you're going to get? When you pray for wisdom you're going to get troubles. And then after you work your way through the troubles, you'll have wisdom. So that was the fundamental mistake we made, wanting to be God's people. Neither of us has ever been satisfied to stay unaware of ourselves and others and to remain incurious about how it all fit in with God.

A year and three months after we were married we had a handicapped child. She had to have brain surgery when she was ten days old or she'd have died. I was twenty-four, Jackie was twenty-one, and we had to decide what to do. Here were these surgeons saying, "Should we operate or shouldn't we?" How could we possibly answer? We didn't know anything. They could just as well have asked a wall that question and they would have gotten just as good an answer. We were like a couple of chips floating on a river at flood stage. We just went along with it, doing what we could. We didn't have any experience to help us make that decision on such a life-and-death issue.

I see now that's why it's such a help not to know the future. If we knew what was going to happen, before it happened, we would be sure that we would never be able to handle it. But by not knowing, we are able to do what we have to when the time comes.

"Do what you think best" was the only answer we could give. And they saved her life. To do this they had to cut away part of the cerebellum of her brain. This damage was in addition to the damage done by the pressure of the spinal fluid that had built up. This meant our daughter had cerebral palsy. That term was just coming into use at the time. The doctors didn't tell us any of this. From experience, they knew we would most likely run away from them to other doctors in a search for answers that didn't exist or in a denial of what we were faced with. They knew we were in for a lifelong heartache, but they weren't able, for some reason or other, to tell us what we were faced with. Our daughter cried day and night for almost a year, and the toll it took on her, and on us, and on our own parents, her grandparents, was immeasurable.

Still, seeing her now at age thirty-four, we certainly are grateful to have her in our lives, and I am sure she is grateful to have been allowed to live her life.

A year and a half after Janet was born, Jackie was reading the story "Karen" by Marie Killelea in the *Ladies' Home Journal.* She realized that Janet was an ataxic cerebral-palsied child. We were living in Kansas City at the time and she went and asked a doctor if this was so. He said, "Yes, that is what she has."

Physical therapy was in its bare beginnings then, coming out of World War II. From descriptions in the story "Karen," I bolted some pipes to our coffee table to make walking bars. I made a harness out of diapers and straps to take Janet outside and help support her while she tried to walk. Two years later we bought her a child's leather football helmet and padded it with foam rubber so Janet wouldn't kill herself falling. We began a rudimentary form of therapy on our own. Later Janet had the best therapy available in the country when we moved back to Minneapolis and she went to Michael Dowling School for Crippled Children. We moved from the suburb we lived in back into Minneapolis so Janet could go to the Dowling school.

Of course in those days, because we were good Catholics, we had more babies. There were two kinds of people who had lots of babies in those days, Catholics and sex maniacs. I was both. In twenty-eight months Jackie had three children, and we added two later after she took time out to have a couple of back surgeries and to see a psychiatrist about why she was so depressed all the time.

Now we'll talk about how I supported this growing family of mine. When I got out of the University it never occurred to me to apply to a good company for a job. Some of my friends were going to work at places like Pillsbury and General Mills, Northwest Bancorporation, Honeywell, and Minnesota Mining. But not me. Not a loser like me. I'd go to some rinky-dink, crummy little outfit to look for work. I also didn't know anything about the world of work. I finally took a job selling market research on straight commission, the most ignorant, stupidest deal in the world.

Jackie said to me, "Before we get married, you're going to have to find a real job." So I got a job in Brainerd, Minnesota, selling newspaper advertising for fifty dollars a week. It never occurred to me to go to one of those fine companies headquartered in Minneapolis and get a job. Looking back now I can see that I would have had a good chance at a job at one of those places. But back then, the way I was, I felt such a sense of inadequacy and insecurity that I didn't dare apply at a good company. I was impressed by my close friends' getting jobs at those companies, but it never occurred to me to apply.

I had another crummy job after I left Brainerd, and finally in late 1951, with two babies and a wife, I got a decent job with a good outfit and they sent me to Kansas City for a year and then brought me back to Minneapolis. I got myself hired in this good advertising agency because I was already starting to be a real student of advertising. The guy who hired me saw the promise in me and they gave me a year of training as a copywriter. Then they brought me back to Minneapolis and made a mistake with me. They thought I could be an account executive, a guy who works with the agency's clients managing the work on their accounts. I had a gift of gab and presented a good appearance, but I was no more capable of doing that kind of administrative and executive work than I was of flying to the moon.

I would make out a list of things to do in the morning—one, two, three, four—but I was so afraid of that work that I'd never get the first thing done. When the boss asked me if I had finished a job, I'd lie to him. Finally in desperation I'd get something done. Everything was late and everything was all screwed up.

At the end of 1953, my wife was in the hospital. She had had a spinal fusion. They got her up after a week or so and the fusion hadn't fused, so she had to go back into surgery again. With the two surgeries, she had about three weeks of morphine and Demerol day and night. They pulled her off that stuff cold turkey. She had the D.T.'s and was generally crazy from all that surgery and dope. In the middle of this, the boss, a very fine man, called me in just after Christmas at year-end bonus time and said, "You don't get a bonus. We should fire you. You haven't been doing your work." But I had written some good copy while I was living in fear and wasn't doing what I was supposed to be doing as an account executive, so he said he'd give me another chance if I wanted to try to be a copywriter.

I made the switch to copywriting and was very successful. But inside of three years I became restless. I very much admired the advertising Leo Burnett was doing in his agency in Chicago. He was coming to town to speak. The night before his speech I got all revved up and wrote out my advertising creed. After his speech, I went up to him and handed him what I had written. It was good enough to interest him. He asked me to come down and be interviewed for a job, and I was able to pass their scrutiny.

My work in advertising had been very productive and well regarded, but what I didn't see then was that my anxiety was so high that I wasn't capable of doing good work when the pressure was heavy. My going into that high-powered agency in Chicago made about as much sense as some little country club pro going on the professional golf tour. He might have a good game in the nice, protected setting of his friends at the country club, playing a course he knows like the back of his hand, but that's not the pro tour. Out on the tour he has to play well without any support. He will come to times when he has to win money so he can afford to check out of his motel. A golfer with high anxiety, no matter how good he is, can't handle that.

Some of those big-time advertising people were good men and some were sharks. I couldn't cut it. I had so much anxiety I could just barely work under that pressure. I wasn't seasoned enough and my big ego that got me down there in the first place was humbled, I'll tell you. After about six months, I was called in and told I wasn't as good as I told them I was and they were cutting my pay twenty percent. Jackie was pregnant with our fourth child and we faced a huge pay cut. That wouldn't do for us in Chicago. I called Minneapolis and got a job at an agency there and we put our house on the market. I was determined to stay out the year so they wouldn't say I was a quitter, but I knew I belonged back in Minneapolis.

Near the end of the year, we sold our house, I turned in my notice and called my new agency in Minneapolis to tell them I'd be there in a month. They said they'd changed their minds and didn't want me now. "You can't do this to me," I thought, but they could and they did. We packed up the kids that night and took the train to Minneapolis. I made some calls and got a one-man advertising agency started. I was quite successful from the first month. I was soon making more money than I had in Chicago. As I mentioned earlier, a hallmark of a neurotic is that they can snatch defeat from the jaws of victory, so the minute things started going pretty good, I had to louse them up. The way I did it was by spending more money than I made. My answer to this was to try to make more money and more money and invest it so that I could retire early from a job I thought I hated. I presented this grandiose plan to a friend who advised me on financial matters. It was just an hour later that I had a heart attack at the age of thirty-five.

In the hospital room, as I lay there and waited for Jackie to come, all of a sudden I saw that I'd poured my life down a rathole trying to impress other people. A strong feeling came over me. I saw that never again was I going to do anything I didn't believe in. The spiritual awakening I had there in that emergency room fell on a lot better ground than some of those earlier spiritual awakenings—not completely fertile ground, but a lot more fertile ground.

I was determined to do only what I believed in. My next shock came when I found out that I didn't know what I believed in. I could just as well have flipped a coin for all I knew about what I believed, but I made a start just doing the best I could. For the first time, I became more receptive and open to the people around me and sought their ideas. I asked my wife what she thought I should be. She said, "I think you should go back to school and be a teacher." I asked a client what he thought and he said, "You should be a teacher." I asked a neighbor what he thought and he said, "I think you should be anything but a business man." I sold my business on the telephone and went back to the University of Minnesota, got a Ph.D., and started teaching there.

All during this time, Jackie and I had tried to be the best parents we could. I had worked at being a good husband and Jackie had tried to be a good wife. We had been very active in our church. I had joined the Catholic Church in 1952, after Janet's birth. The experience of being so helpless in the face of Janet's handicap finally humbled my big mind enough to make me willing to consider the idea that I couldn't do everything myself. This made me more receptive to religion and showed me that there must surely be some power bigger than me. We worked hard to be good Catholics. We did what they told us and we believed what they said.

One of the Catholic magazines we took told us we must not support sin in any form. They said that divorce was a sin and we should not support it. Jackie's favorite brother had been divorced. When he remarried we wished him well, but we said that we could not let our children think we supported divorce by coming to his wedding. Jackie still just dies of embarrassment when she thinks of this.

That's how it was in the fifties and early sixties. Good Catholics were pretty hidebound. Since then Jackie and I have had to eat those words, I'll tell you. Our children have had five marriages and four divorces between them to date. We were sincere, we were well meaning, we were trying to do what we thought was right, but we didn't pay much attention to our hearts. We were so full of what was right, that we couldn't see what was good.

When I had that spiritual awakening there in the hospital, I see now that I didn't turn to the idea a church could help me. I'd belonged to five churches by then and none of them had yielded up to me what I was needing in that hospital room. I didn't think about going to the churches. I just realized I needed to find out what I believed in, and I went out in life and started searching hard for the answers I needed so desperately.

I talked about these things to my friends. I'd puzzle out these things with students in my classes at the University. We wanted to move to Montana, so in 1967 I took a year's leave of absence from the University of Minnesota to try Montana because my wife and I loved the West so much.

After a year or so in Montana, I finally gave up my desire to be rich and famous so I could be somebody. I had consciously made the decision that I was just going to be a little guy, and I was just going to take what life handed me. I bought a little house. In the basement bedrooms, students who had rented the rooms had kicked holes in some of the walls. I was so ashamed of that house for fear of what my rich relatives would think of it when they came to visit. Of course the rich relatives never came. For a guy who always had to have fancy clothes, a fancy house, fancy cars, fancy everything, to have a house in such disrepair was a real comedown. I had nightmares after I put in the bid for that house. But I had decided that I was going to live just a calm, quiet life and that I was going to give up my hard-charging ways.

In May 1969, I said the first book, *I Ain't Much, Baby—But I'm All I've Got*, to a group of nurses. I really spoke out of my deepest heart to those nurses about what I'd found as I'd searched for the things I deeply believed in. The seminar was basically about communication. I told them that the first ninety percent of communication was having a good heart toward another person, it isn't about where you put the commas and periods and about using short words. If you have a good heart toward another person, you have no problems communicating with them. I said that the secret of having a good heart toward another person is having a good heart toward yourself. I told them what I had been doing in the seven years since I had that heart attack to get a better heart toward myself. Seven years of searching, that's what that book was about, a report of what I'd found out.

After I finished that seminar to those nurses I saw I'd said a book. I wrote *I Ain't Much Baby . . .* directly off the tapes of the seminar because by then the discipline of speaking in the classroom had taught me to speak sentences and paragraphs. The book became a huge success and fed that sick ego of mine. I went right back to wanting money, fame, and power so I could be somebody.

From 1969 until 1976 I really went crazy again. I now see pretty clearly what happened, but at the time it was like I was in a hurricane. In fact, one of our favorite authors wrote a book about his "hurricane years." I don't believe anymore that it is the calendar age I was at that caused anything. I think at certain times in our lives we face certain problems and it doesn't have anything to do with our age. At the same time I was going crazy, my kids were going crazy and my wife was going crazy. My kids were teenagers at that time, it was at the height of the Vietnam war, and the drug scene began to race through our sleepy university town. Our kids started experimenting.

My wife was an alcoholic and was also addicted to prescription drugs, but neither of us knew that this was the problem at that time. She was always home, she did the cleaning and cooking and made cookies and cakes for the kids and was there for them to talk to day and night. She was a churchgoer and was going to Mass daily then. On the surface things looked all right. But she was getting quieter and quieter all the time. She had been put on tranquilizers by her doctor way back in 1954 after that awful back surgery. She had settled down with just one or two pills a day, but by then fifteen years of pills had taken their toll.

She was slipping fast from her psychological dependency on those pills into full-blown addiction. She would get scared about taking pills and try to stop. She would then return to her first love, alcohol. Because she was always home, the meals were always on time, and she didn't pass out, I didn't see the signs and neither did she. We both knew we weren't communicating, but we used that to blame each other and to pull apart even more. I call that time in our marriage the Ice Age. Some of our kids were becoming addicted too, and I didn't know that.

I had my own thing going. My addiction was a sexual compulsion that had suddenly erupted like a sleeping volcano. My compulsion was as addictive as my wife's and kids' addictions. In the course of that time I did everything harmful to my wife that it's possible for a man to do to a woman. And then, after about seven years of this, I had another spiritual awakening. I suddenly saw that I was a dependent baby and that I was completely irresponsible. I saw that Jackie was the woman I wanted to be with more than anyone in the world, but if that was the case, why didn't I act like it? I saw that, at any threat of a fight between me and Jackie, I would just tuck my tail between my legs and run like a dog. It was "peace at any price," a complete running away from responsibility. I was this way with not only my wife, but also my children. "I don't want to get into it. I don't want to hear about it. I don't want to see it," was the way I was. So I wasn't a husband to my wife or a father to my children.

In 1976, in the brief space of a few hours, I had that spiritual awakening. I saw that if I made a new marriage, I would soon have it just as screwed up as the one I was in. I saw that I wanted to go back to my marriage and be a man, something I realized I didn't know anything about.

I said to myself, "I don't want to live this way anymore. I'm going to start being the best kind of man I know how to be and be as responsible as I can be." So I cleaned up my act and made up my mind to concentrate my sexual energies one hundred percent on my wife from that moment on. I knew that would be a tough thing to do when I'd lived the kind of life I had lived.

I had a terrible problem in my relationships with women. At that time I sexualized all relationships with women. I didn't know how to relate to a woman in any other way. They were objects to use. They had been objects of fantasy from my earliest years. I was afraid to have them close to me, I didn't know what to do with them. To protect myself from intimacy, I'd turn every relationship into a sexualized relationship, where sexual thinking and sexual fantasy was involved. I related with all women from a sexual standpoint unless they were over seventy or under eighteen, and I didn't relate to them because they had nothing for me.

Well, I set about doing what my spiritual awakening showed me.

I began to be as responsible as I could see how to be. I concentrated sexually only on Jackie to the best of my ability from that day on. Like all beginners, though, we don't do everything very smoothly or very well at first. My wife had to witness a lot of what she now calls my "sexual crap" being acted out between me and other women as flirtations or other types of socially acceptable but uncomfortable behavior.

In the years before, I had been leaving home a lot. Jackie suspected, and did a lot of grieving, but like most women in a situation like that she didn't really want to know what she knew, and that was a hard situation for her.

Now, here was her wandering boy, home and being bossy as hell. I was making noises like a responsible husband for the first time, and then on top of that, because I was determined to keep everything I did out in the open, every time another woman and I connected with each other in a flirty way, Jackie was often around to see it. Jackie thought I was trying to drive her mad because I was sending even more overt mixed messages to her than I had back in the days when my compulsion was more secretive, and I was leaving town a lot.

One of the first things I faced was that my financial affairs were chaos. I had wasted or lost a lot of money by being careless and by indulging myself and the kids in ways that were not good, that were even very harmful. I had serious legal exposures. I had all kinds of loose ends that, in my careless living, I hadn't taken care of.

Our house was a mess. We'd moved from the little house to a beautiful log home up a mountain canyon outside Bozeman in 1971, but I hadn't done one thing to make it a better house from the day we moved in. Jackie got the boys to clean the garage and do some of the "man" things around the house. She and the boys had even stained the logs every year, but the boys had done a typical young boy's job and stained the windows sometimes as well as the screens, so there were messes all around.

The house was in a pretty spot, but we couldn't afford much when we had built it and it had a little, dark cramped living room with hardly enough space for the whole family when we gathered together. I had made enough money over those years to have expanded that house but I hadn't seen the need for it. With my new awareness, I saw that Jackie was a person who needed lots of space and I had stuck her in a cave. So the house needed fixing up and expanding.

Why did Jackie stay around? She stayed around partly because she was a good person and her Catholic upbringing absolutely forbade divorce. Also, family meant everything to her. But it was partly because, as she sees now, she was a dependent baby too, and this was coming out of her own addiction. She was just as sick as I was, and by then things were coming to an end for her too. One of our boys said to her, "Mom, you're going to die sitting in that dining-room chair looking out that window." She heard him and she knew it was true, but she seemed at that time to be just paralyzed looking out that window wondering where I was or where the kids were and what kind of phone call was going to come next. What was happening in our family was eating her alive, and she was starting to want to die.

Here's where a loving God stepped into Jackie's life. That was in the summer of 1977, when Walther Lechler told her she was dying when he came to teach the School of Life with me. She came to the school Walther and I were giving. It started on a Sunday. On Tuesday Jackie quit a twenty-four-year dependency on tranquilizers. She just cold-turkeyed herself off those pills and didn't tell anyone. She's lucky she didn't have a seizure or something worse.

On Thursday, Dr. Lechler was carefully taking the class through a demonstration of scream therapy. He had everyone join hands and scream as loudly as they could for five minutes. The time came to stop screaming and Jackie didn't stop. She couldn't. A combination of withdrawing from those pills and the pain of all the years just poured out of her. It was a terrifying thing to watch. It could have been a very dangerous thing also, except that two highly trained medical men were there—Dr. Lechler and his associate from West Germany, Dr. Horst Esslinger. This is why Jackie is very cautious when telling people about using scream therapy as a tool. The tool is so powerful it is eminently dangerous except in the most careful and qualified hands.

Jackie went to West Germany for treatment and went into the full story about herself and her circumstances in her book, *I Exist, I Need, I'm Entitled,* that she wrote with Dr. Lechler some years ago. The book's out of print now, but you can find it in some libraries.

Jackie finished her treatment in the spring of 1978. On her return home we had our moment of truth. What she hadn't wanted to know, she now knew for sure, because I told her the truth about me. She looked and acted like a different person because of what she had experienced in West Germany. Looking back now, with the benefit of quite a few years, she feels so grateful that she had no more mood-altering chemicals going into her body. She could see so much more clearly that what she had been blaming on herself was my own problem and not hers. This gave her the strength to go through all that was ahead for both of us.

The summer and fall of 1979, three of our kids went through treatment for alcohol and drug abuse. Jackie and I went through family weeks with them and also had a family week between the two of us. The family counselor we worked with said afterward, "Jess, you've got a lot of guilt and your kids are using it on you to control you and get what they want out of you." I could see the truth of that and tried to get rid of my guilt, but I couldn't. Some of our close friends who watched all of this and held our hands through all of the pain could only say, "My God, my God."

It had come to the point now where we'd been working at a more and more intense pace in our marriage. I'd managed to make some amends to my wife. In making amends we can ask forgiveness. She had forgiven me, but it was a lot harder to forget, especially during the years that I was still doing some flirtatious things and she was witnessing them. There were times when she doubted her ability to stay sane if she continued in our marriage, but she kept hanging in there because of her deep belief in commitment.

The day came, about two years after she returned from West Germany, when she was well enough and clear enough to seriously consider divorce. She laughs now and says that all that stopped her from divorcing me was her belief that this was just another way I had of forcing her to do my work. She was thinking that I wanted a divorce, because of my behavior, and was acting that way to try to make her angry enough to file for divorce from me, and that way I could have a divorce but still keep my "good ol' Jess" image. If I wanted a divorce, she figured, I would have to get one myself. In the meantime, she was going to take care of herself and build a life for herself. Jackie was getting over her dependence on me and her fear of being abandoned. She was learning that she was a good person and needed to see her life as her own, not one all mixed up in the lives of me and our children.

I was going through this same process myself. One day on an

early morning horseback ride, Jackie got upset for what looked like no good reason and blew up at me. I tried to find some way to get to the bottom of what was going on but couldn't. We came back and I put the horses away. I came in the house and told Jackie that I didn't want to spend one more day living with her if she didn't want to be with me. I told her I was going down to the office and add up the values of everything we had and that she got half. Or, she could take a regular income, if she preferred that. But I didn't want her to be in the house that night unless she wanted to be there.

As we talked further, I found that Jackie had been low on blood sugar on that early morning ride and that's what had led to the blowup. I said that that was fine but my point still stood, because I felt that we shouldn't be together out of any dependency but only because it was something each deeply wanted. That day was about a year after Jackie came home from treatment and was so important for me, because it was me breaking out of the need for a dependent relationship just as Jackie was doing. For me, this was part of the big step of breaking our neurotic dependence on each other so we could find the real reasons we were together in marriage, which were that we were soul mates and had a deep love for each other and a deep belief in God's grace that was strong enough to help carry us through those hard times.

To say that this was a dangerous time for both of us doesn't begin to tell the story, but with God's grace we survived, and we have learned a whole lot since. This is what makes me such a good teacher of this stuff. I only teach what I have experienced in the laboratory of my own life—and that's a lot.

This is my story up until a year ago. I gave the series of talks this book is based on at Dayspring Methodist Church in Phoenix during late February and early March of 1983. This is my story about as I told it the first night of those talks. But lots changes and happens as I say a book. It's like God is saying, "Okay, buster, I see you feel you're ready for some more self-knowledge on the subject you're going to write about. Well, I'll serve you up a good helping." And that's what God did for me in his infinite love and kindness. He gave me a big new hunk for my story in just the past year, right in the middle of that series of talks on marriage and since then. So you'll find the last year of my story in the chapter after the next one.

4.

〜

Meet the Crazy Mind

YOU'VE HEARD MY STORY. Where did all those catastrophes come from? Why did that marriage survive all those catastrophes when any one of them could have killed the marriage? This book is about a spiritual approach to marriage that Jackie and I have uncovered and discovered in our lives and the lives of the people in the marriages around us. What were the spiritual principles that were operating under the surface, unknown to us, that helped us through all the disasters we got through, and what was our biggest enemy in those early years?

When Janet was about four years old, we helped organize United Cerebral Palsy in Minneapolis. Many of the marriages of the parents of those handicapped children had already broken up. They couldn't stand that pressure. And that was thirty years ago when divorce wasn't nearly as common or as easy. So that was the first hurdle we got across. Others were the addictions of myself and my wife, then of our children, and all the catastrophes that I brought into the family with the consequences of my neuroticism and my addiction. The miracle to me is that the spiritual principles were operating under the surface to hold our marriage together despite all the chaos our crazy minds could produce.

From my experience, the biggest thing that keeps us from being able to practice the spiritual principles of marriage and is the foremost enemy of marriage is: our crazy minds. Those crazy minds of ours are not only the foremost enemies of our marriages, they are the enemies of everything else that is good in our lives. And it is those crazy minds that put us into the addictions and compulsions that rob us and so many people around us of most of our power of choice. Once we are into an addiction or compulsion, we are completely powerless. We have no choice but to go down to the bottom with it until we finally crash hard enough to be willing to give up listening to our crazy minds and search for a better answer. So, before we talk much about marriage, we need to look the enemy right in the eye—the crazy mind.

What was going on in the crazy mind of that little guy you were reading about in the chapter before as he struggled through that life? Why were all the sadnesses in that life? As Jackie and I were going through that life, the people around us who loved us could hardly bear to watch our suffering at times and wanted to get away from us. I even saw some people get angry at us because they had the feeling we must be doing something that caused all those disasters and why didn't we stop what we were doing to cause all the trouble? I now see more clearly what was going on. We were doing the best we could in our marriage with the love and knowledge we possessed. But the spiritual understanding we had of the way life is and how it works wasn't strong enough to help us cope. The spiritual understandings we had worked fine for many of our friends, but those spiritual understandings weren't strong enough to handle the problems of our fully addicted family. We were stubbornly persisting in old ways of doing things, that we couldn't make work for us. Yet I see now our failures were all perfect for us because they were the experiences we needed to finally break us enough to make us open to a new and better way.

Why did we persist so long in those old ways? Where did those old ways come from? Here we have two obvious choices: We can take the idea that is so popular today, one of the psychological approaches, and say we were programmed that way. Our parents, our environment, our institutions made us that way. Or, we can take the old idea of original sin that says we were born sinful and would go to hell unless we got saved.

I've never liked either of those two ideas. But it wasn't until about ten years ago that I finally found a spiritual idea about what happens to us when we are born that finally helped me make sense out of my own life and the lives I saw around me. That idea was the simple statement of the Cheyenne Indians. Their basic idea is that the one way in which all of the People (the Cheyennes) are equal is that they are all born separate and alone from God. From this it follows naturally that the reason for our life here on earth is to make our spiritual quest to God. That was an idea that made some sense to me and fit with the concept I had by then of a kind and loving God.

I saw that God could have created many different kinds of worlds but there were two that were obvious to me. I had earlier railed against God, feeling that if God had wanted me to be good, why hadn't he made me that way? I came to see differently. God could have made us all lovely Boy and Girl Scouts who just spent our time helping old people across the street and singing in the choir. As I thought about that, it didn't take too long to see that that wasn't such a great idea. What does love mean when it is the automatic and forced response? If we were made Boy Scouts and Girl Scouts, we would be no more than puppets—automatons who simply walked mechanically through life. If we have trouble seeing any point in this life, as it is, just imagine living a life like that and finding a point in it.

Love only means something when we have a choice. If a man and a woman were stranded on a desert island and, after a month, he tells her how much he loves her, it doesn't move her the same way as it would if they were both back in the big city.

If we are born separate from God, then coming into love means something to us because it is moving away from something other than love toward what is love.

As I thought more and more about the idea of the Cheyennes, I saw how I had distorted most religious teaching. I was talking about my new understanding of God to Jackie and she said, "I think the first question in the catechism is on that point." I went and looked it up and, sure enough, the first line of the Baltimore Catechism all Catholics learned from was to the effect of: Why are we born? And the answer was: To know God, to love him, and to serve him in this world. I saw the same thing in many other religious expressions of why we were born. In the spiritual literature outside the formal religions, I came to find that a very common expression of our birth was that it was at our birth that we forgot where we came from. One of the most beautiful expressions of this is in a poem I was given by my son Joe.

THE MONUMENT
BY BLAINE M. YORGANSON

God,
> Before He sent His children to earth
> Gave each of them
> A very carefully selected package
> Of troubles.

These,
> He promised, smiling,
> Are yours alone.
> No one else may have the blessings
> These problems will bring you.

And only you
> Have the special talents and abilities
> That will be needed
> To make these problems
> Your servants.

Now go down to your birth
> And to your forgetfulness.
> Know that I love you
> Beyond measure.

These problems that I give you
> Are a symbol of that love.
> The monument you make of your life
> With the help of your problems
> Will be a symbol of your
> Love for me.

Your Father

That seemingly simple little poem is one of the expressions I like best of the understanding I now have about why we are here and what we are doing. I was born like the Cheyennes, separate and alone, and my life is my voyage to God. The problems I have in life come from two sources. The first is from some kind of destiny, so these are problems I need to accept and be grateful for. The source of the rest of my problems is my trying to live separate and alone, away from God and all his lovely children. I get rid of this kind of problem as soon as I stop living so much in myself and start living more with God. So the problems you saw in my life and in our marriage as I told my story were these two kinds of problems:

my gifts from God and my self-created problems as I tried to live a life apart from the people around me and God. Since my idea that I was separate from God was a gift from him also, both kinds of problems I had were gifts from God.

What happened to me because I was born separate from God? I tried to use my head to figure some way out of the chaos and pain I saw around me. Gradually my mind got crazier and crazier as it would find its foolish notions in trouble. Rather than throw away one of its foolish notions, it would just invent new foolish notions to try to patch up the old foolish notion in a desperate attempt to make the whole mess work. My crazy mind thought that it—mind —was all there was. If it was challenged by the feeble voice of the spirit in me, my crazy mind would, like a spoiled child, insist it was right and any other voice inside was wrong. So that is how I see my crazy mind. Of course it blamed people and circumstances for what happened and was happening. But what else can you expect from a crazy mind but blame? A crazy mind will never accept responsibility for what it does. If it did it wouldn't be crazy anymore.

It's my crazy mind that's the enemy of my marriage. What kind of marriage can that crazy mind of mine make? What chance does a person with such a crazy mind have of really seeing another human being, to say nothing of understanding them?

As my crazy mind loses its power in my life and over me, I have less and less problems in my marriage. It is my crazy mind that is the manifestation of my separateness and aloneness. It wants to tell me others are the enemy. There's an anonymous verse that says:

> The world has not forsaken me
>   and set me out to die;
> This world is not the enemy
>   but rather that stranger—"I".

That idea is simple to express but it is the hardest thing in the world to hold on to. That "stranger—I" is my crazy mind. I don't want to know who I really am and where I came from. When I get even a small glimmer of the truth of who I am, I keep forgetting it the first chance I have. All life long, my crazy mind wants me to forget who I am and go back to being crazy full-time.

My first year at Montana State University I was teaching a freshman writing course. I was scared because this was a probationary period for me and I wanted to do everything right. I taught a course where there was a lecture once a week and the rest of the days were writing labs. I was so scared and wanted to do it right so badly that I blew the lecture the first week. The second week came, and I felt rushed and scared and I blew the lecture again.

By the time the third week rolled around, I saw that I couldn't teach someone else's way. I saw that I had to teach the only way I knew how. I explained the mistakes I had made to the class and told them how I was going to teach for the remaining seven lectures. I asked if there were any questions or comments. A kid in the front row raised his hand. I'll never forget him—his name was Phil Lalich and he was from Butte, Montana. "You know," he said, "for a smart guy, you sure make a lot of mistakes." Phil and I have been friends ever since. People from Butte have a straightforwardness about them I love. It isn't a very pretty town but its people are beautiful. It's a mining town with a lot of ethnics. Those ethnics mixed in together and made a lot of beautiful people with interesting names.

Phil Lalich is right—for a smart guy I do make a lot of mistakes. As I finally became more aware of all those mistakes, I finally started studying the mind. That's what helped me learn more about what original sin is, as the different religions call it. As I said, I think original sin might be another way of saying what the Cheyenne Indians were talking about when they said that the one way all people are equal is in their loneliness. I think this "sin" or "loneliness" is the mind. All of us are born with a mind, and for most of us it just kept getting crazier and crazier and crazier. We hate and fear the word "sin." But all "sin" means in its original is "missing the mark." What's so awful about that? Nothing is so awful about missing the mark. All of us beginners do a lot of that in anything we try. Well, then, what's wrong with missing the mark or sin in our spiritual program? Nothing is wrong with missing the mark except our crazy mind. It wants to do everything perfectly, the first time. If it can't do something perfectly, it won't play the game. So there's nothing wrong with sin, just our minds.

The sin we all start out with is the pain of being separate and alone and all the crazy things our minds will take us into in an attempt to escape that pain. The mind is just like a new puppy. We're born with it and it is completely untrained and doesn't know what it is or what it's supposed to do. It starts taking in impressions from the first breath we draw. It doesn't remember where it has come from and it doesn't know where it is or what it is supposed to do. But it's aware and receiving messages right from that first breath, and the one thing it knows from that first breath is that it wants power and complete control.

Have you ever watched a new puppy when it's brought into its first home? It starts to race around and sniff everything. It climbs all over everyone there, it runs into all the rooms of the house, it responds to every word everyone says to it, and then it usually squats and piddles on the best rug in the house. This brings out the rolled newspaper and discipline begins. The puppy is scared to death one minute and licking your face the next. Total confusion. Pretty soon that puppy is in the process of tearing up everyone and everything. That puppy is our crazy mind.

That is why we live in utter chaos. The mind doesn't want to be the servant, it wants to be the master. We're born with these minds. These minds are unbelievably fine things for getting us to the post office. There isn't a single person I know who can't sign their name, who can't accomplish any of the other very important intellectual skills like reading and mathematics. I don't know a single person who can't look out and perceive and observe and use their fine mind to compare and evaluate. We all can make judgments. "Is this color blue or green?" Or, "I've got a pair of red pants on, should I wear a white shirt or a pink shirt?" We all have this function working in our mind so we have the power to discriminate and judge. That's beautiful.

There's another part of the mind that lets us take all that the mind has seen and heard and throw it into that big filing cabinet called the subconscious, where it will lie until it is needed. At some future date, our little computer called memory will bring it out of the subconscious just when it is needed and place it in the intellect ready for use. Under hypnosis one time I saw an adult completely relive her fifth birthday party. She was able to describe everyone who was there. So it's all there waiting for us, everything we've ever done or seen or heard, waiting to be used, even though we don't consciously have immediate access to it.

As a writer, I'm using this function of my mind all the time. It's like everything I've ever done or thought is in a big funnel. As I write, the contents of that funnel are ordering themselves and flowing down into the neck of the funnel in just the right order so they can flow out the tip of my ballpoint pen or through my fingers onto the word processor. The conscious mind can't do such a complex organizing job by itself. I know. I've tried that. But it is easy for the subconscious mind if it is handled lovingly.

We tap our subconscious to draw conclusions and often to have a deep wisdom. We can be very wise in our family life and our occupations. We can be very wise in investments. The mind can work just fine this way.

Where the mind goes completely crazy is in never being content to stay in its own territory. Who has ever seen a puppy come into the house and stay in the kitchen on its newspapers? No puppy has ever done that. They go around and make puddles on the floor wherever they please, the more excited they get the more puddles they make, and they want to chew on everything. I've got a lot of books that have the corners chewed off by puppies that have been in my home. The crazy mind refuses to stay in its territory. It wants the whole house and doesn't want to allow us to give our bodies or our spirits any attention.

This is the story of the first thirty-five years of my life. My crazy mind would be working against me. One of the most beautiful ways I've ever heard this explained was on a tape by an alcoholic named Bob E. from California. Bob E. wakes up in the morning and his first thought is, "I'm tired, I don't think I'll go to work today." Then his next thought is, "But if I don't go to work I'll be fired." So, Bob says, "I'm awake four seconds, I'm too tired to go to work and I've lost my job." His next thought is, "If I don't go to work and I lose my job then I'll lose this apartment because I only have a hundred dollars in the bank." So now he's been awake eight seconds, he's tired, he's out of work, and he's homeless. His next thought is, "My knee still hurts where I hit it on the coffee table. I wonder if I have cancer." Now he's been awake ten seconds, he's tired, he's lost his job, he's lost his home, and he might have the "Big C."

What an illustration this is of how our thoughts beat us up, how our crazy mind can put us down into exhaustion and depression in the snap of a finger. All of the functions that were working for Bob E. in that ten seconds are good and legitimate functions of the mind. It was his mind's ability to perceive that told him, "I'm tired." It was his mind's ability to project from experience that told him, "If I don't go to work I'll be fired." His ability to judge and evaluate told him, "I'll lose this apartment because I've only got a hundred dollars in the bank." But the functions were distorted because the thoughts were allowed to run wild. The crazy mind was in control.

It is so true that we are what we think. All of you have had the experience of having your mind suddenly recall an embarrassing incident from the party you were at the night before. You don't just think it, you begin to blush at the memory. Or, you are sitting at the office and you remember the guy who cut his car sharply in front of you an hour ago and you feel anger again and your heart starts to pound. Or, how about remembering a fight you had last week with your husband or wife? You suddenly feel frustrated and resentful and your shoulders droop, your stomach starts to hurt, and suddenly you are depressed.

The saddest example of this I've heard recently is the story of Bear Bryant. In the years before he retired, several different people all told the same story. When asked when he was going to retire, Bear Bryant always told them that he'd die if he retired. *Sports Illustrated* carried a story about how a writer who had heard this went to see Bear Bryant a month into retirement and remarked that he hadn't died yet. That story just hit the newsstands when Bear Bryant died. Another writer who attended his funeral and wrote a tribute to him made the comment that Bear Bryant often said that if he ever gave up the game of football he'd have a heart attack or die.

Words come true. Our thoughts are things. Our body reacts to a thought just like it was an actual event. I recently was with my friend Dorothy Black, a woman I had grown up with. Her folks were friends of my folks and I'd even stayed with her family three or four months in high school. Dorothy attended the marriage seminar where I did the beginnings of this book. She told me some people had asked her what I was like as a child. She told them I was happy, laughed a lot, liked a good joke, loved to be with people, and was well liked. Now, the way I had perceived my childhood was that I was lonely, not well liked, seldom laughed, and didn't have many friends. I believe Dorothy's perception of me is somewhat closer to the truth than mine. Okay, where is the difference? I was selectively distorting my experience to suit my crazy mind and to suit my needs, because I *wanted* to feel bad about myself. How can you constantly have a low opinion of yourself when you've got a lot of good things going for you? Simple. You constantly distort what you've got going for you.

To me, the distortions we choose for ourselves come closer to telling about us than so much present psychology does in looking for its scapegoats. The problem with scapegoating is that the power resides with the scapegoat. And as long as we choose to believe someone else or something else is to blame and is responsible for the way we are, we are prisoners of our own minds. We give them, or the scapegoat, power over our lives. The truth is, the power resides within ourselves if we are willing to grow up and put down our excuses. It doesn't matter that our foster-mother tried to stuff us in the oven because we were bad. Sure, that was a lovely story to help us feel sorry for ourselves. Sure, the story was good for lots of sympathy down at the clubhouse. But eventually we come to see we are, in a way, prisoners of our sad songs. For most of us our reasons have become our excuses. It is so helpful for me to realize that *I am the problem.* My parents are dead. I can't work out my excuses with them, I can't change how it was back then, and I can't change how it is now, either. *No human being can change reality; they can only change how they choose to experience reality.* That is where our real work is to be done in this life.

I believe that all of us have within us a power to choose how we will live our life today, and that power is the higher mind. For most of us the physical reality of our lives is all right; we just don't want to accept that it is all right. We live dissatisfied and uncomfortable lives because that is how we choose to view our lives. We choose to have anger or resentment or self-pity, and then we get a daily dose of the fruits of our choices.

Our intellect is excellent at discriminating and evaluating in the physical realm. We can find our way to the post office with it. We can do our daily work with it, we know when to get up, when to eat, when to go to work, what to do at work, when to go home, and when to go to bed. We can tell blue from green and evaluate whether blue or green is the proper color for us. Where we get into trouble is when we take the intellect into the spiritual realm. That's when we end up asking things like: "Have the Catholics or the Methodists got the sure path to heaven? I believe it's the Methodists. I've got to find a way to prove I'm right and discredit those false-believing Catholics." And that's the trouble.

The mind as we commonly think of it, the discriminating, evaluating mind, is not capable of making spiritual choices. The questions of who we are, what we're here for, what we're meant to be, those are spiritual questions. They can't be solved by the lower mind, any more than a calculator can show us television. Spiritual questions can be answered truthfully, only by the Higher Mind, that still, quiet voice of the spirit that lives deep within us. If we give the crazy mind a problem like that, it will screw it up for sure.

The crazy mind is a totalitarian dictator. The crazy mind is the intellect plus the ego, and it cannot afford to be wrong. It's like all totalitarian dictatorships. When something goes wrong it excuses itself based on circumstances. The Russian farm program has failed from a steady stream of forty years of unfortunate weather and other circumstances of that sort. Right in Russia they have two farm systems. They have the huge commune system, about ninety percent of their acres, and it grows about seventy-five percent of their food. The other ten percent of their land is the private little gardens controlled by the people and it grows about twenty-five percent of their food. And in hard times these acres consistently produce. No dedicated Communist mind can admit to what this is saying. The crazy mind is noted for its dishonesty.

Chinese Communists evidently don't have as crazy minds as their Russian counterparts because they have recently decided to give farmers and small businessmen more freedom to run their own operations, and they are starting to talk about the dangers of extreme socialism.

I'll never forget a speech I gave to my Toastmaster's club many years ago. It was about six months before my first heart attack, and the title of my speech was "A Dedication to Excellence." In my speech I expounded about how a dedication to excellence was necessary for this country in order to have higher standards, and to keep this economy rolling, and all sorts of stuff like that. Let me tell you what the author of that speech was doing at that time. I was running my own business but I was so depressed I couldn't get any of my work done on time. I was always late. I was spending so much money in my fits of depression I was behind in my bills, and so I was constantly juggling money. Because of this, although I wasn't living on a tight budget, my wife sure as hell was! And, as if this wasn't bad enough, because of my immaturity I was doing business with a crooked guy who was giving me bad checks to pay for his advertising. I was on the hook for that advertising and when his checks bounced, I would have to cough up hundreds of dollars and pray that the next check would be good. As I look back, I can see the tremendous dishonesty I was blind to as I made that speech.

You see this so much in the alcoholic. As I must repeat, I'm not an alcoholic but I go to a lot of open meetings to help me find a new way of life. The practicing alcoholics fall off of every barstool in town. They come to a party at your house and throw up on your carpet. But when someone tries to get them to go to Alcoholics Anonymous they can't do that because they are afraid of what people will think. They don't want anyone to know they are alcoholics. Their crazy minds convinced them they were invisible when they were drinking. Now, their crazy minds won't let them see their true circumstances.

Do you know what happens when a drunk realizes he's alcoholic and joins Alcoholics Anonymous? His crazy mind has to give up its power. The drunk has to surrender and become willing to work a spiritual program to lead him from the grip of his crazy mind into the belief that there is a higher power that can restore him to sanity. I would be a fool to believe that a spiritual way of life like that was only meant for drunks. The longer I study their program the more I come to see that they developed a way of life that is one of the most valid and consistent spiritual programs available to lead us out of dead ways of life many of us have found for ourselves. The AA's have developed a way of life we all have dreamed about and yearned for that has helped them to triumph over one of the toughest compulsions known to man.

I saw that the twelve-step way of life as practiced by the AA's was comparable to the kind of commitment and dedication to a spiritual principle practiced by the first Christians, the ones who lived in Christ's time and shortly thereafter. The only thing that keeps me from that way of life is my own crazy mind. It says, "No, I don't need this. It's my wife that's keeping me in pain. If I get a divorce, I'll be all right." Or, "If my kids would just leave me alone and if they would just grow up I'd be all right." Or, "If I can just find a better job or move to a new town I'd be all right." We have all seen this kind of dishonesty in our friends. Why is it so hard for us to admit that our crazy minds do this to us too? The answer is simple. If I admit these things to myself I'll have to do something about it, and my crazy mind would lose its dictatorship.

When I look at my marriage relationship, I really see my crazy mind. I see how much of the time my thoughts are: "I want, I need, I think, I, I, me, me, mine, mine." I marvel at how little my mind is focused on the other half of my marriage, Jackie, and the other people in my life.

My wife recently mentioned to me a subtle thing she came to see about herself as a woman. Women tend to appear to be more unselfish than men because of their nurturing natures. They are other-person-oriented through motherhood, by its very nature. She came to see that many of the supposedly selfless things she did were for her own wants and needs, like "what people will think," and not selfless at all.

In a marriage relationship, when trouble comes and it is obvious that help is needed, it is usually up to the healthier one in the marriage to go and get the help. When we are out in the woods with a friend, and the friend breaks a leg, we don't ask our friend to go and get help while we sit there and twiddle our thumbs and curse them for breaking their leg. No. We rush out and find help for our friend, and usually find a cup of coffee and a ride back to the woods as the form of help for ourselves in that trying situation.

Sometimes, in rushing to get help for our friend, it could happen that we get chest pains and find out to our horror that we have a bad heart and are sicker than our friend with the broken leg. But we don't curse our friend with the broken leg for the circumstance that brought our bad heart to our attention. We're grateful we found out in time to do something about it.

Why can't we view getting help for our marriage in the same way? Because our crazy mind can't admit the truth. My God, if it did allow us to see the truth it would be out of business! We'd throw off the dictatorship and choose democracy and that would be the end of our dictator mind.

It's an odd thing about the crazy mind: it wants things completely its own way, yet it is a real baby, too. It is dependent on others for its happiness and well-being even though it turns around and shoves away anyone who tries to get too close. What kind of a marriage can two people like that possibly make? As I said earlier, all they can make is the typical neurotic marriage where you take one weak neurotic and lean them against another neurotic and hope they stand up. Not a very pretty picture, but there's a worse picture ahead. That's what happens to us when we try to find some answer that takes away the pain of the loneliness and craziness of living with our sick mind. Then, later, we find our "answer" is our addiction and has us hooked.

5.

Finding My Core Addiction

WE HAVE CRAZY MINDS and there is almost no limit to what these crazy minds will do. But underneath all that craziness, there is always a thread of sanity. Crazy as I was, the thread of sanity in me wanted me to be a good person. Out of the chaos that was in me from my earliest days was a small, quiet part of me that hungered for God. The same was the case with Jackie. One of her earliest memories was wanting to be a saint. So there was a part of us right from the time we were very young that wanted to be God's man and God's woman. We both were pulled toward God before we ever met, both of us seeing, separately, that his was our human journey. We believe what Albert Einstein once wrote: "There is only one road to *true* human greatness—the road through suffering." He also wrote: "The most important human endeavor is the striving for morality in our actions. Our inner balance and even our very existence depend on it. Only morality in our actions can give beauty and dignity to life."

But how was I going to get to God when I had such a crazy mind? Well, the higher power, God as I understand him, had some very ingenious methods to pierce through my craziness. He had to have, because the craziness can get so confused and clouded. I heard a very deep and thought-provoking story one time. A woman prayed to God for wisdom and God sent her trouble. But after she worked her way through the trouble, she had the wisdom. That's a prayer I've said a lot, "God, give me wisdom." And God sure did hear my prayer and answer it.

As I was part way through doing the seminar on marriage in February and March of 1983, God was kind enough to give me a big, fat problem. I've already told you in my story that I came to see I had a problem with women. I quit acting out my sexual compulsion years ago. I stopped making secret trips out of town. In the years since then, I slowly gave up most of the rest of the addictive sexual behavior, like coming on sexually to women, challenging women, attracting women's attention, and stuff like that. All this behavior was very painful for my wife to watch. As I cleaned up my sexual behavior and concentrated my sexual energies on my wife and became more responsible in every way, I began to rebuild trust in my marriage.

As this story about myself unfolds, you will begin to see why I believe in commitment in marriage. Without commitment on Jackie's part, she wouldn't have been able to do and say the things she needed to do and say. Without commitment on my part I would not have heard or acted on what she said and would not be moving toward new wisdom today.

My outward behavior was gone, but it never occurred to me that my sexual thinking was still there so the sexual compulsion was really still there too. I was not acting out but I was still running videotapes through my head of other women from the past. And I was responding sexually in my head to all the sexual stimuli around me. At times, I even sought out sexual stimuli to be engrossed in or to think about. There was lots of sexual fantasy going on in my head. A good word to describe what I was doing is the old-fashioned word lust. I was lusting after women and sexual stimulation, but because that part of me had been with me since childhood, I wasn't even aware I was doing it. That was the only way I had ever lived. I didn't know there was another way. I didn't know that everyone didn't think and feel the same way I did. I was like the goldfish in the bowl. I had lived in water all my life. I didn't know about the air that was just outside my bowl.

My fantasies—including sexual fantasies—had been with me since childhood. They were my way of escaping from anxiety ever since I can remember. One large problem with fantasies is that they take us away from life. That's why we use them, to escape the pain of life. And fantasy is unreal. Nothing real can live up to fantasy because in fantasy we are in complete control. We can manipulate everything just as we want. It's just like going to the movies. We can jump from anything we want to anything else we want. A person who fantasizes sexually can marry a highly proficient and sexually stimulating partner, but no matter if they marry the most adept sexual partner in the world, the fantasies are always more so. In a compulsion, of course, nothing is ever enough, so we always have to return to the fantasies. Fantasies are at the root of the sexual compulsion.

Many compulsive people will give up drinking or drugs or one of their other compulsions and, without a change in attitude and thought, will simply switch that energy into another of their compulsions like work or sex or food. So we have to go for a complete change of personality if we are to live peacefully in this world. Getting rid of the acting out alone doesn't take care of the problem. Thinking about something, I have found, has the same consequences inside me as doing it. So the fantasies are the key part of the compulsion and the behavior is almost just incidental.

When I got married, my sexual compulsion wasn't so strong I couldn't put it aside. And I did. I had "caught" Jackie, so the thrill of the sexual conquest was over, and there would be no more sexual conquests to help me get rid of pain. So I switched to work as my addiction and became a workaholic. I was also a hunting-aholic. I had telephonitis. I was a compulsive spender. I was compulsively seeking power and importance. And all of these thoughts and lesser compulsive actions pushed my wife away. I literally killed any possibility of a relationship with these thoughts and actions. While Jackie could tolerate these kinds of behaviors more easily, there were times when she didn't know what old "spooky Jess" would be up to next.

In 1983, in late February, I was invited to a meeting of sales people. Because of my books, I was recognized by quite a few people. After the meeting a number of people came up to me. One was this gorgeous woman in her thirties who invited me to go to a meeting of the National Speakers Association on the following weekend. I wasn't a member of the organization but I wanted to go because I knew some of the people who would be there. She was very warm and effusive and talked about my books. I told her I thought I could go to the meeting on Saturday but I'd have to let her know and she gave me her card. I felt guilty about the idea of going with her, but I wasn't a member, so going with her was the only way I could go.

Just before we parted she said, "You know, Dr. Lair, I'm just a groupie of people like you." I wanted to go to the meeting. I was very attracted to her. I knew that with my past record there was an inappropriateness in going to that meeting with her. I knew that Jackie would be troubled by it. The intrigue of the situation was, I can see from hindsight, fascinating to me and I was set off.

My wife noticed immediately when I got home that something was up. I act differently when I am set off. She just wondered for a while what was going on, but when we were having breakfast the next morning she asked me about the meeting the day before. She saw by a stiffness in my face and by my shifty eyes when I spoke of planning to go to this meeting on Saturday that I was back in an old pattern. That afternoon she saw this woman's card on the coffee table and the woman's picture was on the card. Jackie knows me so well, and she immediately knew that I had left the card on the table as a signal of my compulsion, whether I knew it or not.

She claims that I always telegraphed a message in some way about what I was up to. She knew I would probably just go to the speech with the woman. But she was also afraid I had the potential to slip back into old behavior and she knew she wasn't going to tolerate any more in the name of commitment. And, even though I wouldn't go back into the behavior with the woman, she didn't like the behavior she was seeing in her own home. She already had the name of a group for the mates of people like me and she made a few phone calls. That afternoon the woman who set me off called and I became uncomfortable and secretive and stopped talking on the phone and covered the receiver with my hand when Jackie walked by the phone. Then she knew for sure that she didn't want any more of the old ways in our life.

The next day she told me I had a compulsion as strong as any alcoholic and I had two choices, "either you do something about it right now—or you get out." She handed me the phone numbers of two men who were working on the same compulsion I have.

I had a deep, sick feeling in my stomach. The only action I had outwardly taken was saying that I might like to go to the meeting with the woman, but my crazy mind, that had begun shifting into fantasy, was so obvious to my wife that here I was with everything all screwed up within me, and between Jackie and me. I went right to the phone and called one of the numbers. The guy told me the problem was in my head, it was my lust. What I was so often thinking about and fantasizing about was the problem. What I was doing or had stopped doing was secondary. Thinking and fantasizing about doing things was affecting me the same as if I was doing them. I called the second guy and he said the same thing. I hung up and had the most overwhelming feeling of relief I've ever had. "My God, so that's what's been wrong with me all these years." It was my constant sexual thinking that was the problem. My sexual thinking for me was like the wine for the alcoholic. Other people could handle wine but the alcoholic couldn't. It was like old Vince said: "Of course you aren't an alcoholic. Wine doesn't do for you what it does for me. Wine took me to the land of impossible dreams. It took me completely out of things."

I saw that fantasy at first, and then sexual fantasy, had been for me like wine was for Vince. It had taken me out of my pain any time reality got unpleasant. It had been my "answer." It wasn't a problem for me. It was my answer. Living with the pain of my crazy mind and feeling separate and alone, that was the problem. As the pain got deeper, it took more and more of the compulsion. And it even took more compulsions. As Vince said of me one time to some people, "Here's a man who has gone to excess in everything." And it was true. Then, as my compulsions had more and more awful consequences, those consequences gave me new, additional things to preoccupy my mind so I wouldn't have to face the real problem—me and life.

I'll never forget that feeling of relief I had when I saw that my problem was lust. I hadn't realized what I had been doing. I knew that I wanted to stop lusting. I knew by my own power that would be impossible. But I knew that with God's help, one day at a time, it would be possible. I am so grateful for the peace I had when I was faced with accepting this deep compulsion in my life. The compulsion had been with me all my life. Because my compulsion was at the centerpoint of my life, my whole life was a jerry-built structure to support my compulsion and all its different ramifications. One of my reactions in the past when faced with looking at my compulsion had been, "How can I be doing something very far off when I'm so much of a success in helping other people?" Now, all of a sudden, that question had a clear answer. I was successful and famous partly out of a deep, lifelong need to get rich and famous so I could be somebody. What I thought was evidence I didn't have a problem, was evidence I did.

At this point it's very important to distinguish between the part of my activities that came out of my addiction and the part of them that came out of my true self. For example, I'll probably keep on writing even if the bulk of the effects of my compulsion are lifted. But if I do, the writing will be freed of a compulsive need to be noticed and freed of the overdriven striving that is so characteristic of compulsion. Jackie has said to me, "I believe it would be best for you if you didn't think about writing another book for a while." I feel moved to take her suggestion. It is a peaceful feeling for me to forget about writing any more books and concentrate on the business of being a human being and the art of living. If a book starts building up in me naturally, we will both recognize it and handle that appropriately. If that doesn't happen, well, I've already written down seven books on my spiritual quest. Anyone who especially identifies with me can find out all they need to about my quest by carefully reading those books and then reading them again in between the lines.

I saw that giving up my compulsion would mean leaving the only way of life I really knew and embarking on a life that I had had many tastes of but wasn't yet a deep reality. I had been able to learn about it from Vince and the other AA's who had tried to help me all through the years. But I knew all along that I was never able to get the fullness of what they were telling me.

Vince had often said of people in AA who were still using pills, "You can't get this program if you're still on any mood-altering chemical." Here, all this time, I had been addicted to a mood-altering chemical and didn't know it. So I finally saw why these ideas hadn't worked for me as well as I had seen them work for the alcoholics. I had been able to know about the ideas. I had been able to write about them effectively. And, I had been able to practice them to some degree. But I hadn't been able to get the fullness I had seen those AA's enjoy.

As soon as I saw that my sexual thinking and lust was my core addiction, I saw that I couldn't do any more of that. It was obviously impossible for me to stop all destructive sexual thinking and lusting through my own power, but it would be simple with God's power, one day at a time. The meditating I had done came to my help, too. I had experienced, from those years of meditating, that when an idea came into my mind all I had to do was use God's grace for the power to gently let the idea go. I didn't need to be afraid of what I was thinking. My experiences in meditation showed me I wasn't a prisoner of my thoughts anymore. I had seven years of experiences of my mind as the servant and not the master. So, with the help of God, I could be free from what I had been a slave to for fifty years and hadn't even known it.

I had the special good fortune to be in a different spot than most people are when they are faced with giving up an addiction. I had been working one spiritual program for sixteen years, another for five years, and I had been meditating and learning from Muktananda for six years. I had freedom from most of my neurotic ways and from needing to be in relationships with alcoholics. That was a great help to me so I could see I wasn't giving up something that was tremendously important to me. I was getting rid of something that was killing life.

Granted, at first I had some occasional regrets about leaving the excitement of the old ways. But those were just fleeting thoughts and were pretty easily laughed away. My overwhelming feeling was one of great relief that the war was over as long as I stayed surrendered. The other overwhelming feeling was of great gratitude to God for the new life I'd been given and to my wife for so clearly and lovingly showing me the need to get rid of the old way. Also, there was a deep gratitude to my newfound friends, who made it possible for me to go to the very deepest gut-level honesty, where nothing I'd ever done couldn't be said—and was. They are the ones who, on a daily basis, help make this new life possible.

I met one of my "new buddies" for coffee that first night and we exchanged stories. These stories hit me in *my* belly. These stories were about me! They didn't give me butterflies in my stomach. This feeling was more like scratching and clawing tigers.

I was told by my friend that the root of my illness was lust and that I had to give it up. He told me that fantasies held me in the grip of that lust. And I knew this to be true. I'm not responsible for the first thought that pops into my head, but I am responsible for entertaining that thought. And every time I lust I am literally killing the present moment and pushing the people in my life away. My brother Jim came to my mind. He had once said to me, "Jess, I don't understand you. One minute you're here with me and the next minute you're gone. I don't feel like I have a brother." I had done this to him since we were children. I had done this to my wife from the very first week of our marriage.

Sexual desire is in all of us. Even monks have sexual desire, at least at first. The difference between sexual desire and lust is that lust is playing with the sexual desire. I see a pretty girl and feel sexual desire. That's just fine. What lust is, is playing with the thought of that pretty girl. If at night, I have trouble going to sleep and bring that pretty girl back into my head and play with it in fantasy, so that I can calm down and go to sleep, that's one form of lust. There are about as many different forms of lust as there are people, but most people can identify what lust is for them when they understand the principle.

Thanks to years of searching for a way to be God's man, I already had most of the tools necessary to make this big step in my life. Thanks to commitment on my part, I had stayed with the marriage at times when there was such a temptation to be leaving. Thanks to my wife's commitment to me and to marriage, she could demand that I do this or get out because she was clear.

She said that she would never divorce me, that choice was mine, but that she would no longer live with me in this way I was living. That was very clear. There was no condemnation, no hatred, no screaming, just clarity. She had recognized that I had a compulsion and would stand by me if I did something, but she would no longer support me in my compulsion by ignoring what I was doing or rationalizing away my behavior and how it was making her feel. She was no longer dependent upon me for her own fulfillment, so she wouldn't go one step further with me in my behavior. This is perfect. This is what it takes. I had no doubt in my mind whatsoever that my wife meant what she said, and furthermore I knew that no denials or protestations were appropriate.

It was no accident that at the sales meeting the woman came up to me. It was no accident that she invited me to go with her, because I attracted that. The woman was no low person. It's like catching trout. How do you catch a trout? You present it with a fly that looks like the real insect and the trout snaps at the bait. Incidents like this are always mutual things. Nothing like this happens by accident. There's no such thing as cruel fate. It has been my experience that we attract these things into our lives.

In a marriage it's often these types of behavior that keep us together! Our guilt, our feelings of being victimized, of being helpless or hopeless are the glue of marriage all too often. What separates the men from the boys and the women from the girls is staying in the marriage relationship and laying down the sick behaviors, feeling commitment so strong that we are willing to grow up together no matter what our age or pain is. My friend

Walther Lechler says: "In most marriages it's babies marrying babies, giving birth to babies, and then raising babies who marry babies, and so on and so on."

It was about four years ago I told Jackie that we should write a book about marriage. She always shudders whenever I get an idea for a book, because her experience has been that we begin to experience huge doses of medicine on whatever subject I'm working on. The week we went through where I had to face my compulsion she was laughing hilariously because I'm the one who had to bite the bullet on this book. She found it a pleasant change from a lot of the experiences she's had with me. After a few days of going through that experience, I told her that I'd scaled down somewhat my ideas of what having a perfect marriage meant, and that I now know that most people probably have perfect marriages because most of them are just right to show us ourselves as we truly are. Jackie laughed uproariously again. I can't imagine why!

The sex compulsion is such a puzzling one because sex is such a deep part of each of us and it is all around us. Sex is like the water the goldfish lives in, which is all around him. Ask the goldfish what he thinks about the water and he will probably say, "What's water?"

I first met the great Indian guru Muktananda in Oakland, California, in 1979. The first thing he talked to me about was sex. He said that the sexual energy was so powerful that just one speck of it could create a whole human being. Because it was so powerful, it should be used very sparingly. He said yogis didn't use their sexual energy. All that energy is available to them to be transformed into spiritual energy. And, he said that he advised his followers who were married to have sex very sparingly, no more than once a month if possible, so they too could have as much of their energy available to them as possible to transform into spiritual energy. I found out later that many of the married couples who were his devotees made a mutual decision to renounce sex for life so they would have all that extra energy to transform into spiritual energy and aid their spiritual quest.

At the time he was saying all these things, I thought it was because I had just written the sex book and he was giving me information in that connection. I see now that he saw my sexual compulsion and was offering me help that I was not yet ready to understand.

Muktananda's advice to me sounds quaint and old-fashioned and strange in today's society, where the general belief is that the more sex you have the better, and if you are having a problem, it's probably caused by some sexual repression or restriction—all you have to do is get freed up sexually and everything will be all right. And the idea of anyone restricting their sexual life is looked at as an idea that doesn't make sense anymore. I'm coming to see now that there may be some people with sex compulsions writing and pushing some of that stuff and that it's just like drunks writing about drinking: they think it's really good and we should all do more of it—it would really fix everything that ails us.

We're in a society where we are so deep in the compulsion of sex, it adds an extra load to people who have the compulsion. We always had alcoholics, even during Prohibition, so we know that cutting something out isn't the answer. But one thing people don't realize is that they had a big drop in deaths due to cirrhosis of the liver then. There is even a drop in cirrhosis of the liver deaths in the states with the highest liquor taxes compared to the lowest. So there is an effect from our society. The more fundamental effect is from our own separateness and aloneness, but this society is a great one for sexually compulsive people to find what they seek.

Sex has always been a problem in the world. We all know it's nothing new. You just have to read the Bible to see that the early fathers and mothers of our religious heritage had the same puzzlements with sex that we do. If you read the religious books of other great religions in the world you see this strain in there also. So sex as a problem is certainly not new.

What is new is that we have adopted a sense of sexual freedom that has become a grave source of harm to us all. More and more we are seeing young people turning for psychiatric care or for treatment of drug or alcohol addiction who get that addiction lifted and then go out and find they also have a sexual addiction that is devastating for them.

A surprising number are also talking about having been sexually abused as children or of having been forced into incestuous relationships. Upon investigation many of these stories are true, but a surprising number of them do not have any basis in fact. Are these young people lying to themselves and others? Are these young people weird or crazy? NO! They are actually sexually abused, but from a source we aren't paying enough attention to. For the past twenty years, in an ever more blatant way, sensitive young children and adolescents are being subjected to ever increasingly more explicit sex in glorious Technicolor in our homes on the television screen and in ten- to fifteen-foot-tall explicitness in movie theaters. Another source of course is magazines, with sexual pictures nowadays of total explicitness.

We are a whole nation of sexually molested people! And I think we have to start asking ourselves what part this molestation is playing in our marriages. How can an average young woman's body and sexual prowess measure up to the perfection and white heat her young partner has seen and read about from his earliest years? How can a young man possibly compare to the passionate scenes she has been tantalized by and been led to fantasize about through movies and magazines? These two young people, by the time they marry, have been sexually overstimulated for anywhere from one to ten years. Anything they have between them is less than they have been led to expect once the "honeymoon" period is over.

Another problem that is becoming more and more prevalent is a large group of young people doubting their sexual abilities. We aren't just a sexually permissive society anymore, we are a sexually promiscuous society, and any young girl over the age of fifteen who isn't on the pill in high school is considered a freak or stupid. The question isn't should we kiss on the first date anymore, it's should we have intercourse on the first date. And young men and women who haven't had sexual intercourse at least some times before they're twenty are looked upon as people with a sexual problem. And these young people are suffering. They have been led to doubt themselves in ways that they shouldn't.

A woman wrote to me from the West Coast and told a poignant story about asking her twenty-year-old daughter what she would want if she could have anything in this world. The daughter answered, "My virginity." In showing this chapter to one of my sons, he said, "Do you know what it was like to see Edith Bunker raped on TV? I thought, good God, even Edith!" Now, of course, they did not actually show Edith being raped, but they might as well have for the impact he felt. He was referring to an episode where Edith was coming home one night and was attacked and how she and the family dealt with it.

Excess seems to be the name of the game these days. That pendulum does swing. And no one in my generation would want to go back to the tight structure that we grew up in. I have total confidence in this generation coming into power. They're going to find answers that will solve this sexual plague. In the meantime, though, we're all hurting from it.

A recent *Time* magazine article said that the sexual revolution is over. The gist of the article is that recreational sex has lost its appeal so that most people want some kind of emotional relationship before having sex. They talk of a new urge for commitment and a big rise in people who don't have any sexual desire. But, three parts of the sexual revolution are left intact which many people who have a sexual compulsion find to be problems: fantasy, masturbation, and sex without commitment.

Most of the rhetoric in the sexual revolution was about right and wrong. People argued against those concepts as being so relative and so culture-bound that the rules didn't make sense from a right and wrong standpoint. But there is a different way to look at behavior and that is from a spiritual perspective. Another way to look at behavior is from a psychological perspective, in terms of the consequences of behavior for the people involved. Much of the sexual revolution was against religion and its rules. People argued that they could do these things and God wouldn't strike them dead. And, they claimed, fantasy, masturbation, and frequent sex in any form was good for them. There wasn't much evidence at that time to support those views. The point of the *Time* article is that a lot of people who have tried recreational sex haven't liked its results.

The lessons I see coming from some of us with sexual compulsions is that a person would be wise to reexamine their use of fantasy, guilt and shame, masturbation, and sex without commitment.

In psychology, fantasy is not only not questioned, it is advocated by many as harmless and even desirable. Yet, there is a substantial body of research which shows that, at a subconscious or unconscious level, we are unable to distinguish between thinking of something and actually doing it. Thinking of giving a person an electric shock produces essentially the same physiological responses as actually giving the person the electric shock. What this body of research suggests to me is that our conscious mind has available to it the minute-by-minute feedback of the five senses. But the subconscious or unconscious mind doesn't have that advantage. So it can't distinguish between the fantasy and the real.

That means that the person who fantasizes something feels all the same feelings as the person who does the thing.

Also, there is another part of fantasy that seems to be a problem. When we imagine or fantasize something that we haven't done, it's like our conscious mind has a need to bring that fantasy about in our life. Bill Russell in his book *Second Wind* tells about learning basketball through his fantasies on tour with a team in his early days. He watched the starting center move on the floor. After the game, Russell would spend hours running those videotapes through his head, seeing himself making those moves on the floor in game situations. He changed from a gangly, awkward guy to the beginnings of his championship form by doing that. So this was an example of how fantasy can bring about what is fantasized. People have reported the same thing in the sexual area. They fantasized some desired sexual scene and the next thing they knew they were acting out that desired scene. Since the forbidden is often the most sexually stimulating, many times their forbidden fantasies became actualities and they were horror-stricken at the progression. So it was the thinking and fantasy that led to the action.

Masturbation used to be surrounded with a lot of guilt by people in religious programs. There has been a lot of reaction to that right-wrong applied to something that is so common for young people. But there is another side to masturbation, and that is the harm it can do to some. Masturbation's necessary companion is fantasy. Put masturbation and fantasy together and there is a form of sex with self that can be highly addictive for some people. For these people, fantasy and masturbation become the preferred form of sex. There is no need to depend on some other person with all the problems that involves. This is a path that leads ever inward until a person is finally lost inside themselves. The shell they built with sex and fantasy has become their prison. For these people, their masturbation persists on into marriage, when they finally have what they thought they wanted all those years and then find they don't. When sex with self becomes a highly dominant pattern early in life, there is a high degree of self-isolation. And there is a preoccupation with the drug that produces a constant daze. How can these effects be considered psychologically helpful? Where's the evidence? Simple. Life offers us evidence on questions like these that haven't yet been raised in the field.

Sex without commitment may also have behavioral conse-quences. There is a chance that the romance we feel in the presence of a loved one is something we can become addicted to just like alcohol. It feels good, but it runs out, so we have to find some new relationship to feel the romance. Eventually, it gets hard to feel the romance. In all these relationships, we use sex, which has the ability to bond two people together for life. We know about that bond by studying fairly simple animals like geese, who bond for life and can't rebond when a mate is killed or dies. So using romance and sex over and over again may rob us of the power we need to bond with another person. Many people in their thirties and forties may be finding that they used romance and sex so much that, if they finally decide they want a lifetime partner, it is almost impossible to find any more romance, or, they find sex has lost its interest for them.

All these consequences of fantasy, masturbation, and sex without commitment are psychological and behavioral. They have nothing to do with right or wrong; they are just the results in people's lives from the choices they made. Those choices may have been made in ignorance, but ignorance of the law doesn't save us from the consequences of the law. The person who is ignorant of gravity and falls is just as dead as the one who knows about gravity. I believe this is a world of justice without judgment. The issue isn't right or wrong but that we reap what we sow. If we don't like radishes, then we need to stop planting radishes.

So without using religion and its rules, there are a lot of reasons to go cautiously with a lot of the ideas that are being thrown around so loosely today. But there is another, bigger reason to look at our sexual practices.

If we have a spiritual program, and I believe everyone does, then we need to look at sex from the spiritual side. As near as I can see it, the core belief of most spiritual programs is living moment by moment in the direct experience of reality as God is offering it to us in that moment. This is the heart of my spiritual program. In that perspective, there is no place for daydreaming and fantasy. That's harmful to me spiritually because I'm removing myself from the world God is offering me and turning instead to a dream world of my creation. So my effort is the opposite of fantasy. It is to live as completely as possible in the moment in full appreciation and gratitude for what I'm being offered. Also, since fantasy is the same as doing something spiritually as well as psychologically, fantasy produces the same shame and guilt as actually doing the act.

Guilt and shame are feelings many in psychology want to attribute to a false sense of should and shouldn't. So people are trying to get over the feelings of guilt and shame by listening to psychologists telling them that what they are doing is all right. One of the ideas that is used to make sex all right and murder wrong is that we aren't hurting anyone in sex with self or a consenting other. It is called a victimless crime, like homosexuality or cohabitation. There's still a problem there. If we are all one spiritually, then when I hurt myself, I'm hurting you too. And if God lives within me as me, maybe my guilt comes when I'm not true to the deep inner self.

I tried to get rid of guilt for fifteen years and couldn't. Within a month after I stopped all sexual fantasy and lust, I realized my guilt and shame was gone and I felt an integrity I had never felt before. I felt like a truly grown-up person. That wasn't just my opinion. My wife and kids were saying, "Dad, you're different." They hadn't said this to me when I was dealing with my other addictions, only when I dealt with my core addiction. Other people who knew me came up to me to say, "Jess, you're different." I know the feeling of being freed of shame and guilt. I like that integrity.

Masturbation is a problem in a spiritual program for a couple of reasons. One, masturbation involves fantasy which takes the person out of life, as I just mentioned. Two, many spiritual teachers teach that sexual energy is part of spiritual energy. The more sexual energy we use, the less energy is available for our spiritual quest. Three, masturbation takes them more into themselves and into self-centeredness rather than God-centeredness. What man of God could ever make the statement "I'm so close to God, because I masturbate so much."

Sex without commitment seems to be at odds, too, with most of the spiritual programs I know anything about. In light of those spiritual programs, it seems to me not to take other people into account very much and seems selfish and irresponsible. I don't know of a spiritual program that suggests we go out and have sex with a lot of women or men but don't worry about making any kind of commitment to them.

These are the problems I see running around today. They are fallout from the sexual revolution and are still here for many of us to deal with. The tight structure I grew up in was an excess of another kind. We were a close-mouthed, secretive generation that didn't allow our neighbors to know our business. This led us to value things like rugged individualism and lifting ourselves by our own bootstraps. This led to a lot of ego and a lack of true spirituality. We gave a lot of lip service to God because that was part of the façade of the self-made man, but underneath we were just as fearful and lonely as the kids of today. And our God was a vengeful, punishing, punitive man on a cloud who kept books on our lives.

I've come to see that this kind of God is the same as the "no God" attitude so prevalent today. And both of these concepts really play some part in the sex plague of today. When that hollow, empty yearning can't be filled by our idea of God, we'll try to fill it any way we can. And sex, more than any other physical expression, has enough deep emotion tied to it to let us feel like we've found the answer—for a while.

Sexual compulsion is no different from any other compulsion. A sex junkie finds out that they're in trouble in just the same way that a heroin junkie or a drug addict or an alcoholic does. It eventually takes more and more to do less and less.

The ancient Chinese curse, "May you live in interesting times," seems to apply to the sex plague. Sexual mores have changed drastically in the past ten or twelve years, but I'd like to make some predictions based on what I've seen and heard.

In the young people today I see a lot of pain under the jokes and the sexual freedom they say that they like. When we're saying one thing and feeling another, it shows. It's like the old line, "What you are speaks so loudly, I can't hear what you're saying." Everyone always knows what is going on. Even if you can't see the fire, you can sure smell the smoke.

My wife sees that there are an awful lot of young women walking around today with terribly old, tired faces. Their lack of self-worth is screaming at us. They are beginning to see that sexual freedom is not the sexual license they have provoked or allowed. What began as a deep, valid need to be freed from the yoke of male dependence turned into domination of another sort. They are beginning to see that sexual promiscuity for free and for fun is no different than sexual promiscuity for pay. They have not found their freedom in being so opposite from their mothers any more than their mothers had found freedom in their opposite ways. There is no freedom in license. And this is good, this suffering. These young women will find themselves, will know who they are in the same way women have found out who they really are since the beginning of time. When the pain is so great, and the deprivation is so unbearable, they will put down this way and try another. No one can do this for them. No one could do this for us. This is life.

My wife has also said that many young men of today have the same haunted expressions on their faces. They have lived through what a lot of older guys just fantasized. They have truly walked barefoot through an acre of bare boobs, and instead of feeling free, they feel neutered. Young men today don't need prostitutes; it's accepted that they can have sex simply and easily if they want it. They are even suspect if they don't want it. And instead of having fun, they are horrified at themselves. An expression that is really succinct that they use is, "I haven't trashed out a woman in a week." Once again, we don't have to see the fire, we can smell the smoke. From promiscuous sex a lot of these young men are questioning their masculinity *more,* rather than believing in it as they thought they would. And this too is good. When the pain becomes so great they hit bottom with it, then they can be restored to sanity, if they choose to be.

We must never sell the human animal short. The young people know craziness when they see it as well as we do. It isn't anyone's place to say, "I know more than you do." And it is foolish to say that the sex plague is worse than the plagues of other days. It just happens to be one of the plagues of our times which is being served up in glorious Technicolor. The solutions are here and it is up to those involved to find them. And they will.

Shortly after I became aware of my sex compulsion, I was taking a walk around the little lake near our apartment in Oklahoma City. I saw a young couple lying there and came home and wrote out this little story:

"The couple was lying on the grassy bank by the lake. The cool morning breeze was blowing across the water. The semi-tame ducks were waddling about in the bright morning sun. He was stroking her arm and she was stroking his leg as they lay there totally absorbed in each other.

"This is the height of romantic love. But there's an important difference here that can't be seen by the outsider. These two people were each 'in love' last month, too. But they were in love with two other people. As their previous 'loves' grew deeper and deeper, their hold on the other person grew deeper and deeper, too. The other person was like a fish who had swallowed a hook so deep they couldn't spit it out anymore.

"As the lover caught the beloved and could spin them around in any direction like the meekest prisoner, all the excitement of the chase and all the wine of the romance went away. All that was left was the dreariness of the morning-after hangover, and all the dreariness of trying to find a way to live with another human being which faced the 'lover' with the ultimate problem for him—how to live with himself. That's what he had been running away from all his life.

"That's why, at an early age, he had turned to fantasy and dreams and obsessions. Sexual stimulation had been his haven and refuge way before that sexual stimulation became localized and focused on his genitals. Most all five-year-olds played doctor. But most all of them had all kinds of other interests and soon went on to them. But not our love cripple. He was already hooked. He *had* to think about playing doctor, over and over again.

"Like alcohol for the alcoholic, sexual stimulation and sexual fantasy did something for him it didn't do for most of his companions. But he didn't know that then. How could he? He wasn't inside anyone but himself. And it wouldn't be until his life was way more than half over that he would find another person who was desperate enough to be honest and tell how it was with himself. Then our love cripple could see that he was not alone. But that was for a time way in the future. This was now for him and he had to have what he had to have, no matter what the price. What true addict ever asks what the price is? No, our addict was already hooked. He was addicted to sexual stimulation and feeling. 'Lust' was the old-fashioned word Jimmy Carter used for it in the early days of his Presidency, and was laughed at for his honesty.

"But lust isn't funny to lust's prisoner, just as wine isn't funny anymore to the wino. Lust is the constant chase for romance, the constant search for sexual excitement and stimulation. But just like any drug, the more you use it, the bigger the dose you need to achieve the same effect. That's why women across America are mystified, then hurt, as they see their husbands quickly becoming dissatisfied with plain sex. They are asked, then begged, to get into sexual clothing and other assorted rigs so there can be enough excitement for the poor, sick love cripple for whom nothing is ever enough. She feels like she is being tortured, that the man must hate her. But he doesn't. She isn't the issue. Addiction is the issue, and both are prisoners."

Here is a beautiful quotation on lust from a book by one of my wife's favorite authors:

THE HINDRANCES
EXCERPTS FROM THE BOOK
A Gradual Awakening
by Stephen Levine

A hindrance is a blockage to the light of the wisdom mind. Rather than calling it "sin," it can be seen simply as an obstacle to understanding which attracts the attention, causing identification, and distracts us from an even-minded awareness of the flow. Hindrances are the basis for much compulsive reactivity, the seeds of much karma.

Though there are numerous hindrances, they are commonly divided into five major categories, five enemies, if you will, of the balanced mind. They are lust—which is a form of greed; hatred or anger—which is a form of aversion; sloth and torpor; agitation and worry; and—perhaps the greatest obstacle to investigation and clarity—doubt . . .

Greed is often a desire for pleasant states, for "more, sooner, quicker." It isn't necessarily sexual lust, although that certainly is one, easily recognizable aspect of it. It could even be lust after understanding, greed for certain subtle states of mind or peak experiences, or grasping after complimentary self-images like "I'm a good meditator." The problem with this, as with all hindrances, is that it directs attention outward and therefore seldom recognizes itself. And, of course, without awareness of what's happening, it's very difficult for purification, for letting go, to occur. In a much subtler form we can recognize the quality of grasping as we drive down the road and notice that the eyes, without being directed to do so, are reading signs, are reading billboards, that there is a conditioned grasping of the mind at stimulation.

This is one of the predominant energies we notice in the mind—a grasping at objects, a thirst for experiences. Lust can be extremely painful to ourselves and often to the object we lust after if the object of our wanting happens to be another human being. Lusting either sexually, or, more subtly, for someone to serve as a reflection of who we think we are, causes that being to become an object of gratification, an object devoid of its wonderment, of its own intrinsic value. We are altogether separate from such objects of satisfaction, we feed from them, we use them. This is not to say that we cannot dance lightly with our desires, but the music must be heard by both and the hearts kept open . . .*

I've come to see that this addiction to lust is just like every other addiction. A lot of people want to say that there are physical addictions and that there are psychological addictions. I believe they are all one thing. They all start in the mind and are all the belief that *something outside ourselves can make us whole.*

Carl Jung once wrote a letter about an alcoholic in which he said: "His craving for alcohol was the equivalent on a low level of the spiritual thirst of our being for wholeness, expressed in medieval language: the union with God."† I believe that all compulsions are the equivalent on a low level of the spiritual thirst of our being for wholeness—the union with God.

Later in that same letter, which is printed in its entirety in chapter 10, Dr. Jung went on to say: "I am strongly convinced that the evil principle prevailing in this world leads the unrecognized spiritual need into perdition, if it is not counteracted either by a real religious insight or by the protective wall of human community. An ordinary man, not protected by an action from above and isolated from society, cannot resist the power of evil . . ."

When people get hooked on sex and have a whole society turning to it more and more through the various media, the isolation, the fear, the guilt, the loneliness simply grows and grows because sex has become a substitute to us just like alcohol and drugs. It is our substitute for our true and all too often unrecognized need for wholeness, for God.

The problem has been beautifully stated in these words: "We were addicted to the intrigue, the tease, the forbidden. The only way we knew to be free of it was to do it. 'Please connect with me and make me whole,' we cried with outstretched arms. Lusting after the Big Fix, we gave away our power to others . . . we were driven ever inward, away from reality, away from love, lost inside

* Anchor Press/Doubleday, 1979, pp. 58–59.
† Carl Jung letter to Bill W., January 30, 1961. Alcoholics Anonymous archives. Also in *C. G. Jung: Letters*, vol. 2, Princeton University Press, 1975, pp. 623–25.

ourselves . . . first addicts, then love cripples, we took from others to fill up what was lacking in ourselves. Conning ourselves time and again that the next one would save us, we were really losing our lives."

I have faced my compulsive behavior in other areas of my life. I believe now I had a sexual compulsion from my earliest days. I felt inadequate, unworthy, alone, and afraid. My insides never matched what I saw on the outsides of others. I hated the pain of that. Rather than facing the pain and working it out as many in our little town did, I looked for an escape and found it in fantasy, sexual stimulation, and lust. In high school and college years there was the chase and then the loss of interest once there was a conquest. When I got married, the chase was really over and there were no more conquests to be preoccupied with so, as near as I can see now, I immediately switched addictions and became a compulsive worker. In the next twenty years, my sexual compulsion was gone except for a couple of minor incidents, despite living in the midst of all kinds of potentially sexually stimulating situations. Then, all of a sudden, the sexual compulsion flared up like a volcano that had been progressing and growing for twenty years.

As I am faced with this deep compulsion in myself, I'm coming to a much better understanding of compulsions. I can see so clearly how my compulsion helped me run away from the pain of my separateness. And I can see how my compulsion led to a tremendous distortion of reality so that I was unable to really see the craziness of what I had been doing, what I was thinking, and where I was at.

I was reading what a young actress was saying about herself. She was about five feet seven and weighed one hundred and ten pounds. She was saying how she looked so much better when she was ten pounds thinner. She said, "I'm no anorexic, I just know how I look." I thought, "Well, maybe she isn't anorexic," but as I thought further I thought about us compulsives and our distortion and denial of reality.

Here is a woman with a figure most women in America would give anything to have. Yet she's not happy with it. I used to see this as just part of the perpetual dissatisfaction of the neurotic. But I think there's something else working here. This woman thinks of herself as having too much weight, that she's fat in places. So when she looks in the mirror, she sees fat. What is so striking is that her reality is probably already distorted. If she is an anorexic, her reality will become progressively more and more distorted to the point where she can be a walking skeleton and look in the mirror and see fat. Or, perhaps she won't look in the mirror, there's no need to, she knows she has some fat she needs to get rid of, and if she can starve herself a little longer, that's what's needed.

And all the time she will be living in this peaceful cocoon where people are taking care of her and urging her to eat but she is slipping further and further into the same peacefulness people feel as they are freezing to death.

This distortion of reality is hard for the outsider to understand. This might be the case even though we ourselves are distorting reality in some other way that we aren't even aware of. But as we attempt to deal with our compulsions and those of others, we need to be aware of how distorted the reality can be for the compulsive and what a slow process it is to recover any semblance of a more reasonable reality.

I think this is why intervention is so needed and is such a help in the compulsions. In the early days of AA, it was believed a person had to lose everything and get so desperate that they were at the very bottom before they would be ready to even consider AA's new way of life.

Gradually AA came to see this didn't have to happen. People could be talked to and the progressive nature of their compulsion pointed out to them. From this, they could see they didn't have to lose everything before they came in. These were what they called the "high bottom" drunks, meaning they didn't have to go so low before they quit. Some of these high bottom drunks went back to drinking because they felt they could get away with it after all. Many of these found they were wrong and then came back to AA. But not all the low bottom drunks stayed sober either. So AA found that the more help you could give a person as an aid to breaking through their distorted reality, the better. Today, this process has been formalized as an intervention and it can be taught to people around the addict who need to intervene for their own peace of mind.

My case is almost a classic in intervention. Jackie, all of a sudden, had information I didn't have. She then shared that information with me and I was completely ready to use the information. I didn't need much intervention, but it's always better to have overkill than underkill.

A big point about intervention that I make to people when they are wondering if they should intervene is this one about information. It's not fair to someone we claim to love when we have information they don't have. We need to give them that information so we can feel right about ourselves. It's easier to appreciate that when we understand how distorted reality is for the compulsive. Something that looks so obvious to someone around the compulsive, isn't that obvious to the compulsive. An alcoholic can be sitting at a bar getting so totally drunk he's falling off the barstool and still think that no one sees him. He thinks he's invisible. When he decides to come to AA, he sneaks into the meeting place so no one will see him and think that he's an alcoholic! Usually he is the only one in town who doesn't know he is an alcoholic. All the people around him knew he was an alcoholic a long time earlier.

The intervention process for the compulsive person is a process where a massive amount of reality is piled on them at one time. Every person who is important to them gathers together with a counselor and rehearses what they want to say, and then they gather to confront the compulsive. All this is needed to break through the distorted view of reality the compulsive has built. Sometimes an intervention might have been successful without as many people or as much preparation. But when it is understood what a distorted view of reality the compulsive has, then it's easy to see it's not worth taking the risk of underestimating the seriousness of their situation.

It helps us compulsives to see that, at first, there are many things we don't see clearly because of all the ways we gradually distorted reality. That's where honesty comes in. We think we can get honest quickly. We can't. Most of us have to realize we were never honest. Maybe we didn't steal money, but that's just cash register honesty. The real honesty is honesty with self, and no addict I ever knew was ever honest with themselves. If they had been, they would have grown up instead of lying to themselves and looking for the answer to their living problem in addiction. So we shouldn't be too surprised at ourselves at how hard and slowly honesty comes into our lives.

I was playing golf awhile back and hit a ball that rolled in some bushes around the equipment shack in the center of the course. It was only when I got down there that I realized the bushes were out of bounds. I didn't want to go back and hit another ball because the group behind us was on the tee already. I had taken some penalties on myself and didn't want to take another. Some of the guys I played with had kicked balls out of the weeds, so that's what I did. I didn't feel comfortable about it then and that night it hit me hard about how dumb it was. I didn't care what the score was, or at least most of me didn't. But my old competitiveness and self-pity flared up and honesty lost. If I'm going to keep score, then there's only one way to keep score and that's following the rules as well as I know how. But I didn't do that in that moment. I was dishonest on that hole. Honesty is coming to me, but it sure is gradual.

The most beautiful story of honesty I ever heard was about a guy I knew out in California. He was in AA and another twelve-step program. He was a retired contractor. After he had been in the program for a few years, he saw that he had to do something about how he had cheated on his income taxes. He went down to IRS and told them there were years when he had cheated on his taxes. He had $400,000 in the bank as his savings he retired on. He turned all that over to IRS to settle his account and lived happily on his Social Security checks until he died. I didn't hear this story from him but from a mutual friend who knew of it. He was a beautiful example to all of us of what it means to come from such a distorted view of reality back to true reality.

It might seem like it would be easier for us if we would face our pain of being separate and alone right away and start to do something about it rather than go through the pain of cultivating an obsession and then suffering all the consequences of the obsession just for the purpose of running away. It does seem more logical we would face our separateness right away but we don't, so the pain of the addiction must be less for us than the other pain.

The reason the addict stays in their pain is not because they love to suffer but because the pain gives them another variation of the same kind of relief the high from their obsession gave them. The preoccupation with the next drunk or the consequences of the last drunk are just as compelling as the drunk itself. The preoccupation with planning the next drunk and the drunk itself, both keep the mind of the addict from being aware of their pain, "the hole in their guts," as one famous Alcoholics Anonymous speaker calls it.

Compulsions that work great are food, work, gambling, sex, alcohol, drugs, buying, shoplifting, crime, housecleaning, white-collar crime, social climbing, sports, hobbies, being a bleeding heart, almost any good thing can be carried to excess and made into a compulsion. Because certain people have a talent for creating compulsions, we often have more than one compulsion. And most everyone has at least one activity that serves to take their minds off what's happening.

The line between something being a legitimate interest and taking that interest into compulsion is what it does for us. When we are skiing just for the fun of it, we pick up our skis, go skiing, come home and put down our skis and turn to the next thing at hand. The obsessing skier thinks of skiing, puts his or her full being into skiing, even when the skiing isn't there. Everyone has some light memories of anticipation or of reliving pleasant experiences. But obsessing is when those memories are a strong-enough preoccupation to serve as an escape.

A very interesting compulsion is false piety. This is the compulsion where a person pretends to be with God as a way of running away from the fact they are one with God. False piety looks a lot like real piety at first glance. But the people around the falsely pious aren't fooled for long. They eventually come to see that there is something wrong with the life of the falsely pious person; their life just doesn't lead to peace for them or the people around them. Their lack of peace can be explained away by them and others for a while, but eventually the explanations break down. Until they do, the people around them get plenty frustrated, having so much trouble attacking the "pious" one.

All the compulsions I've talked about here are the compulsions with self. Sex, drinking, gambling, eating, working, and lots of others are in this category. But there is another bunch of compulsions that these things don't cover and they are much more common. Almost every marriage suffers from them. They are the compulsions that I see as falling into a different category, which I think of as compulsions with others and their lives. That's next.

6.

———— ⌣ ————

The Compulsion
with Other People's Problems

IT WAS ALWAYS PRETTY EASY FOR ME to understand my compulsions for work, power, sex, or what have you. It was much harder for me to see another kind of compulsion I had. That was my compulsion with other people's problems.

I was flying home on an airplane about five years ago after having a confrontation with my daughter. As I was looking at my life, I was all of a sudden overwhelmed at all the alcoholics in my life. There were alcoholics in my family. Three of my five friends were alcoholics. There were alcoholics among my associates in every area of my life both in Bozeman and in Phoenix. The question I asked myself was: "Why are all these alcoholics in my life?" By this time I had come to realize that the things in my life were there because I had attracted them to me. Why was I attracting all these alcoholics into my life? What were they doing for me that I needed to have done?

Right on that plane, in the space of an hour or so, I got over my long-standing need to be involved in other people's problems. It was just like an alcoholic when he sees that he doesn't want to drink anymore and starts seeking sobriety, a day at a time. Well, I got over my need to lose myself in others' problems and became ready to start living my own life instead of escaping by losing myself in others' lives. By then I knew enough about the neurotic side of myself to admit to my responsibility for bringing those things into my life, and I knew I had a choice.

A choice I made on that airplane was that I didn't need alcoholic relationships in my life anymore. I didn't need any more disasters. I got over that on that airplane.

As soon as I got home I took a couple of steps. I saw I needed help in putting my decision into practice by finding some people I could talk to who had a similar problem. I did that. I also went to work to clean up the relationships. I got my horses back from the practicing alcoholic I had loaned them to and he dropped completely out of my life. I went to another of the people with whom I had had a problem and had a very clear talk with him, telling him how I felt about his breaking a couple of promises in our relationship. I told him to do as he pleased with the rest of his life but that I didn't want anything like that in my life anymore. He hasn't broken a promise since. That relationship changed into one of the best I have. He also took a look at his life and saw what some of his drinking was doing to him and made a change in the way he was using alcohol. A number of other relationships with recovering alcoholics changed from alcoholic relationships to non-alcoholic relationships.

The big point is that all this happened because *I* changed. All of a sudden there were a whole new set of relationships in my life. So this experience has given me a good understanding of having a compulsion with others. Our society is permeated with this compulsion. The compulsion with the alcoholic is just one of the most common and is really the reason we know so much about the subject. That's partly because the behavior of those of us who have a compulsion with alcoholics is so bizarre. The most bizarre story is one I've told a lot, but it needs to be retold here.

A friend of mine is a doctor and a recovering alcoholic. A woman patient of his married an alcoholic who beat her up and put her in the hospital. She divorced him, married another alcoholic who beat up on her and put her in the hospital again. She divorced him and married a third alcoholic who beat her and put her in the hospital a third time. The doctor finally tried to point out to her the pattern of her behavior, but she wouldn't hear a word of it. She was outraged that he would suggest such a thing. "What do you mean telling me I had a hand in this behavior?" She was content playing the part of the victim and wanted to go on playing that part.

Where this problem gets more subtle is when a home is started for battered women by people who see themselves and other women as the victims of men. They take in two kinds of women. One kind of woman is the one who married into a battering home without much awareness of what she was doing and she needs help and doesn't want to go back into that home. She is very ready to look at the choices and is willing to become aware that she made some poor choices. Now, with an increased awareness, she is ready to make some healthy choices for herself.

But the other kind of woman is like the one my doctor friend confronted, and she is the one who will do the same thing over and over again in the firm belief that the world is a cruel, vicious place, and she stays blind to her own part in it. No way is she ready to have the awareness that she is choosing, over and over again, the same trouble for herself.

What is so subtle is that the workers in the home for the battered women have to be very careful as to why they are helping. They can be helping because they are like St. Francis and are seeking to love rather than be loved. Or they can be just like the woman whose story I told you and be in the battered women's home because they have a compulsion with others as a way of escaping from their own lives.

Most men and women I see working with others in the so-called "helping professions" have no idea how hard it is to deal with the part of themselves that needs their compulsion with others as a preoccupation to run away from their own problems and get lost in them. So they stay lost in their own problems and, without knowing it, help those around them to do the same.

The point of all this isn't to criticize or condemn anyone. The point is the pervasiveness of the compulsion to lose ourselves in others. What a weird compulsion! But part of the beauty of the compulsion is that it works so well for the person involved. Who would dare challenge us on our behavior when we are so busy working for mankind? We say, "If you want to challenge someone, go after the alcoholics, the sex maniacs, they are the ones who are really hurting people, not me." But you see, that's not the issue. The issue is how we hurt ourselves when we use any compulsion to run away from the pain of facing ourselves as we really are.

The people in the alcoholism field have come up with the word "enabling" as a word for what the wife or the husband of the alcoholic does to help the alcoholic stay in their behavior so the enabler can stay in their compulsion with the other person. The wife will get a job to support the family and buy whiskey for the alcoholic so she can feel superior as a way of covering up her own sense of inadequacy.

This compulsion with others is a big problem in marriages because it causes such confusion about who is doing what to whom for what reasons. It makes family relationships one big tangled mess.

When marriages go sour, one of the most frequent things we hear is one person explaining how they are perfectly all right, it is the behavior of the other person that is wrong. We all want to believe that we are perfectly all right and that it is the other person who is wrong.

I have had a number of years to look at my compulsions. As I have been forced by life to deal with the compulsion I have to get involved with other people's problems, I've learned a lot about the more subtle compulsions. It all goes back to our own sense of our own inadequacies. Most people have never been forced to look at that aspect of themselves. But I see in marriages, as in the rest of life, a big hesitancy on the part of the partners to look at the part of their lives that is all tied up in doing for others. There is the old saying, "They are the kind of people who give their lives for others. You can tell the others by the haunted expressions on their faces." There are two big problems in the doing for others that many people aren't aware of.

The first problem in doing for others is that it distracts us from seeing ourselves as we really are and getting on with our spiritual quest. The other problem in doing for others is that it "enables" the others to stay in their sick behavior. The wife who goes to work because her alcoholic husband can't hold a job, and then ends up supporting the family and buying the husband's whiskey for him, isn't doing him any favor. She's obviously really hurting him. Why would she do something like that? Why would she continue doing something like that even when she is made aware of what she is doing? The problem is so clear in the alcoholic family and we see it so often in the wife. Up until recent years, most wives of alcoholics stayed with the alcoholic husband. But most husbands of alcoholic wives didn't stay with them and got divorced. I'd guess those statistics are changing as more and more women are able to get jobs and support their families. But I'd guess it's still a long way from an even split because of what I see as a deep desire in many women to do what they have to do to keep the home together. That's the good part of their motive. There's a troubling part of their motive that they become aware of when their husbands come into AA and sober up. Then the women find that a part of them enjoyed their feelings of superiority and having an alcoholic who was dependent on them. When the person sobered up and started bringing home all their paycheck and paying bills and being responsible, the wife wasn't in the driver's seat anymore. That's when she had to start looking at her own problems and what she was running from. But that's where we all have to get to one way or another when our sick games stop working for us. That's when a lot of us are forced to look back in our lives and try to see where things went wrong.

Being separate from each other and from God is very painful. Our crazy mind tells us we aren't good enough. But most of the time we can fight off that pain. So we're reasonably happy and free of deep pain when we're children because we don't have that much consciousness. We do have enough consciousness to have our times of pain. But as we get to be six and eight and ten and twelve, we get more and more consciousness, so we feel our separation more and start to feel the pain more deeply and more consistently.

We try to solve things but we also try to cover up pain through other intense preoccupations. When we find a preoccupation that works for us, we use it to run away from our pain into the stimulation of the obsession. Eating is an easy example. Eating makes us feel good. When we are in pain, we can turn to eating to take away the pain. Eating takes away the pain because it's hard to be in pain while we're eating. But we have to stop eating eventually because we get so we can't hold any more or we are full enough that eating doesn't work to take away the pain. So we can stop eating or we can make ourselves vomit so we can eat again. But eventually there comes a day when even that stops working. But then we have a new preoccupation, the consequences of our eating. So we can be intensely absorbed in the consequences of our eating. That seems to be suffering, but it works fine to take away our sense of our separation, because all we can think about is how fat we are or how awful it is that we just binge on food and then vomit.

But usually one compulsion isn't enough. A person who has a

compulsion has found it works to stop their pain and so they tend to get other compulsions. As I said in the previous chapter, direct compulsions like eating, drinking, lusting, drugging, etc., aren't as dangerous to the person who has them because the person is finally faced with the consequences of the compulsion. Compulsions are usually progressive, so eventually the compulsion gets so bad something has to be done about it.

What we're looking at here are the compulsions with others. These compulsions work the same as alcohol but they are more dangerous because the consequences are more subtle. My compulsion with the alcoholics in my life served me beautifully. I could feel superior to them by comparison. My life wasn't screwed up like their lives were. I was superior in that they had to come to me and ask for help and I could give it. Or, I could volunteer my help if they didn't come ask for it often enough. And my own personal sense of inadequacy wasn't threatened because these people around me had all their obvious inadequacies. There was no danger they would call me on mine. Here is where we teachers, doctors, nurses, social workers, counselors, all have to look at ourselves to see if what we are doing is coming out of a compulsion with others' problems and our need to feel superior to them. And this is something we have to do for ourselves because our compulsion with others is so above reproach that hardly ever will anyone call us on what we're doing. Who tells the doctor, or nurse, or psychiatrist that they are crazy in the way they are trying to lose themselves in other people's lives.

What's so clear to me now is how I set all this up at an early age. I remember one day in college, one of the other big men on campus I ran around with asked me, "Jess, how come all the people we know are neurotic?" I passed his question off by saying that it was because those normal people weren't near as interesting. But it was just that they weren't as interesting to us neurotics. But also, those dull people weren't interested in us. Why would a reasonably normal person want to be around us neurotics who were constantly in trouble? We thought it was exciting. They thought it was dumb.

I heard a good story that powerfully illustrated how far our preoccupation with others can go. The woman telling the story was about twenty years away from the situation so she had the benefit of many years of hindsight, reflection, and self-acceptance. Her husband was an alcoholic. As his alcoholism progressed, he stopped coming home for supper. But each morning, the wife would say to him, "You're coming home for supper tonight, aren't you?" and he would say he was. About five-thirty she would take up her station by the window and start watching the cars, waiting for him to drive up. By then she had started keeping the shades drawn all day long so the neighbors couldn't see what was going on in their house. So she would be standing at the side of the window with the shade pulled back a little ways so she could watch the street but still not be seen.

She would stand there for hours waiting for him to come home, and he wouldn't be there until midnight or later and then there would be the fight and the promise it would be different in the morning. Then in the morning the pattern would start all over again. From the outside, such a story sounds insane. But we get used to our own insanity; it's progressive, and most of us can't see how insane it is. The point is, the preoccupation with her husband's problem worked great for her.

The clincher to her story was her answers to her kids when they would come up to her as she was standing at the window lost in her watching. They would wonder when supper would be ready or would need help with their homework. She would pass off such requests with, "Don't bother me. Can't you see I'm busy?" And she was busy, very busy.

About a year after I had my heart attack at thirty-five, an acquaintance of mine in advertising had a heart attack at thirty-six and died immediately. He was exceptionally active in community affairs. He had been president of the JC's and was in many other organizations and had a young family like I did. A friend who knew him told me that in the month before he died, he was home only two or three evenings. The rest of the evenings he was busy with his activities. The college started a scholarship in his honor, but I always wondered how his wife and kids felt. There is a possibility that at least some of those activities were an escape for him. Things like this were hard for me to figure out until recently. Now I see why I need to avoid something like that.

I need to put down the idea I'm separate and alone and inadequate. God lives within me as me. The idea of my inadequacy comes from my crazy mind's need to be perfect. When I see I'm not inadequate, I don't need to *do something* so I can be somebody. I'm already somebody. I'm the best Jess that God could make. All I need to do is live in that. All my crazy doing was also supported by another false idea. I thought there were lots of things in this world that needed to be done and if I didn't do them, they wouldn't be done, or at least they wouldn't be done right.

What I see now is that God made this world perfect and there is nothing I need to do to make it go. It went well before I was born and will go well after I'm dead. All I need to do is any little task that is put before me purely out of love for God rather than to build me up or to do something no one else could possibly do as well. Who would do the "work" in a world like this? Simple. The work would be done out of love by people who don't think of it as work. I'm an advertising man. I write advertising for hybrid seed corn and other seeds. I've been doing that for thirty-two years and I'd love to do it again this next year. A friend of mine in Bozeman loved to haul away people's garbage. There's no job that some people aren't doing out of love. Yet there's no job so neat that everybody doing it just loves it. It's all in our attitude toward God and the world and ourselves.

As I see it now, there's only one thing for me to do in this world and that is to wake up and know that God lives within me as me. Once I wake up to that, then I just go home and be a householder. Then it doesn't matter if I'm doing the dishes, making the bed, fixing the house, writing an ad, or writing a book. It's all holy, it's all God.

My friend Bill Gove has a beautiful story about that. He tells about the businessman who was watching some bricklayers. He walked up to one of them and asked him what he was building and the bricklayer said, "A wall." The man thought the guy didn't have much vision so he went up to the next guy and asked him the same question. His answer was, "A building." He thought to himself, "Well, that's more like it." He asked a third bricklayer what he was building and he said, "I'm building a great cathedral that will soar to the skies." You know what, they fired that third bricklayer because he was supposed to be building an Esso gas station!

These are the kind of things we do when we don't know who we are and are constantly caught up in our preoccupations so we won't have to take off the covers and look at ourselves. Now I see why my preoccupations were so harmful to me. When I would experience some feeling that was unpleasant, I would turn to one of my preoccupations for relief. I would think of an elk hunting trip and plan it. Or, I would think of some financial project and think about possible ways of handling it. Or, I would eat more than

I needed and eat between meals and then be preoccupied with the scale and fat and my belly sticking out and not looking good.

I recently had a spiritual awakening on food. My need for a snack before I went to bed was taken away. It happened one day when I watched a neighbor deep in her preoccupation with her weight. I was so mad at her. Then I realized that she was me. So I was all of a sudden over it. I haven't spent many thoughts since then on fat, I haven't been on a scale for months, and I don't think so often of food.

A dentist spoke some years ago about taking three hundred and sixty-five little vacations a year. He went on at least one big hunting or fishing trip each year. Then, each day, he would take a break from his work and replay his past vacation trip or anticipate the next one. I thought that was a great idea. I see now he was a hunting-aholic. "But," you say, "that was just a harmless preoccupation." That's what I used to think, but I see now that he was out of his present reality just as I so often was.

The book *Zen Keys* helped me with this understanding. It described Zen as the direct experience of reality. That means that wherever we are, that's where we are. When I drive a car, that's where my mind needs to be. When I'm taking a break, that's where I need to be. My mind does roam some, but I don't send it off to roam in certain spots anymore like a hunting or fishing trip or some other preoccupation so strong it can take my mind off something unpleasant.

There was an interesting point in the book about energy. It said that in Zen the experience is that we lose energy through anger, hate, envy, jealousy, etc. A Zen monk can tell how he is doing in his spiritual development by how much energy he has when he comes to the evening. He may be physically tired but he has his good energy as completely as he had it in the morning. I haven't reached that point yet but I have got to the place where I have most of my energy at the end of most days. In the old days, I would come home from work with my energy gone. After supper, I would sit down in my easy chair and I couldn't get out. Often I would fall asleep in the chair because I didn't have the energy to get up and go to bed. I haven't been that low on energy for years except in serious illness or a rare disaster.

I sit down after supper to read the paper, then get up and go do something else, then sit down again. I'm not glued to the chair anymore by emotional fatigue even after two or three days of the most intense business conferences. We have these indicators in our lives. As our awareness increases, we see we really are making progress. It isn't the big leap into instant sainthood that our crazy mind wants, but it is progress; not perfection, but slow, steady progress. That's the same path any person on a spiritual program has to follow. Humility about where we're at, patience about the way we're progressing, and gratitude for all we've been given, those are the qualities we gradually gain.

This need for a constant awareness of our moment-to-moment reality is the reason any preoccupation with anything but what's at hand is harmful to the spiritual life. Maybe other people don't need to live this way, but the people I know and read of who are working spiritual programs don't want any preoccupations, obsessions, or compulsions. It all has to go, and good riddance to all of it. In *The Miracle of Mindfulness*, Thich Nhat Hanh tells us how to set aside one day a week to practice a quiet, unhurried pace and to always be where we are.

So this is the harm from having a compulsion with others. They are doing just fine. God is meeting them just where they are. And God is looking after the work that needs to be done, so all I need to do is what is put in my hands to do. I used to be so filled with self-importance that I had to sleep with my feet in the air to keep the sky from falling. Now I can take a day off once in a while.

When a person finally comes to see that their addiction with others or with some substance has taken over their lives, they start seeking help and they begin to see how powerless they really are. When they finally see this powerlessness, they have four problems: 1. They have the habitual, compulsive way of thinking that has developed in their addiction. 2. They have the consequences of their addiction. 3. They still have the initial problem of being separate and alone, the problem they used their addiction for. 4. They are deep in the denial that was necessary for the addiction to develop but that now makes it hard to see and accept the facts of their present situation.

It takes a super-powerful program to solve addictions like that. The twelve-step programs like Alcoholics Anonymous are probably the most overlooked phenomenon in psychology and religion today because those programs are the super-powerful programs needed to help people do the big job of freeing themselves from the iron hand of addiction.

How do you stop an addiction that you used your religion on and prayed to be released from, or an addiction where you went to the best that psychiatry and psychology had to offer and they gave up on you and told you not to come back? You obviously have to find a God with more power than the ones you tried. Granted, many people were able to make a regular-power God or a regular-power psychology work. But for others, the worst cases, God or the psychiatrist wouldn't work no matter how hard they prayed or how often they went to the psychiatrist. Even their mothers couldn't help them. They needed to find a higher-powered God or a higher-powered psychology.

For these people, a new way has been found to increase the effective power of God. While God has all power, what part of that power an individual will let into their lives is the effective power of God. So it is effective power that counts for the individual.

I think the secret of increasing the effective power of God is this: You shine God's light through a fellow sufferer, a fellow addict. God coming to you through a fellow addict so magnifies God's power you can finally see it and feel it and it lifts the addiction where everything was hopeless before. One of the first people to apply this principle was St. Francis, the rich and noble kid who had to give away everything and be the poorest of the poor so God's light could shine through him as a poor person so he could touch the other poor.

Centuries later, in 1935, the alcoholics first found that a fellow alcoholic could so magnify God's power that it could cure the fellow alcoholic. Later some drug addicts found they were enough different from the alcoholics that they needed the fellow drug addicts in Narcotics Anonymous to magnify God's power.

At this point I need to repeat something I've often said: I'm not an alcoholic. But sixteen years ago, an old alcoholic named Vince saw how crazy I was and he and Betsy and Jack started teaching me how to live. So I owe my life and much of what I have learned to these alcoholics. If it wasn't for them, I couldn't speak so familiarly of the twelve-step programs. Because of them I got to go inside Alcoholics Anonymous in a way few non-alcoholics have ever had the chance to go, through open meetings, state conferences, and personal sponsorship.

Once AA had showed the way, the other twelve-step programs came along like Alanon for the spouses of the alcoholics, Gamblers Anonymous, Emotions Anonymous, Sexaholics Anonymous and all the others. But it is so easy for us to get tradition-bound. Many in

AA who had to fight to win acceptance for their program turned around and locked in on their own program as a cure for anything, including hangnails. If one of their members had one of the "other" problems like a food problem or a sex problem, they were told to just work their AA program on that problem and it would go away like their alcohol problem. Use AA to solve it. And for many people, their AA program worked well enough to solve a food problem or a sex problem. But the AA's who stood on AA as a cure-all for all problems maybe forgot their own history.

Before AA, most of the twelve steps were used by their co-founder, Dr. Bob, for five years in the Oxford Movement, but those steps and the Oxford Movement God didn't get Dr. Bob sober. It was only when God came shining to Dr. Bob magnified through a fellow alcoholic that he could get sober. And the same for the other alcoholic in that twosome, Bill W. God shining through other alcoholics was so powerfully magnified it sobered up way over a million hopeless drunks. Powerful as this was, it still wasn't powerful enough to bring to recovery the worst of the overeaters in AA or the worst of the sexaholics in AA.

Men and women in AA who worked the best AA program they knew how, still found themselves helpless over their eating or their lust after ten, twenty, even thirty-odd years of AA. They found they had to go to their fellow food addicts to find out what food abstinence was or go to their fellow sexaholics to find that all they had to do was stop their sexual thinking. They found they had to go to their fellow addict so that God shining through him or her could be magnified enough to free them from that other addiction. What many in AA often didn't realize was that a sexual high was a "drug," a mood-altering drug. They wouldn't let a newcomer drink a lot of cough syrup but didn't see that a sexual high produced its own powerful drugs internally and was just as addicting.

Does this mean an endless proliferation of programs among twelve-step-program members? No. But it does mean that those most caught in their addiction will probably need a fellow addict who shares their addiction to free them.

There is an organization patterned after AA using the twelve steps called World Anonymous. It wants to roll all the obsessions and all the other problems up in one package and solve the whole bagful at one time. It might face the difficulty I have discussed that it isn't just the twelve steps alone that are the answer, it's seeing the magnified power of God through their fellow addicts together with the twelve steps that is the answer.

There is a second part of the twelve-step program that is just as little understood as the first part. The first part of the program is where the compulsion is lifted by the power of God shining through the fellow addict. Sometimes the compulsion is lifted and the addict returns to normal life free of the compulsion for the rest of their life. These cases do happen, but they are rare. What is most always the case is that the compulsion is lifted temporarily, long enough for the addict to start to build a new life free of the addiction.

But here is where the second part of the twelve-step program comes in. And this is the part of the twelve-step programs that many have such a hard time understanding. The addict needs to stay in frequent association with their fellowship, to keep the addiction lifted, as the addict goes about building a new way of life that works for him or her. This second part of the program is where God shines through the fellow addict and God is so magnified in the process that the addiction continues to be held at bay while the addict learns what they had put off so long: how to live.

This second part of the twelve-step programs is just as hard for people to understand as the first part. They see the alcoholic's need to stay close to the fellowship and can't understand why the alcoholic isn't cured and doesn't walk away. They can't see that the addict's cure is only a temporary one and that the addict needs to stay in the warmth and protection of the fellowship for the recovery to continue so he or she can build a new way of life that works for them without their addiction.

Many people outside the program and some new to the program scream against this. They see it as a new dependence, a crutch. But it is no more a crutch than food or water is a crutch for a well person. It is something they need, but it doesn't restrict their lives, it enhances their lives.

As a person goes on in the program and gets better and better, people have a harder and harder time understanding this continuing need for the program. When they see a person like old Chuck who has been sober thirty-eight years and is leading a beautiful life, they can't see why this person should stay in the program. But what they find so hard to see is that the program is one of the finest spiritual programs we know of today. Alcoholics Anonymous has its fiftieth anniversary in 1985. It has been proposed for a Nobel

Peace Prize because of the extent and revolutionary character of its work. Over a million alcoholics are sober today in the program, hundreds of thousands who achieved sobriety in the program died sober, and hundreds of thousands of others are finding relief from their addictions in companion programs.

The people in the programs find they have a way of life that keeps leading them closer and closer to their brothers and sisters and to God. Why would they want to give up such a spiritual program? Why would they want to give up a way of life that has satisfied their deep need for wholeness and unity far beyond what they ever dreamed possible? So the issue for them isn't just freedom from their addiction anymore, the issue is living a new spiritual way of life they had always hungered for and had not been able to find. When one's feet are finally planted on the path to a God they had been seeking all their life, why would anyone who now is in their right mind want to leave such a path? But an onlooker who doesn't understand spiritual paths can't be blamed for not being able to make much sense out of the seeming riddle of someone who isn't drinking, yet insists they are alcoholic and will be for the rest of their lives and that they will never be cured, even though they know God, as each of them understands him, has given them the freedom not to drink today.

So these are the contributions the twelve-step programs are making to the lives of addicted people who turn to them for help. I mention these experiences of the twelve-step groups because so many people have found they can apply the twelve-step principles and practices to their problems, whatever they may be. And I think these ideas from the twelve-step groups are especially illuminating on the spiritual quest that marriage is where a spiritual program is so necessary to make sense out of some of the difficult times in marriage. For many of us entering into marriage, it was a case of babies marrying babies. In this sort of situation, we all have such deep dependency needs that we usually stood by and just watched each other continue on in the way we were going rather than face the fear of abandonment.

In standing by and watching me be in my compulsion for as long as she did, my wife had to face what her need was in our situation. She had an overwhelming fear of abandonment. It had ruled her life. I had to face what my need was in our situation and found that I had the same fear. From seeing how strong this fear was in our own lives we began to pay attention to others who came into our lives. We soon saw that an overwhelming fear of abandonment was the driving force of most of the personalities we met. This fear is just another way of stating how alone we feel, and a great many of us find maladaptive ways to overcome this. All of these ways are our attempts to control our lives and the lives of others.

These attempts fall into two categories in my opinion. We choose either power and manipulation or people-pleasing and being victims as our control devices. The way we play out these roles is as varied as the people involved, but all of the ways we choose are ways we enable ourselves and others to give us the illusion that we will not be abandoned. Psychiatry can bring us an understanding of this, but in my experience it can give us no solutions.

It is only in spiritual programs that I saw a solution being offered that could bring a person out of their maladaptive ways and give them a new way of life. The reason for this is so simple that we oftentimes don't even see it. Fear of abandonment is simply a lack of faith in any power greater than ourselves. It is showing us that we have no belief that there is any purpose or reason for our existence on this earth, and that there is no such thing as a higher power who has his "eye on the sparrow."

Now, we can continue to live in this way, and if we do, we will be faced with having to look into the mirror each day knowing that we are looking at all the power there is in our lives.

Is that what we want? Is that knowledge going to bring us peace and joy and love in our daily life? Is that knowledge going to teach us to live and let live? Is that knowledge going to show us how to live one day at a time with trust and happiness in each day's daily bread? I think not. I think that the knowledge that we need comes from an ongoing support system and a true spiritual awakening in our lives in order to have the change of personality that Carl Jung was speaking about in the letter cited in the previous chapter when he told the hopeless drunk that his only chance for change was in having a spiritual awakening and that there was no hope for him in further psychiatry.

Carl Jung was such an inspired man, and perhaps he could foresee that the world would soon be caught up in an epidemic of this type of problem. This need for a change in personality has become commonplace rather than exceptional in our lifetime, but that's okay. For fifty years there has been a fellowship perfecting this kind of support system, and they have now generously allowed the steps of their fellowship to be used in other support systems that can help every kind of "nut" there is in this world.

But, more applicable to most of us, the twelve-step groups have demonstrated the importance of a spiritual program in dealing with our crazy minds and all our compulsions. We can learn from the example of the twelve-step groups the need for a rigorous and honest spiritual program to deal with ourselves as the imperfect beings we are. Now that we have faced our imperfections and see that we are relieved of the burden of seeking or assuming perfection, let's look at the idea of commitment in marriage.

7.

Commitment
Is a Marriage's
Security Blanket

As I mentioned earlier in the book, the experience of Jackie confronting me on my sexual compulsion came right in the middle of the seminar I was doing on marriage. The seminar was six weeks of two talks each Sunday night at Dayspring Methodist Church in Phoenix. Here I was right in the middle of talking to a bunch of church people about how to have a perfect marriage, and I was faced with seeing my sexual compulsion and all the wreckage it had wrought in our marriage. The irony of the whole thing was not lost on Jackie. In fact, the first talk the Sunday after our Thursday confrontation was on commitment. And the name of the church was Dayspring. For me, too, the irony and symbolism was so deep, I had to laugh at the whole situation. But it was just perfect for me to be faced with talking commitment in that circumstance because that is what commitment is all about.

My discussion with Jackie at the time went something like this: "Guess what? The chapter I'm starting to talk about next is about commitment, and the second talk Sunday night is about the sex plague in America."

"Well," she answered, "you know about those things first hand, don't you?"

"Yup," I said, "a person can't teach what he doesn't know."

"Good Lord, how you do rationalize," was her reply. I looked at her to make sure she was smiling. She was.

The first and most important commitment in marriage is to God. We need to say to ourselves, "Hey, God, I'm going to marry this person and I'm going to stick with this marriage for life. Even if this person tries to kill me, I'll still maintain a relationship. I might move out of the house, but I'll still stay in relationship." This is a wild statement, but I say it to show the deep level of lifelong commitment that's necessary. This vow has to be solemn, and made to God as each of us understands him. Just saying it to the other person isn't strong enough to stand up. It won't cut the mustard when the marriage is faced with what Jackie and I dealt with that week and at other times in our marriage.

The second commitment should be to ourselves. We should tell ourselves that we'll stay in this marriage for life in order to find our natural being, our true self.

The third commitment is to the other person so that they know that they too will have room to grow, to give up their own childish ways.

The fourth commitment is to mutuality. No mutual agreement on this, no marriage.

There is no way we can marry and have a family without this commitment. We may marry and have children, but with divorce as an option, we cannot have a family. We are just a bunch of babies sharing a roof. Commitment in marriage is the *morality of marriage* that Albert Einstein spoke about.

You have heard my story and my views on marriage. As I was doing some research on an article on Peer Group Therapy for the new Encyclopedia of Psychology, I had the good fortune to talk to the late Sidney Jourard's widow, Toni, and to his good friend Ted Landsman. Jourard believed in self-disclosure. I was asking about the consequences of that disclosure on the lives around him. I found to my surprise that he had died in 1974 at the age of forty-eight. His wife, Toni, told me that he had addressed the annual meeting of the American Association of Marriage and Family Counselors and the National Council on Family Relations just three weeks before he died when a car he was repairing fell on him.

Toni sent me a copy of his address and I was interested to see it went along many of the same lines I have discussed with you. So to give you another perspective on this same general approach to marriage, in this case from an eminent psychologist, I'll give you the first third of his speech.

MARRIAGE IS FOR LIFE
by Sidney Jourard

"I feel rather honored to have been invited here, and I am rather dismayed and delighted in a way to see how many people there are fighting the good fight. And it is, indeed, a good fight. I'll throw in my ten cents' worth or whatever denomination you might want to put after it.

"The title of my talk has nothing to do with chronological time. When I chose a title 'Marriage Is for Life' I meant that marriage is to enhance life, and it is not so much an answer as it is a search. I want to direct my remarks to that search, the search for life itself.

Ideal (and False) Images of Marriage

"The image of the good marriage is perhaps one of its most destructive features. The ideal marriage is a snare, a trap, an image the worship of which destroys life. The ideal marriage is like the ideal body or any other ideal, useful only if it engenders the divine discontent which leads to questing and authenticity. Whose image of a way to live together will guide a relationship? This is a question relevant for a president and his electorate, a doctor and his patient, a parent and child, a researcher and his subject, or a husband and wife. Shall it be an exercise in the concealment and display of power or a commitment to dialogue? Failure of dialogue is the crisis of our time, whether it be between nation and nation, us and them, or you and I.

"I had thought of putting together a book of my several writings on marriage, education, psychology, politics, and business and entitle it 'Disaster Areas,' for that indeed is what they are. The state of marriage and family life in this country can easily be called a disaster. I think it stems in part from unrealistic expectations and in larger part because of a culturally induced arrest of growth in adults. Perfectly good marriages are ended because something has gone wrong. Actually, I would say they are ended right at the point where they could begin.

"There are two fallacies perpetuated which keep the disasters happening. One is the myth of the right partner. The other is the myth of the right way to act so as to ensure peace, joy, and happiness. People believe, or are led to believe, that if they just find the right partner, the right answer to the riddle of their existence will be found. Once having found the right person and the way of relating that is satisfying at this time, the partners try to do everything to prevent change. That's tantamount to trying to stop the tide. Change, indeed, happens, but it happens underground, is concealed, and then it's introduced and experienced as a catastrophe. Instead of welcoming it, the partners find it devastating. Each may then seek to find someone who will not change, so that they never need face the need to change themselves.

Marriage as Dialogue

"Marriage at its best, according to the image that is making more sense to me, is a relationship within which change is generated by the way of relating—dialogue, so that growth as well as identity and a sense of rootedness are engendered. Change is not so much a threat as it is the fruit of a good marriage, according to this image. Marriage is for growth, for life. It's a place to call home, but like all homes one must leave it in its present form and then return, and then leave it, and then return, like Odysseus, leaving Ithaca and returning.

"Kierkegaard refused to marry and thereby defied the nineteenth century. I have refused to divorce, and I defy the twentieth. When one marriage in three is dissolved, or maybe it's 2.6, to remain wedded to the same spouse is virtually to live an alternate life-style. If so few marriages endure, then something is nonviable about that way of being married. I have tried in the twenty-six years of my marriage to be married in the ways designated by tradition, by the mass media, by my friends, by textbooks on marriage, by my wife's image of a good marriage, and none of these ways were for life. None were life-giving, but were rather images or, better, idols. To worship idols is idolatry, a sin. To worship marriage is like any other idolatry, the expenditure of one's own life, time, and vitality to enhance the image. That such marriage is disastrous is self-evident. When it endures it becomes a major cause of psychological distress and physical illness in our land.

"Conventional medicine, psychiatry, and psychotherapy and, for that matter, marriage counseling and family counseling frequently function very much like combat surgery. The illness and suffering which reach the healers stem from the stress and 'dispiritation' engendered from inauthentic family relationships. Laing and Esterson documented the way a family image can be preserved at the cost of one member being scapegoated as a schizophrenic (Laing and Esterson, 1965). The wards for cancer, heart disease, gunshot and knife injuries, suicide attempts, and other stress ailments provide evidence that nondialogic family life engenders unrelenting and destructive stress. To be married is not an unmixed blessing. If marriage is hell, and family life is a major cause of disease, which indeed it is, why stay in it, or get in it?

"Is the family dead, as David Cooper observed (Cooper, 1971)? If it's dying, should we then kill it, put it out of its misery?

"What do people do who have tried marriage and then gotten out of it? The overwhelming majority remarry and try to live the second, third, or seventh marriage in a way that is more life-giving for the self and others than the first. Frequently these marriages 'fail,' as did the first, and I put 'fail' in quotes, because I don't think marriages fail; I think people fail marriages.

"*Wherever I go in this country I get uncomfortable. I think it's more so in California than elsewhere, and it's not with smog or even the inhabitants of Orange County, but with the people one encounters everywhere. I am a trained and rather experienced psychotherapist, tuned in to the nonverbal expressions of despair, loneliness, anguish, and need. So many of the adults I encounter casually or in depth are suffering a rupture of their last lawful or common-law marriage and are desperately looking for a new one or despairingly avoiding all but superficial relationships in order to avoid risk. The silent shrieks of pain deafen me. To be married is for many boredom or hell. To be unmarried, legally or unlegally, as many experience it is hell and despair. Is there an alternative?*" (italics added).

"Everything depends on the model or metaphor which defines the marriage one will live, seek, grow in, or die from. There are lethal images of marriage and family life, and there are life-giving models. I take it that enduring, growing relationships are essential for truly human life and for personal fulfillment and growth. I take it that happiness, pleasure, or growth if sought as ends in and of themselves will not happen. They are by-products of a fully lived life. A life lived in continuing dialogue with some few others will encourage, even force growth.

"I take it as true that there is no way to go through life without some pain, suffering, loneliness, and fear. We can help one another minimize the shadow side of life; none can avoid it completely. To seek to avoid pain at all costs is to make an idol out of pleasure or painlessness. To avoid solitude at all costs is to make an idol out of chronic companionship. To avoid anxiety and depression at all costs is to make an idol out of safety and elation. To have to achieve orgasm with somebody in particular is to make an idol of that person or of the genital experience. To sacrifice everything for the breathless experience of being in love is to make an idol of breathlessness.

"Many people live in such idolatrous fashion. They marry for those ends and divorce when the other side of reality creeps or bursts into the magic circle, only to seek another playmate or protector in relation to whom the idol may once again be worshiped and the sacrifice of life continue afresh.

"Marriage as dialogue through life is for me a viable image, one that engenders life and growth as the conversation unfolds (italics added). Dialogue for me, as for Martin Buber (Buber, 1937), is the appropriate way for human beings to be or to strive to be with each other, not imposition, power plays, and manipulation. Family life is an appropriate place for dialogue to be learned and practiced. And through dialogue it's a place to grow in competence, self-sufficiency, and self-esteem.

"To me the great failure in marriage, as in American education, is that neither institution as lived and practiced fosters enlargement of self-respect, respect for others, or growing competence in the skills that make life livable. Deception, manipulation, bribery, and threats are as American as apple pie and mother. These skills are learned in relation with Mum, Dad, the teacher, or the teaching machine.

"There is, as near as I now know, no assured way to practice marriage as dialogue except by living it. As soon as a relationship becomes habitual, dialogue has ended. Predictable, habitual ways for people to act with one another are simply nonverbal ways to say the same things to one another day after day, year after year. Habit is the great anesthetic, the annihilator of consciousness.

"Nondialogic ways of being married are either exercised in a chronic struggle for power and control or they are harbors to escape those aspects of life that would engender growth. Some people stay married so they will have someone to control. Some people stay married so they will have an ear to talk into. Some people stay married so they can suffer or make their partner suffer. Most curiously, some get divorced when their partner will no longer be controlled, will no longer listen, or will no longer consent to suffer. The other's changes may be, indeed, a sign of the other person's personal growth. The one who gets a divorce may find yet another partner with whom control can be practiced or who will listen to undisciplined chatter with apparent interest or who will accept pain.

"All this is by way of saying that I think in America, and in the countries that follow the example set by the American way of life, we expect more out of marriage than it could ever deliver and we expect the wrong things. God, in her infinite wisdom, so designed us that we are of two kinds and we find one another irresistible at various stages in our lives, so much so that we decide to live together. So far, so good. It's joyous to find another person attractive who finds you attractive, then to make love, even to have children.

"Then the honeymoon ends and the marriage begins. It is at this point that I think most divorce happens. We are hung up on honeymoons. My honeymoon was a disaster. I knew next to nothing about tenderness and solicitude, sex, women's sexuality, my bride's sexuality. I was incapable of dialogue. I wanted to be seen in a certain way. I needed my wife to be a certain way, and obliging girl that she was, she obliged. She seemed to be the kind of person she thought I thought she was, the kind of person she felt I would like. We carried out this double masquerade for about three years. It took me that long to cheat. By seven years I was an accomplished dissembler in the realm of my sex life, not my love life, where I was a truth-teller in all realms except that.

"With our first separation I had a modest collection of female scalps, so to speak, to my credit and my wife, to her credit, after the shock of disclosure wore off discovered the dubious joys of semi-guilty infidelity. Through some fluke, though, within a month of a decree of divorce, we decided to resume our by now somewhat scarred relationship, rather wiser and more honest with one another about who we were. This openness for those not practiced in it was pure hell. It was painful, I assure you. It was painful for me to learn that my wife had a mind, a perspective, and feelings of her own different from mine. She was not the girl I married; in fact, she never was. I married my fantasy, and so did she. She had some coping to do, discovering that I was not the saint I had once seemed. She learned I was, and still am to some extent, a scarcely bridled privateer, a pirate, and adventurer, barely domesticated to her or American conceptions of married males.

"How do two or more eccentric and energetic people live together? With humor or not at all. I did not become selectively gelded upon marriage. The more I reflect upon it, the more I like myself, having had the courage to pursue those ways of keeping vital and alive as nondestructively as I did. I could have done worse. I could have sought a divorce or have been divorced by my wife. If the first three years were the honeymoon—actually only about one year was honeymoon—boredom and pretense at joy in our sameness is a better description of our next two years. My cheating was the beginning of a marriage with some authentic companionship, some lying and getting with the career, and the experience of living with several very young children. This marriage or this way of being married lasted seven years, until I experienced the death of my father, the completion of my first book, and the dreaded disclosure of my rather complicated affairs with several other women. Here was a real opportunity to be taught a lesson or to learn a lesson. I didn't divorce, however, nor did my wife divorce me, because we retained some recollection of affection between us and we had some children to care for and a vast amount of anger and mutual reacquaintance to go through. It is, I assure you again, a painful experience extended through time to make yourself known to the person with whom you live and to learn aspects of her experience, attitudes, hopes, fears, and so on which shatter your image of her.

"But my marriage and family life were not all my life. I had friends, other interests, and I pursued these, as did she. My life did not begin when I met her nor end when we were out of contact with one another.

"My third marriage to her began with hope and resolve, as we struggled to find some enjoyment in living and to care for our children. I suspect we were growing in experience, self-sufficiency, and self-esteem. I hesitate to use certain words, but I'll say them. The point I was going to make is that marriage and family life is a wonderful place to learn shit, fecal detritus, because if you don't know shit, you have not lived. But if that's all you know, you have not lived.

"I don't know how many marriages I have had by now, but I am married at the present time to a different woman of the same name in ways that are suited to our present stage of growth as human beings. I am not breathlessly in love with my wife, nor is she with me. Now, she read this and there are some asterisks in her handwriting. It says, 'Maybe not breathlessly, but I do love you now with more intensity and depth and true caring than I ever have in my life.'

"When we spend a great deal of time in one another's proximity, we can both know irritations, even rages of astonishing intensity. It is difficult for two strong and passionate and willful people to share space and time without humor and respect for the other, even though she is wrong, as from my point of view she is. It would be so much easier for me to divorce her and to live with, even marry, some younger woman with firmer breasts, a smaller waist, who is as sexy as a civet, who worships me and wants to have an intense and meaningful relationship with me, who would attend to my every word, and think I was the Messiah or at least worthy of the Nobel Prize. Many of my colleagues have done that. I could never see—except when I was most exasperated with my wife and fed up with being a father—why these friends of mine, otherwise sensible, wished to play the same record over again. I find someone whose perspective is smaller than mine, or who wants me to be their father, or who is but an echo of my own perspective, rather boring. Flattering, but boring. And I don't want to father anybody because I've been a father. I find a grown person of the opposite sex incites me much less to rape or riot than a young girl, but more interesting by and large, at least to listen to."

Well, there you have Jourard's view on this same subject. You see how similar this is to what I've found. I hadn't read this article until about a year and a half ago. That was two and a half years after I presented the basic ideas for this book to Doubleday. What is so interesting to me is how two people coming from very different perspectives come up with such similar views. Just a little later in his speech, Jourard quotes another writer whom I have not read who has similar ideas too:

"A book on marriage which I have read—and I have read many, including the O'Neills' (O'Neill & O'Neill, 1972)—which addresses this mystery of growth with some of the respect that it deserves is a small volume written by Israel Charny called *Marital Love and Hate* (Charny, 1972). Compared to his vision, many of the other books fail to acknowledge, I think, the depths of misery and destructiveness which are the other side of personal growth. Charny sees the family not strictly as haven or a place for fun and games, although it can be that, or as a place for sexual delights, but as a place where that most savage of all creatures, man, can learn to share time and space nonviolently and nondestructively. Armed by his vision, as well as by my own, I can see that many so-called successful marriages and happy families are that way because someone is repressing his perspective or is colluding with others in the destruction of his own perspective.

"According to this view, marriage is not for happiness, I have concluded after twenty-six and a half years. It's a many-splendored thing, a place to learn how to live with human beings who differ from oneself in age, sex, values, and perspectives. It's a place to learn how to hate and to control hate. It's a place to learn laughter and love and dialogue. I'm not entirely persuaded that marriage and family counseling is a profession with any particular contribution to make to the quality of life. There is so far as I now know no way for people to live alone or with others that God endorsed as *the way* that she intended. (Laughter) Why is that funny? Certainly she intended that we cohabit to conceive and then to rear children, but the exact way we should live with one another was never specified. We have to grope and search, according to this view. As near as I can see, such groping for viable, nondestructive ways proceeds best within a context of dialogue.

"Dialogue takes courage and commitment to honesty. When people find they can no longer live with their partner, it is not divorce or separation that is indicated. This is in some ways like suicide. The person who tries to kill himself is being unduly literal. By his act he is saying that he no longer wishes to live in the way he has been, and he is also saying that he can imagine no other way to live. He doesn't necessarily wish to stop living, just to stop living in that way. His failure is a failure of imagination as much as it is a failure of nerve.

"Divorce too frequently means that one partner or the other refuses to continue living married in that way. The divorcé then finds someone with whom some other dimension of himself can be expressed. This looks like change or growth. I have wondered whether hitherto unexpressed dimensions of self could not have emerged in relation to the spouse because with the new partner an impasse will arrive and there will be the necessity to struggle with it.

"If there is growth in serial marriage—and there is—one wonders why there could not be growth in the first. I know of many marriages in which one partner or the other refused to acknowledge or value the change in the other. The unchanged one ordered the changed one to revert to the way he or she was earlier, on pain of divorce.

"The failure of marriage is the failure of our culture to provide models and reasonable expectations about human relationships. Because we lie so much about our relationships, especially to our children, and because the breadth and depth of authentic experience is not presented in movies, comics, books, and TV, nobody knows what is expectable or what is healthy or life-giving or potentially life-giving in marriage. People think that if they get angry or bore one another or fail to respond sexually that the marriage is finished, that they are out of love. Perhaps the overestimation of romantic love is one of the more pernicious patterns in our society."

After Jourard's speech, he was asked what he meant by dialogue. He said:

"The image of dialogue that I speak from is dialogue as expounded by the philosopher Martin Buber in rather poetic terms. As a conversation between I and Thou is the way he put it. But to put it in prose, dialogue is to speak your truth in response to the other person's truth, with no effort in a concealed way to lie or to con or to manipulate the other person to be in some way what he is not. It's speaking your truth and then waiting to hear the other person's truth, which you can never predict or control. As soon as you try to predict or control it, dialogue is ended. Out of it, incidentally, comes growth. Without it there may be change but it's not necessarily the change you would call growth."

I was struck by what Jourard had to say for a number of reasons. One was the way he put the necessity for commitment, which was as a lifelong search for life. Another was the fact that he and Charny are some of the few I have found who see the pain and even savagery in marriage that I see. When I was preparing to give the marriage seminar in February 1983, I stopped at a Waldenbooks store and talked to the manager. We went to the section on love and marriage and we found only two books on marriage. Almost all the books were on how we can get the hit or the fix of sex, or the romantic love so many of us are looking for. The rest of the books were on divorce. That, to me, was a beautiful statement on marriage today. I know you could go to a religious bookstore and find a number of books on marriage, but the ones

I've looked at, I have trouble relating to. They seem to be written for nicer and more in-control people than I'm able to be much of the time.

The chapters I wrote on the crazy mind and on our many and varied compulsions, to me, make it a wonder that we are able to hold any marriages together. Yet how can we really let down our guards and be ourselves without the protective wall of commitment. That's why the young people who decide to just live together for years and then decide to marry have so much trouble. They think they gave marriage a try. They didn't. They gave living together a try in their fear of marriage. They both had to be on their good behavior or the other would leave. It was only when the marriage was made that there was a real commitment. Then they could each relax and be their savage selves. So we need to really look at commitment and see how it helps us.

I see many men who wouldn't think of entering a business relationship without making a real commitment to giving it plenty of time to work out. They wouldn't dream of running at the first sign of trouble. What I'm talking about is making at least the same commitment to our marriages for our *own* benefit, not simply because of some religious principle or because we're totally ruled by "what will people think?"

Twenty-two years ago I really began my commitment to this marriage when I said to myself, "I'm never again going to do anything I don't believe in." That's when I began searching seriously for my God-created natural being, my "truth" as Jourard calls it. To do that I've had to get rid of all the garbage that's become stuck to my being as a consequence of some very neurotic and sick and destructive choices that I've made. My journey has been a little more harrowing than most people's because part of my sexual compulsion was a hunger for power and conspicuous success. That was one of the many reasons for my books being written. They gave me power and attention that most people don't have.

I see now that I started the School of Life in July 1977 by bringing in some people to teach with me more as a means to find help for me and my family than to teach the students. Some very helpful things came from that. Some of the ideas I found I abused by twisting and using them against my family. But, on the whole, the contributions were very important. Some things I tried were fine tools that have benefited our whole family. Because of this, my wife had the experience in Germany that she wrote about in her book. My kids have had a lot of things and ideas that would never have been available to them otherwise. Some of these things and ideas were very detrimental, but many others helped them a lot. And all of this has led most of us to spiritual programs which have given us all tools of spiritual growth beyond measure.

There's a theory that alcoholics and addicts come out of dysfunctional families. The only problem with that theory is that it is a "which came first, the chicken or the egg?" theory. No family, no matter what its strengths, can continue to function with addiction in the family. And a large group of psychologists and therapists now believe that approximately ninety percent of the families in America are dysfunctional today. So what's the point of the theory? It just adds another burden on families to overcome. All this labeling is heaping burdens upon burdens on families already bowed down. Most psychiatrists and psychologists that I know who are worth their salt go to extremes to avoid labeling anyone with a negative label. The feeling is that the negative label then gives them still another thing to overcome. I tend to agree with that.

How can we categorize each human soul without thus putting a limitation upon it? Our young people are having such a tough time already without being offered such labeling. I think that Albert Einstein saw to the heart of the problem we are just beginning to see when he wrote a letter to Dr. Otto Juliusberger on April 11, 1946:

"I believe that the horrifying deterioration in the ethical conduct of people today stems primarily from the mechanization and dehumanization of our lives—a disastrous by-product of the development of the scientific and technical mentality. Nostra culpa! I don't see any way to tackle this disastrous shortcoming. Man grows cold faster than the planet he inhabits."

And in so much of the field of psychology, severed from philosophy and any redeeming spiritual concepts, the labeling and use of technique instead of a holistic approach is making man grow colder ever faster.

The people I respect in the world today are the ones who recognize the need for spiritual beliefs, and there are a growing number of them, like Einstein, who see that this physical, material, scientific world does not present the true reality of our being. The deeper we get into the intellect and the more we begin to think that all of the answers are there, the more lost we become. And, of course, it is marriage and family that have paid the biggest price.

The intellect isolates us; it makes us truly narcissistic. A selfish, self-centered, fearful person cannot understand commitment. We're too busy protecting our little egos. We're too busy seeking comfort in the myths of pleasure or security or material possessions or change. Most of us cannot conceive of the concept "There's no place to go and nothing to do." We don't understand the surrender to God that is required in order to live in a relationship. We cannot act, we are reactors. We live in fear of reprisal because we demand at least half of the action. I cannot be captain of my own ship because I want *your* ship under my control too. I've come to see from this that lifelong commitment is the only way for me. The inability of our puny, little, self-serving ego to accept commitment is the only explanation for the many people who live together for years, then get married and within months are divorcing. It's as though they immediately stop thinking of the other person, stop "putting in" and start "taking out" of the relationship once the paper is signed. This condition is an epidemic today.

I can't think of any other arrangement in the world that requires lifelong commitment, except maybe the priesthood. All other arrangements are partnerships, and they can afford to be at the pleasure of the two people involved. In the married relationship we must choose what is beneficial over what is pleasurable most of the time. This is our lifelong journey. As my old friend says, "My duties become my pleasures." So, what we are talking about here is moving from selfishness to selflessness.

When we are driven by our intellect, when our mind is our God, our senses are in control. When the senses are in control, pleasure is the only goal. To understand how we are a nation in the grip of sense-pleasure all we have to do is watch TV for a few hours and go to a couple of movies. It is all too clear then that we live with sensory overload all the time, and from this base how can we come close to lifelong commitment? And it is not just the younger generation that is living this way. We all are.

Our minds find many ways to deny the importance of commitment. I'll never forget a young student of mine a few years ago. We were sitting in class talking in the circle about marriage, and Tom said, "Jess, there's one thing I don't understand in this marriage business. Why is that gal so insistent on that little, old piece of paper?" I said, "Tom, if that's just a little old piece of paper, why don't you just give that little, old gal that little, old piece of paper?" Tom turned white. Why? Because that is not just a little, old piece of paper, that is a great, big, awfully strong piece of paper. A powerful piece of paper. There have been many times in my marriage when I've been so glad my wife is committed to me and that little, old piece of paper is about all we have holding us together through the turmoil. And I'm sure there are times Jackie feels the same way.

To have a lifelong commitment, it has to be mutual, of course. We can't afford to be interested in a partner who is not willing to base their life on this degree of stability. This lifelong commitment is to each other, and includes any children we have up to the age when they must remove themselves from our families and begin their own journey to God. All too often, once the children are gone, a lot of us are ready to put down the marriage. We must see clearly that the marriage commitment does not begin and end with children. It is not a convenience to give the children a stable home life. It is a lifelong journey.

I cannot subscribe to the belief that our young people today are of some low character compared to us older folks. No way can I criticize their character. Fewer of us older folks got divorced, but that's just outward circumstance. Plenty of us got divorced inwardly and just continued to live in the same house. I don't like the argument of us older people that we're more stable and more willing to work things out. Nor do I agree with the argument of younger people that they're more open and liberal and willing to try again. I've talked to too many young people who after a second or third marriage have acknowledged that it would probably have been better to have stayed in that first marriage and worked it out, because they have found consistently that the same problems reappeared in each succeeding marriage. They've had to face the same lessons over and over again. And to me there's some special value in that first partner that the next ones can't match. Besides, I've never seen a second or third marriage that didn't carry with it forever the ghosts of the previous mates. We can't put marriage down as easily as we would like to think.

I don't believe there are many of you reading this who can honestly say that you don't know what I'm saying deep down in your hearts. Everyone who has ever married someone, recognizes that they might have married someone because they were cute or attractive, but in my experience there is a lot of *soul mate* in this business of who we marry. God works in mysterious and powerful ways we can't begin to understand. The feeling of soul mate we have with that first marriage is a lot more common than can be explained by cuteness or attractiveness. It's deeper than that.

I've seen some unlikely match-ups and they've shown me that deep down the people involved really did know what they were doing. It's like Stephen Gaskin from "The Farm" in Summertown, Tennessee, says, ". . . God gave Moses the Ten Commandments and then he gave him an eleventh commandment. The eleventh commandment of God is: 'You do too know what I mean.' " I think we do too know what we're doing when we marry. We know when we stand up and say those vows that God's got something to do with that marriage.

I don't give a nickel for what we call the reality that more than one third of those marriages won't work out. Reality is the screwed-up way we've run the show. Reality is what we choose. There is only one reality I recognize and that is the possibility of how things can be when we get in harmony. And the one third or more of marriages that don't last are going to cause excruciating pain to the people in them, and they will split and do it all over again. It is my experience that life keeps pounding on us until we learn. This life isn't a free ride, where anything goes. Life has its order and harmony. When we are out of tune with that order and harmony we pay the price. I don't spend five minutes worrying about this problem, however. I don't have any power. Why should a powerless human being like me think that I can solve your problem when it takes God to solve mine? It would be a real egotistical thing on my part to think that I have answers for you when I don't have answers for myself, wouldn't it?

Now, so far I've said I can't see where there is really any such thing as divorce. No piece of paper I know of will ever undo the vows we made. No piece of paper will ever strike your present mate out of your life forever. But if you have to divorce—go ahead. I would like to see every state in the country make marriage counseling mandatory, but if you don't want to learn your lessons with your present mate, get a divorce. You will learn your lessons someplace else, in some other marriage or relationship.

The depth of commitment needed for marriage cannot be taught in my experience. You can run young people through all the pre-marriage courses in the world and they won't understand.

When you are hot to get married, you will agree with anything so that you can have your dream. All that any of us can ever have before marriage is what I would call a commitment to the ideal of commitment. Where lifelong commitment before God with another person comes into play in marriage is when you come home and your mate decks you with a major fault you've been committing all along and tells you to change or get out. I'm not talking about a spat, a little brush fire, I'm talking about nuclear war, the kind that pulverizes the bones. That's what separates the committed from the noncommitted. At times like that a healthy dose of commitment is like money in the bank.

As I told you earlier, when I was twenty-four and my wife was twenty, we had a handicapped child. A marriage can hardly survive a thing like that. It takes commitment under God to transform, to transcend a thing like that. At the time we began going through that experience, we had only been married a few years. We still didn't understand commitment but it was operating in us at some deep level without our understanding it. With a vow, a clear understanding of a higher power, with God in our lives, it has been my experience that there is nothing so horrible that it cannot be transcended. Some psychologists have begun to say that every relationship can be fixed. I go a step further and say that every relationship should be fixed. It's never too late and we're never too old.

Every once in a while I see a couple who are both exceptionally stable individuals with marvelously tuned physical bodies and a real, mutual *joi de vivre*. They are so rare, but they do exist. I find great joy in being with them and at the same time I am anxious and ask myself, "My God! What is wrong with me that I cannot be more like them?" Then I become more rational and realize that these kinds of people have always been the exception rather than the norm.

In marriage, there comes a time for some of us when our mate is persisting in a behavior that is destroying the relationship. We have all been taught that we cannot change another person, and this is true. The thing we can do, though, is offer that person a clear choice. That's what Jackie did for me when she confronted me with my sexual compulsion. She didn't say I had to change, she just said that she would no longer live with that behavior. For her to have continued on in the way we were going, feeling as she did and knowing what she knew, would have been *enabling* me to continue a pattern that was destructive to her. She would have been doing something that she did not believe in. She would have had to ask herself what sort of dependency made her live such a lie. She showed deep love and commitment to me in saying, "Do something or leave." In order to do this for me she had to be willing to risk my leaving.

All too often it is dependency on the other person that stops us from being able to confront a tough situation. Dependency is not love. We must not confuse the two. When we are dependent babies we dare not risk. We put up with a lot of bad behavior when we're dependent. We exhibit a lot of bad behavior when we're dependent. Dependency is an excruciating weakness; it tells us we're babies.

Jackie had gotten over being dependent on me, so it was possible for her to be clear. She told me that she wouldn't live with my behavior anymore. This is different than trying to change me. She told *me* to change myself or leave. There is a difference there. You have to think about it. If Jackie was trying to change me, she would have taken upon herself the God-like role of trying to control and manipulate me so that I would stop doing that. She would have kept the power with her. Instead she handed the power to me.

When Jackie was using tranquilizers and alcohol I didn't see clearly what was going on. It was such a subtle thing. She never fell off of barstools or tore up the house, she was just out of it. Today, seeing her addiction as I do, if she chose to go back to that behavior I would say to her what she said to me. I would tell her she could drink if she wanted to but I wouldn't live with her. I wouldn't divorce her, but I wouldn't live with her under those conditions. Do you see the difference? If I believed I could do something to make her stop, I'd become a controller and a manipulator. When I see clearly that the choice is hers, and that I am powerless, I get out of the way and allow her to choose.

A whole person is a very clear person. They see what behavior is acceptable in their lives and what behavior is unacceptable, and the message is there, not in a rigid, demanding, harmful way, but in an easy, flowing, loving way. There is no power play in it, it is all just love—just God. That is the true commitment. And that is where I believe it comes from because it's sure obvious to me that no human being ever figured this thing out. My old friend used to point to the partially wooded hills rolling up to the mountains outside his picture window. "Ain't no landscape gardener figured that one out," he would say. Same with life. There is a deep harmony working here beyond any power I could ever imagine. I have found that when I fully trust in that power, I have all the commitment I need.

8.

───────⌣───────

If Your God
Doesn't Work for You,
Fire Him!

IT WOULD SEEM LIKE IT WOULD BE NICE if each of us had a good understanding of the way the world worked before we had to make all the decisions we faced early in life. Why does it take a lifetime to learn to live a lifetime? Because that's what a lifetime is for. So simple—and yet so difficult for us to comprehend. That means all our seeming mistakes are a valuable part of the learning process. I also believe that we don't really screw things up as badly as we think we do. That's just our crazy mind being childish because it can't do everything perfect the first time.

I just read a letter recently from a woman named Elizabeth who is sixty-five and is coming to the School of Life that I give in Phoenix the last week of January and in Bozeman the last week of July each year. She said she had been going to talks and seminars for twenty years and hadn't felt she had got much out of them. When she ran across Jackie's and my books, she felt a ray of hope. I don't know why it is that we have to hear a message from a particular voice that reaches us but we do. I don't see anything special about what Jackie and I are saying. It seems to me that the only thing special is our particular voice and the way it touches people who need that voice or one like it. So now, the woman says, she feels a ray of hope.

What's happening here? I think that woman has not tuned in yet to the God who lives in her as Elizabeth. Maybe coming to the school will put her in touch with her God within. Maybe not. The big point is that this life is for the search for God and the movement toward God as we understand him. It isn't a footrace. It doesn't matter that she is sixty-five and still looking. I'm fifty-eight and I'm still looking too, in my own way. It's like we're all making our spiritual quest on a circular running track. We're all walking along together on our spiritual quest. Some people we are walking beside have made great progress and are very close to God. Others of us aren't as far along. Yet we're all walking along in the sun or the rain enjoying each other's company and mutual help and we're making progress. What more can we ask? It seems to me that gratitude is what we need to concentrate on.

I had the good fortune to walk beside some great souls and enjoy their company and counsel and example. There were many people who taught me how to live by living. I had the experience of seeing the great Baba Muktananda and being in the same room with him for a while. But great as he was, do you know what his message was? It was wake up, realize that God lives within you as you, then go home and be a householder. He didn't tell us to go do some holy thing, because nothing needs to be done. God is all-powerful. Anything he needs done, he can do. All I need to do is do the simple work that is put before me.

I'm primarily an advertising man. That's not the kind of work that people are usually attracted to when they are looking for spiritual-type work. Jackie is primarily a housekeeper. That usually isn't much thought of today as spiritual work either. But we're both pretty clear about what it is that we are doing and where that work comes from.

Now, I also write books and teach a School of Life that is thought of as spiritual by some. And Jackie is very good at taking tapes of my talks and turning them into books that are much more beautiful than before when I wrote books with only God's help. But the teaching and book-writing, which many would think is spiritual, isn't. It's only spiritual in the same way writing a sales letter or doing the dishes or mowing the lawn is spiritual. Either it is all spiritual or none of it is spiritual. It seems to me that, with a true understanding of life, it is all spiritual, even the breathing. Or especially the breathing.

As I was writing this, I couldn't figure out why I was saying these things here. I considered moving this material to a later chapter. Then I realized it belonged here. The reason I think it does is that the minute we start thinking about God and the higher power, we figure we've got to get holy. In the early days of writing my books, there was always a chapter on sex. Many people would tell me that when they got the book, that was the first chapter they read. Each of those books also had a God chapter and I'll bet many readers hit that chapter and skipped it or read it with an attitude of "this is holy so I need to feel pious while I read this."

Maybe the reason I am telling these stories is to keep us all from tightening up or getting a false holiness when we approach the subject of God. If God lives within us as us, then everything is God. Here is a book on marriage and there is no chapter on sex. There doesn't need to be. The whole book is on being our being. Sex isn't something we do, it's something we are.

The most manly man I've ever known renounced sex for life when he was fourteen years old. The least manly men I know are the ones who have sex all the time and when they aren't having sex they are running sexual fantasies through their heads, planning their next sex, thinking about their last sex or preoccupied with the consequences of their sex. When I talk to such a man and talk to him about looking at giving up that lust, he looks at me like I'm trying to rob him of his most prized possession—his manhood. He says, "I can't give that up. I'm a sexual being." To him giving up sex would make him nothing. He can't see what an addict he is. He can't see that there is no way he could stop being a man. And he can't see that his addiction is robbing him of experiencing the very manhood he claims to prize.

Every line in this book is about sex because it's about being women and men, being our being. And, every line in this book is about God because God lives within each of us as us and this book is about each of us being our being. There is no way we can escape the God problem. The harder we try to escape the God problem, the more we are caught in our own snare. So we need to come to grips with the higher power. And all our life experiences up to this point prepare us for this. There hasn't been a single moment that is wasted. There is nothing we should have done different or earlier or better. We don't regret the past or blame it. I don't care if you're on death row an hour away from dying. There is plenty of time to do what we need to do. In that hour are thirty-six hundred seconds. That's a lot of time when it's used well.

The most helpful idea I've ever run into in this God business was that I didn't need to live with that punishing God I had. What I was told was that if I didn't have a God who worked for me I should fire him! I could have as good a God as I wanted. The most valuable idea I've found is that God lives within me as love. Beginning to have the experience of that has been the most powerful help I've received.

In order to explain a higher power, a God of my understanding, I guess the best thing to do is give you an analogy.

When I get my car stuck in the mud, I've got some choices. I can attempt to get out by myself and sit there and spin my wheels and dig my car deeper into the hole. Or, I can call a tow truck. Here I've got some choices too. I can call a company that has a little old tow truck that is weak and breaks down a lot, or I can call the biggest tow truck in town, the M&W semi-tow truck in Bozeman that's used for pulling semi-trucks out of canyons.

In the old days when I was in trouble I used to sit in the car and angrily spin my wheels feeling that I could take care of myself. If I ever did think of God, I didn't think of him and her as having any power to get me out of the mud.

Today, if I get stuck in the mud, I call in the biggest tow truck I can find and I put all of my faith in that tow truck and let it do the work. I don't call in a little Volkswagen tow truck, I call in the biggest and the best. You say, "But Jess, Jess, that's overkill." No. If I get stuck in a spot where he can't get within a quarter of a mile of me, he can just pay out the line and hook onto my little car with whatever force is necessarily to get me out of there very quickly. It doesn't take me any more time to call Bozeman and get M&W's big tow truck than it does to try to get one of those halfway tow trucks.

I've just explained my concept of a higher power to you. My higher power is just like that tow truck, all powerful. It was a revolutionary concept to me that I could have a tow truck like that. It is a revolutionary concept to most people who hear the concept. In fact it is so revolutionary that, in my experience, most of you will have trouble understanding it. Or, even if you think you understand it, you'll have trouble applying it. Oddly enough, many of the people who will have the biggest problems with the idea are churchgoing people. Most of you are what is commonly called "God-fearing people," and that definition is a little too close to the truth.

In my experience, agnostics are far easier to work with on this point than churchgoers. Agnostics are more open to a concept of a higher power who has all power and who is kind and merciful and loving.

Vince told me the story of an alcoholic on skid row in Utah who had a Ph.D. in theology from Notre Dame. This guy was from Chicago, and his father was a prominent judge. When this Ph.D. was drinking he was so obnoxious no one could stand him. He would pass bad checks off on his father's friends, and other things of that sort. The family finally got fed up with him. They told him they'd pay him four hundred dollars a month as long as he stayed out of Cook County, Illinois.

Vince came off skid row into AA in Ogden, Utah, with the drunk theologian about 1945. When it came time for the two of them to start getting the spiritual part of the program of Alcoholics Anonymous, Vince said, "You're going to have an easier time understanding this God stuff than me, with all your education at Notre Dame." The Ph.D. answered, "No, Vince, that isn't so. My head is full of so many things that just aren't so. I'm going to have a lot harder time than you because I've got so many useless, harmful old ideas I have to get rid of."

I find that most of us are like that Ph.D. Our minds are so full of ideas about God and we think that we know so much about God that we can't hear or see anything new. There is only one thing, in my experience, that has the power to open up our closed minds. That is when a crisis comes and our concept of God won't do anything for us. Then we are opened up a little. In crisis, when we start using the tools we have and they don't work, we begin to question.

For many of us our present concept of God is like a cheap set of socket wrenches from Taiwan. Every time we put them on a bolt and twist hard, all that happens is that the inside of the socket smooths out, those sockets won't turn anything. So we skin our knuckles trying the cheap things and finally say, "I'll never buy another set of those cheap sockets again." And we don't until we see another set for $6.95 and then we buy them again.

The higher power idea I'm telling you about comes from the most powerful psychological experiment that has ever existed in the United States. It is one of the most unnoticed by psychologists even today, although this experiment has been an ongoing one for fifty years. It is a spiritual experiment that is largely unnoticed by the churches also. A few theologians have noticed that the participants in this experiment come closest to living and believing and acting as the earliest Christians did. That's when the apostles were still alive to write about that experiment. This is the psychological and spiritual experiment of Alcoholics Anonymous. As I have mentioned before, over one million alcoholics who were absolutely hopeless are now sober and living productive, healthy, spiritual lives. They aren't just sober. Many of them are leading lives that make most of ours look rather sad and dreary.

The churches had given up on these people, the doctors had given up on them, the psychologists and psychiatrists had given up on them, and the justice system had given up on them. Many of these alcoholics had sunk so low that even their own mothers had given up on them. And we all know that when a mother gives up, that's the hardest thing of all. Jails, prayer, hospitals, mental hospitals, losing everything—nothing would work, and then finally one thing did: Alcoholics Anonymous.

The powerful essence of this idea happened in Akron, Ohio, in the middle 1930s when two men came together with the idea that the only way they could ever be sober was if one drunk helped another drunk. That was a new idea that had never been tried before. They also had the totally new and really very revolutionary idea of allowing each person in the fellowship to have a God of their own understanding. These two powerful concepts of drunks helping drunks and each of us having a God as we understand him are, to me, the secret of how this program came to be and, more importantly, the secret of how it has lasted and managed to reach suffering alcoholics so far gone that no other way worked.

The idea of helping another person in order to help yourself and not that other person, I believe, is a key force in mental health. It controls the ego. It keeps us from a self-importance that would soon lead to a "rules" concept which would eventually begin excluding those who did not think as we thought or believe as we believed. From a spiritual standpoint it keeps us from assuming virtues we do not have. The idea that we can have a God of our own understanding who can work in our lives opens up an ability to come to believe for thousands upon thousands who had lost any ability to believe in God any longer and other untold numbers who had never believed at all.

By now, that crude little experiment begun in 1935 has been replicated over one million times successfully. It has proved that a set of ideas giving a new spiritual way of life to over one million hopeless drunks over a fifty-year period has solved one of the most difficult problems known to man. This is how to rid a person of a compulsion that has been unsolvable for thousands of years. Certainly most of these people prayed to God for help without success. It wasn't until they went to another suffering alcoholic and met God through that process that they were relieved of their addiction. I could not deny these facts, and this is where my higher power comes from even though I'm not an alcoholic. It comes out of that living experiment in that tough, tough situation.

It doesn't take much of a higher power to work for you on a sunny day when the bills are all paid, the kids are in the Honor Society, your wife's loving you, and everything is peaceful. But you get into a day when things are so tough between you and your wife it's like you are in a vise and your bones are being crushed, or when one of the kids has just been hit by a car or picked up for drugs, or a daughter had been jailed for prostitution, or when you have just lost your job and they're foreclosing on your house; then is when you'd better have a powerful God working for you or you aren't going to get any results! The God I am talking about is the God who produces results under those tough circumstances. I have never seen a desperate person make contact with that kind of God and not get an answer.

I started out just like most people do in this area. I started out with a Sunday School God. My old God was a God whose primary function was to sort the sheep from the goats. The goats went to hell and the sheep went to heaven. As near as I could see, while the climate up in heaven was pretty good, the company wasn't so good, because it was composed of a lot of people I didn't care for much. It looked like all the dull people went up there. So it was heaven for the climate but hell for the company.

All the people I enjoyed, the ones who made me laugh and feel good and who taught me things like fishing and hunting and things that weren't necessarily for my "improvement," were all bound for hell. They didn't seem to take that church business very seriously. But that's just a reflection of the kind of God I had in those days, not a reflection of the truth. It was a reflection of a God who was preoccupied with judging me. That was a God I had created by making a series of choices about what I was learning in my church and my school and from my family.

Late in 1966, I finally found some people who were looking for a better kind of God for themselves. I was a brand-new psychologist with lots of theories, but I was seeking something for myself. Walking into that room full of people was like walking into a warm room on a cold day. I felt their God. I didn't know at the time that's what it was, but there was something there. I could feel it. I was calloused by my misuse of life, but even my calloused self could feel something. There was something there that even a person as hardened as I was at that time could feel, and so I stayed with that group of people.

From that group, I learned about open Alcoholics Anonymous meetings that would let a non-alcoholic like me come and listen and sometimes partake in their meetings. My hunger for what these AA people had kept driving me into their society.

A lot of those people accepted me. They saw that I was crazy without the benefit of alcohol. We had just moved to Montana then and old Vince had compassion for how crazy I was even though I wasn't an alcoholic. He began to teach me a new way of life. One of the first things Vince saw about me was that I was way off in my concept of God. He is the one who came off skid row with the Ph.D. from Notre Dame.

One thing he told me was: "I'd rather have a whore in the family than live with the myth of perfection and false pride." That statement meant a lot to me. It made me think about my own myths of perfection that had ruled my life for so long. Not only the myth of my own need for perfection, but the myths of perfection I laid on the people in my life. I saw how this myth of perfection also caused me to have so much false pride. And these two aspects of my personality kept me from seeing the truth about myself and about my life for so many years.

Vince said to me, "Jess, your God is a God only of the hereafter, that God who judges you on the other side. Since that's the only experience you'll have with that God, he's no good to you here on earth and you can't test out your concept of God on this side. You would be better off if you took a look at that. You have to realize that you can have any kind of God you want." At first, I couldn't understand him. My idea was that God was God and I was stuck with it. It took me a year or two to see that my idea of God was my own mind filtering the idea of God given me by other human beings in my life who had filtered their God through their own minds ad infinitum back to the beginning of time. I thought I was stuck with my old idea of God. "How can you change what's unchangeable?"

I had also been looking at the results that I saw that the members of Alcoholics Anonymous were getting in their lives from working their program, and I liked what I saw, so finally I said, "Okay. I'll try it. And as long as I'm going to build a new idea of God, I'm going to take one who's like that M&W tow truck. I'm going to have a God who is all-powerful, one who is all-loving, a God who does nothing that isn't total love. I'm going to leave out all the scary parts. And I'm going to have a God who wants nothing but the best for me in all parts of my life and who will be there to guide me at all times. He will be my constant companion and friend who I can talk to all day long as I go through my life."

I have been able to turn my life and my will over to a God like this. I couldn't turn my life over to the kind of God I had before. Who in their right mind would? Why should I turn my life over to a judging, condemning, angry God?

I had a funny reaction to making my decision to have an all-loving, all-powerful God. I felt guilty about it. I felt, "Jess, you can't do that. That's cheating. You can't have such a good kind of God." It seemed almost immoral to do such a selfish thing. That's how deep I was in my old concept of God. But, I had seen it work for so many AA's, and what I had wasn't of any use to me. So I did what so many had done. I took the first leap of faith because I trusted what I saw and felt in the people who were offering me the idea. So I had the courage to allow myself that all-powerful God because by then I'd listened to enough stories around those open AA meetings to know that such a God existed for most of the people who were successful in Alcoholics Anonymous. I began to see and believe that there was a way out.

From our earliest years, most of us have never been willing to learn how to live. When we are faced with a problem in life, we solve the problem by running away into our heads or into alcohol or drugs or sex, or some other compulsion. We get worse and worse in the mind from the neglect of learning how to live, and finally we end in what I call the skid row of the mind, if not actually on skid row. Once we come into spiritual awareness of our true condition we have to see that we must work a little bit each day to get our mind off our own personal skid row. We have to begin to see that what we are seeking is a new way of life, one that will serve us and those around us in a new and kinder way.

I saw that it was the depth of honesty and humility required of alcoholics that they had going for them. They needed a God who was all-powerful to break the iron hand of their compulsion. And they needed to surrender to that God in order to live. I said, "All right, I need that idea of God too. It's just that alcohol isn't a part of the problem for me." And I started working with that kind of God and going to AA open meetings and state conferences and my new God started producing some results for me. So I now had a God I could test in my daily life.

The basic key was for me to see that I was powerless, and then I could come to believe in a God who is all-powerful. I just had to surrender to this idea one day at a time. To me, this is the total opposite of what I thought my church was teaching. What I've finally come to see now is that God is unchangeable. God *is* God, it was only my incomplete understanding of God that had fouled me up all these years. So what it gets down to is only one issue, and that is: What kind of incomplete understanding of God do I want to have? I can have the *incomplete* understanding of a God of vengeance and judgment, and death and disaster and destruction and chaos. Or I can have the *incomplete* understanding of a God who is nothing but love, and who has all power to work for good in our lives even in the midst of what seem to be horrible catastrophes. In both cases my understanding of God is *incomplete,* but one *incomplete* understanding of God works better than the other.

I can have a God who will help me to transcend all problems and pain just like Christ transcended the cross. So there isn't a single thing in my life I cannot transcend by seeking God's help. This God, whom I have slowly learned to seek and whom I am slowly surrendering to, won't help me transcend a cross next week, or help me to transcend someone else's cross, nor will he change some difficulty in my past, he'll only help me to transcend the cross I have this moment, and give me rest and peace and joy in this moment. He gives me only my *daily* bread. But even this understanding of God that I have is an *incomplete* understanding of God. Who can comprehend God but God? If I could comprehend God I would be God.

My wife, Jackie, came to a spiritual understanding for herself recently. In the phrase "God as *you* understand him" there is automatically a program for spiritual growth which is limited only by the choices we make. The potential for spiritual unfoldment is limitless and is in direct proportion to the amount of surrender and openness brought to the concept.

She came to see that God can only act in a person's life in direct proportion to that person's belief in God, in that person's mind and heart. She saw that total faith in God's power is what we call miracles. She saw that total surrender to God is what we call God-realization or transcendence. And she saw that she can have all of this for herself only when she gives up wanting it for any reason of her own.

She suddenly saw that it was right here, right now for herself or for any human being who lives. The secret, as she saw it, lies in the nothingness of it. To her, it is "no-thing." "Some-thing" it cannot be. She saw, for herself, that this is what Christ meant when he said, "unless ye become like little children . . ." When this realization came, she said that it was something she felt rather than something she thought. It was like she had tapped into something that had always been there but she had forgotten about it.

One of the problems that I see many of us have in this business of living and finding a new way of life, one of the things we cannot bear, is to be the essence of our humanity. To me, the very essence of our humanity is that we are imperfect. This brings us into fear, and fear makes us angry and aggressive or makes us withdraw from life in many different ways. We turn to something outside ourselves to solve our problems and we find we do escape for a while. But gradually the escape stops working and we need to find stronger escapes and we finally find the escape doesn't work anymore but we can't stop using the escape because we're caught in the web of addiction. We're hooked. We are constantly being broken by these things, yet we continue our search in ever wider, ever more destructive ways. We build up defenses, become harder and more self-willed, we push and push, and live our lives in turmoil.

The essence of the surrendered life, the peaceful life, the truly God-like life is when we are finally broken and because of it are then transparent and vulnerable. The saints in all religions, the truly great men and women who have left their mark on this world throughout recorded history, all had this in common: they were all broken, transparent, and vulnerable. They had nothing to hide, nothing to defend and therefore no fear. There is no faith and no love and no trust where there is fear. Love is the absence of fear.

The concept of the power of being broken, transparent and vulnerable did not come from me. I first heard these words from a Franciscan priest named Richard Rohr. He had been watching alcoholics for quite a few years and he came to see that this was the power of their recovery and of their program, the fact that they had become broken, transparent, and vulnerable. Father Rohr saw that they had a program that helped them to see the power of powerlessness. They had found a spiritual truth as far as Father Rohr was concerned.

Hearing Father Rohr reminded me of what I had heard someone say about coming into a twelve-step program compared to coming into a church: "Those churches—when you come into them, you have to assume the virtues. When you come into AA you have to assume the absence of the virtues—and you can't fool anyone, or you'll get drunk and die."

It is hard to finally be broken, transparent, and vulnerable. I believe all of us have experienced moments of this. Our first love is one example. We are so much in love, we are completely open to the other person. We are broken, we are just a little thing who seeks our joy in the love we feel we have. In doing this we are also transparent to them and vulnerable to them. But that frightens us, so we try to hang on to the romantic feeling, yet still be more protected. We start trying to control the other person. And then of course that is the end of being broken and transparent. It usually stops before we get very far into vulnerability.

Another time when we have experienced this feeling is in a terrible crisis. When our plane is going down over the ocean, we put aside our fear of others and are completely open to them. But when the crisis is over we usually close up again. The secret is to stay open and not close-up again.

The toughest thing there is in this world is to *stay* broken, to *stay* transparent, and to *stay* vulnerable. My wife, Jackie, has a thing she always says to people who seek her help, and it is a very profound statement in its simple way. She says to these people, "I don't doubt your sincerity when you are hanging on the cross. What I want to see is how sincere you are in the weeks and months after the crisis when you are feeling better and your life is getting easier again. Then you and I will both know if you are really ready to start living in a new way."

The way we human beings seem to be constituted is that we will only seek a truly new way of life when the pain of our present life is so intolerable we are truly nailed to a cross of mental and emotional pain. But sadly, for most of us, the minute the pain eases we go right back to the ways that are familiar to us, because the pain was only *momentarily* bad enough to make us seek help.

There is a saying, "A person who can't remember his last drunk usually hasn't had it yet." Until we human beings really hit bottom, we only go to half measures to change our lives. Most of us have to run our string out to the very end before we truly want to put it down. The minute we get any little measure of success we start patching up, and covering up, and holding up the mask again, and getting back under cover because we hate to be out in front of the world with our underwear showing.

It isn't until we've finally hit our bottom and truly never want to live that way again that we are able to come out in the open and exist as we truly are, imperfect human beings, content to be broken, transparent and vulnerable. Then we are perfect in our imperfections and truly *human* beings, not a bunch of egomaniacs trying to act like gods. Only God is perfect. We are imperfect, and our egos can hardly stand that.

I was uncomfortable with my experience in the Charismatic movement. I saw us all have this wonderful experience and then many seemed to immediately feel we all had to be well instead of trying to get better. I would see many people in that movement be completely transformed by their experience of receiving Christ as their personal saviour. You could see it on their faces, the light just shined. They looked like the medieval paintings of the transfigured saints. You could not doubt that something had happened to these people, you could see it and you could feel it. They were truly broken, transparent, and vulnerable. They were God's people. But in my experience, working in those circles, the next thing you knew you would be talking to them, and their faces would be dark, their bodies tense, and they would be saying: "Everything is beautiful with me. I've got the victory. How come you haven't got the victory like I've got the victory?"

Now, I grant you that not all of the new Pentecostals are like that, but in the circles I traveled, I found people who had problems with me when I said I was still troubled in some areas of my life. I couldn't seem to find people dedicated to staying broken, transparent and vulnerable. I grant I had a lot of problems in those days, but, since then, I have also had many experiences that show me how hard it is for us to stay broken. I'm constantly wanting to put on the cloak of virtue and act as if I have found the virtues. I am constantly amazed that living a life of love is so much harder than living a life of law.

It is no special criticism of the Charismatic groups. I hear people in AA expressing the same concern. One old guy on a tape I heard was saying that one of the things that horrified him the most was seeing so many people who are destroyed by their compulsions, come into AA and pretty soon try to be well. They just get started on a spiritual program and pretty soon they're "well." You ask them how they are and they say, "I'm fine. I'm just fine." They go around trying to pretend to be well instead of being open to getting better. So it isn't just in churches that this happens. AA's tell me they have to be especially aware of the danger of "being well" because the person who thinks they are well is just one short step from going back to their old behavior. When a person assumes the cloak of virtue and stops being open, that's when they go out and get drunk. It is easier to see this principle operating in AA because getting drunk is something you can't hide from other people. In some other spiritual programs we can pretend to be well and fool a few people, plus ourselves.

This has been the special advantage of my study of AA. AA's can't very easily get away with a spiritual lapse without its showing by their getting drunk. So they, and everyone around them, see where they're really at. Those of us in the other spiritual programs don't have this helpful indicator. We can forget our program and go back to pretending to be well and all that happens is our insides go crazy and we get miserable, but there isn't the obvious external behavior for all to see, at least at first. Later, our faces and bodies start to show it so clearly there is no fooling other people, even though we may keep on believing our own lies.

So AA has a long history of understanding the surrendered life versus the unsurrendered life or the pseudo-surrendered life. That's why people in AA never say that they are recovered. They only say that they are recovering. Many people think that it is negative to choose to live your life that way. By that attitude, they just show that they don't grasp or understand the success of this fifty-year ongoing experiment.

As I started writing my books and stating this supposedly heretical concept I had about God as I was coming to understand him, I began to hear from preachers from many denominations who said that they thought I had a good concept of God. I was so surprised! I didn't know that this was fine theology. I just took it because it struck me as being eminently practical. I was taught it by people who said it worked and I could see the results in their lives, and I'm a very practical person, so I tried it. It was that simple.

Now, you ask, how does all of this apply to marriage? This too is simple. You can't be working on a marriage as a key part of your spiritual quest without a spirit you're questing for. Who would quest for a punishing God like the one I used to have? The divorce rate today, just like the rate of alcoholism and drug abuse and a lot of other abuses, is but a reflection of where we, as a people, are spiritually. The divorce rate is decreasing a little but is still much higher than it used to be. Does this mean that the younger generation is less sound than us older folks? No. It just means that things are more out in the open now.

I grew up in a little town of six hundred and four people. In that community there wasn't any divorce, no divorce through the courts, that is. But when you live in a town that small for the first fifteen years of your life you know all there is to know about people there, and they know all about you, too. Plenty of those folks "divorced" early in their marriages and just continued to go on living in the same house because of the social stigma, and because there were no jobs for women and times were too tough to be able to afford a legal divorce. They stayed together hating it and each other because of the pressure of the town and the churches. Marriage to them, and to most of us still, is like having a horse with a broken leg. You shoot the horse, but that doesn't fix the broken leg.

Marriage today is just like it's always been. We're aware now exactly how it has always been because life has come to the place where we're freed up to do anything we want. And we're finding out real fast that all that freedom isn't what we were seeking. The secret of a happy life is still out there somewhere.

One of the things that happened is that most of the states changed their divorce laws to no-fault divorce because it sounded like such a fine idea not dragging in a bunch of right and wrongs. But some of the lawyers who fought for no-fault divorce laws are changing their minds. They don't like some of the things they see happening. They don't like the idea that a fifty- or fifty-five-year-old woman can be divorced by her husband and given five years' alimony while she rehabilitates herself and learns to work. Some women can do that, but many can't. The idea of no right or wrong was attractive at first, but the lawyers are beginning to see that justice is based on the idea of right and wrong coming out of the society's standards and there is no escaping that fact. So, we threw out the baby with the wash water. Now we have to go out and find the baby, dust it off, and bring it back in. We'll change the laws again so they are nearer to something people want to live with rather than some bright ideas that didn't work out very well.

For most of us, and for our families for as many generations as we can go back, the secret to happiness for us seemed to be that, if we just had enough money to live comfortably, then we'd be happy, God-like people. Well, we got there and decided that didn't do it, so maybe education was the key. So now we've got that, and it didn't do any magical thing, so maybe physical fitness is the key.

Here we are now, in the 1980s. We're reasonably affluent, well-educated, physically fit people suffering through divorce, drug addiction, alcoholism, workaholism, and the like. There's hardly a family alive today that hasn't been touched by these things. So now treatment centers are springing up all over the country, each positive they have the answer. It's big business. American families are dysfunctional and they can't get well without professional help. That's it. That's family life in America today. We'll all go to treatment centers, scream our guts out at each other, and then we'll all be well! I hope that you can see the wry humor in this paragraph.

I was talking to Rita Davenport recently, before I was to be on her Phoenix TV show. She said that she had been married for eighteen years and was happy and that she wanted to talk about the sadness of all the divorces among the young people. I was kind of aggressive that day, so I said to her, "Let's not talk about the young people. If your marriage is happy today maybe there are some things you're not dealing with. Would you tell me how you can possibly juggle a marriage, a home, children, a television career, writing books, giving seminars, all of your civic-minded commitments, and your God?" She said, *"Touché!"* I'm surprised she didn't hit me or tell me she didn't want to interview me. But she's a gentle woman who is kind to people like me and so she let me be.

It's always interesting to me to see that most of us need to be so heavily defended. We claim that everything is all right with us. Let's talk about the other guy. None of us wants to say that we're not okay and please help me by sharing the truth of your life with me so that I won't feel so all alone in my reality. The older people want to complain about the young people and the young people want to blame their parents, and none of this has ever gotten us anywhere. Each of us has our own personal quest and it's better if we get on with it rather than talking about and blaming each other. No human being has ever had any sort of spiritual awakening as long as they continue to stay in blame.

People who don't understand AA often think it is negative the way they say that they are alcoholics and always will be. AA's talk about their own problems and how they brought them upon themselves. The funny thing is, though, they talk about having problems, unsolvable problems, really, and yet they live sweeter and sweeter lives every day.

It's like Tom Watson, the golf pro. When he's being interviewed he seldom talks about his good strokes, he talks about his strokes that were passable and the strokes that were poor and you soon realize that out of seventy strokes, let's say, Tom Watson considers maybe sixty-six of them to be just passable or less than passable. Any one of us would give our right arm to shoot any one of those sixty-six shots. Tom Watson is a top pro because he knows we don't grow except by being out on the growing edge, out where the problems are. So we aren't being negative when we are facing our problems and working on them. We are being very positive.

One of the most positive affirmations we can make is to say, "I'm an alcoholic," if that's our situation. It seems a paradox that a seemingly negative statement can be so positive, but it is. It is the million people who admit they are alcoholic who aren't drinking today. Yet the guy falling off the barstool isn't alcoholic. If you don't believe that, go ask him if he's an alcoholic. He'll sure tell you that he isn't.

We came into this world separate and alone. We immediately started building a shell up around ourselves to protect us from life. Finally the pain of the aloneness got to us and we started taking off little pieces of that shell and people started seeing inside us. We got panicky and started trying to put the pieces back on. And we think that this is the only sensible thing to do. We don't understand that our job is to crack the shell of our separateness just like you smash the shell of a hard-boiled egg and start picking off all those little pieces. That's our voyage to God. We don't get there until three days after we're dead. Until then, we're just picking off pieces. That's why we can't have any kind of a marriage until we come to grips with the God problem and our sense of being separate and alone. That feeling of separateness makes us think it's love or power we need. But it isn't those things. It's God.

I've gotten so many phone calls and letters from people who are having problems in their marriages. I tell them we need to take a look at the God in our lives. Often they say, "Oh, but I've got my church!" That's beautiful, but what does a building and a religious practice have to do with God? Most often, nothing. A church is a place where you go and meet a lot of like-minded people. It's an opportunity to make a contact with God. If you've really got that contact, you can't have problems, you simply have opportunities to transcend something or grow from something. That sounds weird or impossible, but I occasionally get a letter from a minister asking me how he can solve some problem. He has been talking religion all his life, yet he hasn't made the connection to the source of the power. No, having a church isn't the answer. God is the answer and he answers some funny prayers. An irreverent person hollers out, "God, if there is such a person, I need your help!" Or, "God, I know you don't exist, but I need help anyway." That's the kind of prayer that gets answered.

The late George Gallup did a big national poll on religion. He found there were two groups of people: the *churched* and the *unchurched.* He found there were an awful lot of unchurched people in America. They just sort of go it on their own and listen to Robert Schuller and the like on TV or go out like Hipshot in the comic strips and talk to God under the sky or in the mountains or whatever. What was so interesting about this is that the poll showed that more of the so-called *unchurched* believed they had had a born-again experience than the *churched.*

Don't be surprised by this. The answer is simple. When we are in church we are comfortable. What do we need a personal contact with God for? We've got our *church.* We've got a nice, steady routine. The minister is up there in front of the church doing our work, he's making all of the appropriate noises, and we aren't even having to pay him all that much to do it. We've got a choir director who's making some heavenly music for us, we've got a pastor's wife who's working hard being holy for us. The whole thing's set for us. Why do we need to do anything? That's what we're paying them for. Furthermore we're getting a bargain because we aren't paying a lot. What's to push us to the growing edge in that deal?

Just in case the ministers and choir directors and ministers' wives think they're getting off scot free, they aren't. Doing these things for us is *their deal!* And sometimes doing their minister or minister wife or choir director thing is their way of running away from the hard, scary work of making their spiritual quest. It's their bag to do this for us because it's their idea of what's holy and good. They're into taking care of people as the way to God. And this is good. Somebody's got to do it. But it's important for them to keep in perspective that it is *their* choice they are making. No one is forcing them to play the martyr. We all do our thing for our own reasons, so there are very few martyrs in this world, including me, even though I like to think that I'm a holy, Christian martyr sometimes.

Well, I really don't want to poke too much fun at church people. That's hardly fair. We could do that with any institution we've a mind to. But, as I said earlier, in my experience, I'd rather deal with an agnostic than a church person when they are in a tough jam and really need a God who can work for them to get them out of the ditch. The church person has an idea of a little bitty God who often can't do much for them. Their idea of God often couldn't lift a flea out of a mud puddle and they don't even realize it. They're just hanging on to that little idea of God even though it isn't working for them when their crisis is tearing up their life.

When I get letters from ministers saying, "Jess, I'm having a terrible problem here, have you got any ideas?" I want to say to them, "You know that God you're talking about all day? He's really great at solving problems for me, I know he could do something for you. He's transformed me on four or five occasions. He's changed me enough inside that I'm awed at some of the things I'm able to do through the power of God now." But those guys couldn't hear that at first. They had to go out and suffer enough before they were ready to see what many of their parishioners had been forced to see. Once they've suffered enough, they won't even have to ask me. They'll let that powerful God into their lives.

God gives us exactly what we expect from him. That's called justice without judgment. If we plant carrots, God's not going to give us tomatoes. If we tend to believe in a puny God, we're probably not going to get anything more than puny results.

If we believe in a God who does nothing but sit on a throne up in space somewhere separating sheep from goats, a God of judgment who is waiting to send us to hell because we are a terrible, sinful soul, how can we possibly surrender to a God like that? We can't.

All we could ever do is give him lip service and go on doing our damndest to try to keep our life in order by ourselves.

In marriage, when trouble comes, if one or both of us have to keep complete control of ourselves, the other person, and the marriage because of our negative attitude toward God, nothing positive can happen in that marriage. Every marriage comes to this. No relationship can escape crisis at some time or other. If we haven't had it already, just wait. It's going to come because that's life. Living separate from God is hard whether we're ready to admit it or not.

But eventually, when the hard times come, there is a spiritual principle that is going to work either for us or against us. In today's psychology, which is rapidly becoming "family" oriented because that's where the crisis is, there's something they teach people in therapy. This is: "As you view your family, as you are with your family, so you view the world, so you are with the world." These same words changed a little are the spiritual principle: *As you view your God, as your relationship is with him, so do you view your family and so do you view your world.*

In Jackie's and my relationship these many years there has been a lot of crisis, a lot of pain. I believe now that I'm powerless, that my life is unmanageable. The shambles I faced in my life proves it, and it wasn't until I found one who had all power, one who could restore me to sanity, one to whom I could turn over my will and my life completely that I could make any progress. Now, only an idiot would turn his will and his life over to the care of the God that I used to have. Who would turn his life and his will over to a God who was bent on the destruction of his people? Why should I turn my will and my life over to a God who, I felt, condemned me since I was a little child? How could I surrender to a God who, I believed, considered me a miserable sinner from the day I was born? How can I possibly say, "I'm yours, take me and do with me as you will?" when I see him as a wrathful, condemning God who is keeping books on me?

Okay, so we need a higher power and a really potent one to get us out of the many troubles we get into in a marriage. To me, it doesn't make any sense to talk about marriage in any other perspective than a higher power perspective. If we believe that we have a marriage that's all positive, a marriage that's filled with joy, a marriage where we're appreciated and loved at all times, where all we have is just a lot of fun, then we don't have any need for a book like this. This book is talking about the kind of marriage that brings us pain when we are off the spiritual path or ready to see to new depths within ourselves. We're concerned here with the kind of marriage that works to show us the parts of ourselves that none of us wants to see. It's for us folks who are in the kind of marriages where we no sooner see one tough part of ourselves than our marriage will show us still another tough part of ourselves. This book is anti-divorce in all but the most extreme cases and is going to tell us what *we* need to do to change, not what the other person has to do to change.

I couldn't have seen that I was the one who needed to change and be changed, if I had a puny God. It took a powerful God to give me that insight. That's what is needed in marriage, a God who had all power. We need to understand that we are incomplete, and we need to know what it means to go to God. We need to know that we are imperfectly perfect and that a committed relationship is one of God's tools to lead us toward our inner perfection. That's what marriage and family is for and we must stop running from this.

The new God for so many people in our society today is psychology. An awful lot of people are using psychological programs to solve their problems. People are saying, "I've got to do things for me. I've got to get at my emotions. I've got to stand up for my rights. I've got to learn to express my anger." Those ideas are fine up to a point, but it's helpful to compare them to their counterparts in spiritual programs.

When you know that God lives within you as you and within the other person as them, this suggests many different courses of action. In traffic, I'm learning to give way more and more to other people who seem to need that space much more than I do at the time. They are God too. I know that now and I need to act on that more.

Old Vince used to speak of giving a problem he was facing a spiritual treatment. How do we give a problem we're facing a spiritual treatment? As I said, I remember that that other person is God. I remember that I don't need to fight for what I need; God, as I understand him, has already found ample ways of providing for me and will obviously continue to do so. I don't need to watch like a hawk to see my interests are protected and fight like a tiger to protect what I have. I need to do the opposite. I need to surrender everything I have before it can truly be mine.

More and more I'm finding I can practice part of one of the most frequently seen spiritual rules, the prayer of St. Francis. It asks God that I may seek to love instead of to be loved, to understand instead of being understood. I used to think that was impossible. I also saw many people who tried to do those things and ended up feeling like they were martyrs. I see now that might have been because they were trying to follow St. Francis' prayer through their own power. But I can't follow that prayer through my own power. Only God's power is sufficient to help me follow a spiritual program like that. Now that I fired that old idea of a God and am in much closer touch with the God within, my spiritual program has a lot more power behind it than it used to have when it was just my power. I'm beginning to be transformed by God.

9.

Me and Scrooge—
Transformed by God

"It is not within man's power to place the divine teachings directly in his heart. All that we can do is place them on the surface of the heart so that when the heart breaks they will drop in."

HASIDIC ANECDOTE

I believe it is not the spiritual teachings that transform us. I've seen that I can read and study spiritual teachings all day and all night and nothing happens. I believe it is like the old proverb says: we need to have our hearts broken before the spiritual teachings will fall on fertile ground and sink in and transform us. Once the heart is broken and opened to God, I have seen people transformed so often that I have come to expect it as a commonplace. It is that transforming I need because of the personality I am. My personality needs healing, transforming, and I can't do it. That's where the God who transforms me and restores me to sanity comes in.

What do I mean by transformed? I mean having a spiritual awakening. I believe now that a spiritual awakening is a change in personality. When we have a change in personality we are a different person in that way than we were before. Many of our great stories are about people who have spiritual awakenings and are transformed by them. We all love Dickens' Christmas story about Scrooge. He has a spiritual awakening and stops being a Scrooge and becomes generous.

We can't change our own personality. If we could, think of our ego. I believe only God, only a spiritual awakening, can change our personality. And this is the promise of the spiritual programs—that we will have changes in personality. The twelve-step programs promise it. The twelfth step starts off with the words "Having had a spiritual awakening as the result of these steps"—and those steps are available for any of us to use. What better remedy for a person like me who has suffered from a number of compulsions than a spiritual awakening like Scrooge had? His spiritual awakening took away his greed and made him generous. Maybe I can take the necessary steps to having a spiritual awakening and my greed for power and lust will be taken away just as Scrooge's was. Wouldn't that be lovely? Then I could go wake up Dickens and say, "See here, we've got a new story for you."

Jackie and I were talking to a close mutual friend the other evening. Jackie was saying, in reference to my sexual compulsion, "Two weeks after I married him, I thought I'd married a spook. He courted me and showered me with attention, but right after the marriage it all changed. It has taken me our entire marriage to understand that the change was not caused by something wrong with me but rather because of the nature of his own compulsion. Up to the time we married I was his fantasy. When we got married, that ended and he moved into other fantasies."

How many of us, in our marriages, suffer from taking upon ourselves, as Jackie did, this God-like role of assuming the responsibility for another's problems by feeling that there was something wrong with us? It leads us into so much confusion and heartache and is harmful not only to us but also to the person we live with.

I see now that I started using the drug of sexual preoccupation and fantasy at five. By the time I was twelve I started to use it heavily. Any time I was faced with the pain of growing up, I could go to my drug and escape the pain. I used women as objects so I was isolated from them. Men I wasn't that interested in, so I was isolated from them too. So finally, at fifty-eight, I face this mess. How do I get out of the isolation I'm in? What do I do with the personality I've failed to develop? That's where the transforming power of God comes in. My heart is broken. All I need to do is let the spiritual teachings come in and God can transform me and I'll be a new person. That's how I see the transforming power of God.

Those ancient ones, those old Hasidic Jews, knew a lot about hearts breaking.

The parts of me that give Jackie the most trouble are the parts of me that I most hate to have called to my attention. The parts of Jackie that give her the most trouble are the parts that she most hates to have called to her attention. This is a stalemate, of course. And this is the thing that causes the most pain in marriage and leads all too often to divorce. These are the things in us that need to be transformed by God, changed so we can be together without so many of our defects working against us.

A large proportion of married couples have gone to one form of counseling or another for their marriages. In most cases, each of them is going to try to show the other person where they should change. Another stalemate, still more pain, and, all too often, divorce. What is this? Where does all of this come from? I do believe that it comes because we marry a fiction and all too soon after marriage we are presented with the true facts. We marry believing in the myth of perfection here on earth. We see perfection in our chosen one, or at least the possibility of perfection, and we call this myth love. The myth called love and the power of sex join us in "connubial bliss" until we wake up one morning and see that it just ain't so.

We are all born separate and alone. We all too often relate to a puny God or no God at all and the family we were born into is all too perfectly imperfect, so by the time we are in our teens we are more and more aware of feeling separate and alone. Then our hormones start clicking and we think, "Aha, I've found the answer. All I need to feel whole, to be able to put down my loneliness and fear, is one of those opposites I see out there." We start dating each other and soon we find *the one*. Because there is, as yet, no commitment, each of us shows only our best side to each other. We do this because we don't want the other person to leave us. Some of us even live together a year or two to see if we're compatible, and we are. Why? Because, without that piece of paper called a marriage license we still reserve the dark side of ourselves from each other to keep the other person there.

Marriage arrives and we go through the honeymoon period and wake up one day and realize we've married our total opposite. And that's painful, but oh so beautiful, because now the learning can begin. We have to face the full catastrophe. She didn't get a knight in shining armor on a snow-white horse, and he didn't get "Mom." Now, to understand the pain of this realization, we really need to see how opposite we are and what that is all about.

Earlier I mentioned the idea that a man is made up of a dominant "man side" and a recessive "woman side" if he is a complete man. The dominant characteristics a man should have are first, and foremost, that he is responsible. He must be responsible first to his God, second to himself, next to his wife and family, fourth to his work, and last to the rest of the world. From a base of responsibility, a man's dominant characteristics are that he is creative, outgoing, logical, philosophical, energetic, a dreamer, a planner, a lover, and a caring, giving human being. His recessive side is that he is receptive, nurturing, gentle, aware, emotional, open, and tender. This to me is a whole man.

A woman is made up of a dominant "woman side" and a recessive "man side." The dominant characteristics a woman should have are first and foremost that she is receptive. She must be receptive first to her God, second to herself, third to her husband and her children, fourth to her work, and last to the rest of the world. From her base of receptivity, a woman's dominant characteristics are that she is nurturing, gentle, aware, emotional, open, and tender. Her recessive side is that she is responsible, creative, outgoing, logical, philosophical, energetic, a dreamer, a planner, a lover, and a caring, giving human being. All of these characteristics for the ideal man and woman should be a blend in the mature person so that they can tap and have available at will any of the characteristics they need at a moment's notice in complete spontaneity.

Now we'll return to the place where I wrote that the honeymoon was over. Remember that I said that she expected a knight in shining armor on a snow-white horse, and he expected "Mom"? The reason I say that is because who is more responsible than a knight in shining armor? Who is more receptive than Mom? You see, what we are each looking for is our other half, our recessive side, so that it can flower and we can come to wholeness through each other on our mutual journey toward God.

Let's pick men apart first. I think that's only fair because I'm male. A woman's basic, tribal, instinctual need, going back to the beginning of time, is to have a responsible man who will feed her, keep a roof over her head so that she can be assured that she can give birth in safety and perpetuate the race. This is an animal instinct that is built into the female of every animate species that God has created. We can want to deny this instinct with all the power of our being now that we are affluent, free, educated human beings, but that need lies deep in the soul of every woman.

Okay. That's woman's basic need. What does she get instead of her knight in shining armor? She gets a dependent, unsure, selfish, mewling baby who doesn't know the first thing about being responsible first to his God, second to himself, and third to her and the family. She gets a man who doesn't want to know anything about commitment on a daily basis, let alone for life, a man who understands only selfishness and domination and competitiveness with her and his own children, and a man who soon flees his home mentally, emotionally, and physically in any way he can.

How does a woman react to all of this weakness in men? She may have been the most receptive and nurturing woman in the world, but faced with overwhelming irresponsibility on the man's part she soon becomes responsible and creative and outgoing and begins to assume a male role in order to protect herself and her children, if she has any. She feels sure she has to do this. Self-protection is a basic need. So our young bride, as soon as the honeymoon is over, must subjugate her dominant side and raise her recessive side to prominence.

Now for the ladies. A man's basic tribal, instinctual need, going back to the beginning of time, is to have a receptive, nurturing woman who will receive his energy, his life force, his food and home so that he can be assured that she will give birth in safety and perpetuate the race. This is an animal instinct built into the male of every animate species that God has created. We can want to deny this instinct with all the power of our being now that we are affluent, free, educated human beings, but that need lies deep in the soul of every man.

That is man's basic need. What does he get instead of a nurturing, receptive mother figure? He gets an aggressive, distrusting, selfish woman who is going to take care of herself and have a nice home and nice clothes and a fulfilling job and share the pants in the family if she can't wear them, because who can trust men to do anything right and responsible? She is going to take care of herself and he had better know how to take care of himself because she isn't going to be home all that much, and she isn't sure if she even wants children with all of the irresponsible men she's seen in this world.

And there you have it. This has been going on for generations, each generation passing on to the next generation these attitudes of fear and suspicion and how to manipulate the opposite sex because by now we don't even recognize instinctual physical and emotional needs and drives. For the last four generations at least, which are the only ones I have personal knowledge of, Father's behavior has taught girls to distrust men and Mother's behavior has taught boys to fear women.

I tend to go along with the different groups of people who believe that war is the root cause of this continually widening and deepening gulf between men and women. Starting back four generations ago with the Civil War, men went off to live through horror which destroyed them as men if it didn't kill them. Torn from the security of home and family, from village or town or neighborhood, from the peace and routine of school or job and order in their lives, these men, from the Civil War through the Spanish-American War, World War I, World War II, the Korean War, and finally the Vietnam War, were thrown into horror beyond words. Their terror and loneliness and despair took away all belief in order, in truth, in values, in home, in security, and they became babies—horrified and needy babies.

On the home front, the women had their very foundations shattered when their husbands and fathers and brothers marched off and left them to care for all they held dear. The women were forced into responsibility with no warning. They had sole care of the home, the family, the paying of the bills and in a large share of the cases were required to go to work. The women were forced to take over the men's role.

When these wars were over, the men came home and they wanted someone to take care of them, to tell them it was all right, that the nightmare was over. The women, faced with these shattered men, were first of all afraid to turn the running of their lives back over to them. Why should they? They had no reason to trust these returned, devastated strangers. And besides, a course had been set, woman's role had been reversed for her, and by the time World War II rolled around women no longer had any reason to believe that life was ever going to be any different. It had been that way since her grandmother's time.

How do men and women, earnestly wishing to live a whole life together in order to journey toward God, change this catastrophe? How can they undo the harm which has been done to the sexes? First of all, by recognizing it. It no longer matters whether the man has gone off to war literally, the mores and values of men and women by now have been completely changed because of peer pressure and the knowledge that has come about in the last hundred and fifty years. There is no going back to some ideal. There is no longer any place for the "hero" and the "little woman." It is inappropriate by now. But what is appropriate is to recognize these deep needs in each other and to allow each other space in which to be a "man" and a "woman" without confining each other to stereotypes. I believe it is impossible for us to do this in a way that would be equitable to both men and women in today's society without a deep need and understanding and surrender to an all-powerful, loving God who wants peace and joy and love for us. We have to have a God whom we can trust enough to become like little children again and start a new way of seeing marriage and all the rest of life.

Now, I've just given you the esoteric, philosophical reasons for why we all are how we are. In real life, of course, none of us knows that's the name of the game, really. All we know is that we are married to someone so opposite from us that we barely have an understanding. We flounder around, we love each other, we're angry at each other, we hate each other, we love each other again, we put up with each other, we rub and rub and rub against each other. And all of this is so that we can learn who we are in the mirror of the other person's eyes and face and words and actions.

Who else can show us who we really are. Our mothers? Our fathers? Our friends? No one else can tell us in the same way that a husband or wife will. You take two men living together in a bachelor pad. They're like ships passing in the night. They might party together once in a while, but their life together is deadly dull. Have you ever looked at a bachelor pad? It's colorless, it's messy, there's no life there, it's just where two people hang their hats. Each person goes his own way. They live under the same roof but they aren't involved. But what's most important is that they aren't opposites, and they aren't committed.

In marriage, when two people are committed, in the day-to-day living together with the intensity only opposites can bring to a marriage, there is pain. Most of the pain only requires little adjustments from the man or the woman or both and the relationship calms down once again. But for ninety-nine percent of marriages there comes a crisis here and there that has the power to blow that commitment out of the window. It doesn't matter how long we've been married, it doesn't matter if there are children involved, that crisis has the power to destroy that marriage, and from the divorce statistics we know this is happening with more and more frequency.

The power of crisis to destroy a marriage comes because in crisis each of us is seeing more of ourselves than we want to see, and the need to change ourselves is evident. The crisis is asking us to give more of ourselves than we're ready to give, or it could be asking us to forgive the other person and we don't want to forgive. It could be asking us to forget about ourselves for a while and concentrate on the other person, and we don't want to do that, or it could be asking us to stop doing that which we are doing and we don't want to do that. Or, horror of horrors, the crisis could be telling us that we have to have a change of personality if we want to stay in the marriage, and of course we *know* we can't do that. These are the things that cause divorce, not the things that are written on divorce decrees.

All of these things are the reasons I know that I have to have a belief in a higher power who has all power because who else can remove my defects of character and transform me? When I realized that this much power was needed, I wanted to kneel down and say, "Here, God, change me altogether. Take away every defect of my character. I give it all up." Well, so far it hasn't worked that way for me. God usually hasn't removed anything unless I've first acknowledged it in myself and become ready to give it up. If I don't know I've got it, why should it be taken away? No, that easy way doesn't work. Transformations, in my experience, come one at a time, and only when the pain of having a defect is so great I don't want it anymore, and I humbly kneel down and ask God's help for that specific thing on that specific day.

When I had my first transformation twenty-two years ago at the time of my heart attack, I was so tense all the time that I wore my shoulders somewhere up close to my ears. My shoulders were up high like you put them when somebody's going to throw a snowball at you. I used to have to have my suit coats altered by cutting out material below the collar in the back. I thought it was because I had high, square, manly shoulders! No. That's wasn't so. As I began to find a more spiritual way of life, my shoulders dropped slowly until they're now down to where they have some slope, and the tailor doesn't have to alter the suit coats. I see now that my shoulders were up in the position of defense. When I was in fear that the world was going to come down on me, that's the way I carried my shoulders. High shoulders usually do not come from anatomy, they come from tension.

Another change that's taken place for me is that my voice has changed. A coronary voice is loud and aggressive. I used to have that kind of voice all the time. Jackie used to call for me at the University and the secretary would say, "I'm sure he's not in, Jackie, I haven't heard him in the halls." My voice was so loud that the secretary made that reply without even realizing what she was saying. She wouldn't say that to Jackie now. My voice has softened a lot since I've been working a program of turning my will and my life over to the care of God as I understand him.

Just like Scrooge in Dickens' *A Christmas Carol,* I had a transformation on stinginess. One day my eyes were opened and I suddenly saw how selfish and stingy I was. I had been giving my wife money to run the household. She could always pay the bills and have a little left over. What I had refused to see was that out of that little left over, I had kids who needed allowance money, a wife who would just as soon have a new dress once in a while, and a house that needed some new furniture sometimes. Those things weren't being taken care of and my wife and kids were going without. My kids had the best ski equipment, they had shotguns and rifles for hunting because that's what I was interested in. But they never had very many nice clothes, and I questioned every purchase my wife made in that department. I suddenly saw that my wife had lived in a house that was way too small and far less of a house than our means would allow. I was generous in the things that meant something to me, but I fought or refused to give the things that I didn't care about but were important to my wife.

I knelt down and asked that this stinginess be removed and slowly over the next few years I began to be more generous. The first thing I did was give my wife some money of her own. I made other changes, and just a few years ago I added a big family room onto our house. I know myself and I know that I couldn't have done these things by myself. God had to step in and help me or these things wouldn't have gotten done.

I have had another transformation that was very dramatic for me. Some years ago I suddenly realized that my wife was the woman I most wanted to spend the rest of my life with, and if this was so why didn't I act like it? I had spent most all of my life sexualizing relationships with women.

So seven years ago I asked for God's help in this compulsion and started on the road back. I came home from a trip that hadn't been on the up and up and I determined to be a responsible man. One thing I didn't do was tell Jackie that I had had this particular spiritual awakening, and she thought I was trying to drive her crazy. I started being responsible the only way I knew how, and it was pretty heavy-handed and controlling. Jackie's drinking and pill-taking got worse and she had her own spiritual awakening and she stopped taking her pills cold turkey and went to treatment in West Germany. She wrote about this in her book, *I Exist, I Need, I'm Entitled*.

When I told her about the other women, she was in deep pain and confusion. One of the things that I had seen earlier was that while I had once again become committed to Jackie and all of my sexual energy must be concentrated on her, I was still getting into sexual deals because the compulsion was so strong and had been with me since I was a child. I knew that I had to have this out in the open or I'd slip back into my old ways. As a consequence, Jackie was witnessing a lot of behavior that was horrible for her. At the same time I was trying to be responsible and I was putting forward changes I wanted her to make, and the combination of that made her angry enough to kill me and confused enough to doubt her sanity. She'd push back, naturally, because she's no dummy who was going to take this lying down. There were times when all I could do was surrender one minute at a time. It was impossible to surrender on a daily basis, things were so tough.

Now you can see a little better, I think, the tough stuff true transformation is made of. Since those days I've talked to lots and lots of people who've gone through a lot of the same kinds of transformations I have, and their experiences are similar to mine. Some people have the miracle-type transformation where they are instantly different. If we're lucky, we might get some of those, too. But it doesn't matter whether the transformation is fast or slow, the point is that it happens.

There is a story about an old cowboy who walks into a bar and says, "Let's get drunk and be somebody!" I always was touched by the pathetic tone of the story. And I could always see that the old cowboy already was somebody but, as he started in on his drinking, he was on his way to being much less of a somebody than he already was. I never really saw how much that story was me until very recently. As I have faced my addictions more and more deeply, I see that the sickness at the core of my personality is just like that of the old cowboy, but my addiction is not drinking, a big part of it is making something happen. I so much need to make something happen so I can feel like I'm somebody. Without making something happen I feel real uncomfortable. When I watch an ineffectual person, it drives me crazy. I want to grab them and show them just how to make something happen because I'm so good at doing that.

I'm recently beginning to see that there is a common thread running through the different addictions and compulsions and obsessions that have so dominated and characterized my life. I can see I have a great greed that shows itself in many ways other than in lust. There is my greed for money and for power. It was that greed for power that made me seek out conspicuous positions on the University of Minnesota campus. That was why I was a president of an organization or two and head of a number of committees. I was greedy for power. It was why I sat down to play Monopoly with an overwhelming desire to win. Sure, everyone wants to win at Monopoly, but most don't want to win as badly as I did. I would practically kill to win. And the people around me could feel it. I'm finally beginning to see these things about myself. And I'm seeing where the problem comes from: my fear.

I see this so clearly because I had two totally different kinds of educational experiences. Right out of high school I went into an Army Air Corps college training program at Coe College in Cedar Rapids, Iowa. There were two hundred of us from Minnesota, Iowa, and the Dakotas. We lived in one big room beneath the college gym. We were in five groups of forty, arranged according to our academic test scores. I had been a good student in high school and was in the top group. We took a pre-engineering curriculum with lots of science. Our days were filled with classes, some military drill, physical education, and study halls.

The routine worked beautifully for me. I was happy and did good work in my classes primarily because I loved the work and the teachers. The competitiveness in me was really quieted down because there was so little fear stirred up in me. Students who were having trouble with their subjects came to me for help in the study halls. I have a talent for explaining things simply, so it helped them learn the subject. But it also helped me a lot, because in teaching the subject I ended up overlearning it, so that tests were duck soup.

A friend of mine was a real comic and another was a fine musician. We had the idea of putting on an Army show so I sat down and worked with some others and put the show together. Sure, I got noticed for it, but that was such a small part. It was done mostly for free and for fun. I was liked and respected by my fellow students and didn't cause any of them any grief and didn't get into any trouble with anyone.

When I switched to the University of Minnesota, I was lost among twenty-five thousand students, I had no routine and companionship, and fear was driving me all the time. That fear is what was working to make me seek power, position, and lust to help me run away from the fear.

Here is an area I'm hoping will be transformed. As I mentioned before, I was recently introduced before a talk I was to give as "a man who has gone to excess in everything." There was the sting of truth in that because almost everything I've done in life I've taken into excess. If a certain amount of an activity is good, more of it is better. That shows clearly my greed. As my old friend says, "Moderation never was my dish."

My excesses, and the constant preoccupation with them that was the payoff for me, used to be a source of amusement to me and my friends. Some of my excesses were even humorous to my family. But mostly they were the cause for deep pain to them because they paid the price for those excesses. One of those prices was the loss of the husband or father because of his constant preoccupation with those excesses, and the fear of the consequences of those excesses for someone with my kind of health history. And that health history in itself was a fruit of those excesses of mine. People who are relaxed and easygoing and just do the work that is needed with an economy of effort, don't get heart attacks at age thirty-five. I had the youngest heart attack in my crowd.

By going out and making something happen, I can have a feeling of power that helps numb the pain of my sense of inadequacy. I recently noticed that I even feel better when someone asks me what time it is and I can tell them. It's really a charge when someone asks me for directions to somewhere or how to do something. The part of me that feels so inadequate that being asked for the time makes me feel more confident is the part of my personality that has been such a problem to me all my life. That's the part of me I'm now beginning to see more and more clearly.

As I see it now, making something happen helps me in two ways. One way, like alcohol, lets me focus so hard on something that it completely takes me out of myself and helps me forget my pain with myself. The other way helps me escape my sense of inadequacy by giving me the feeling of control. When I go out and start a business, I really feel like I'm in control. Same with so many of my other activities—they give me a sense of having power and control. Some people who are into sexual addiction tell about the sense of power and control they feel by making a conquest of a woman or a man. And, oddly, the ultimate in control is fantasizing because no one else is involved who can screw things up by not doing just exactly what they should be doing at just the right time. So in the fantasy world we are in complete control.

There's a fine line between doing things to help me escape from myself and doing things because I love being competent at something, just like a good ballet dancer loves to make the moves just right, often for no other person's satisfaction but his or her own. One of the deepest hungers in me is for competence in the things I do. There's nothing wrong with that. It's a good part of me. But a deep striving for competence doesn't help me lose awareness like alcohol does for the alcoholic, or like "making something happen" does for me. Achieving a fine competence demands a clarity and an awareness that is the opposite of what I get when I lose myself in one of my compulsive activities where I'm trying to make something happen. When I'm in compulsion, I have lost my awareness and I'm like a blind man just focused on the one thing in front of me and oblivious to all else in life. "Making something happen" has a power component in it that is almost sexual and clearly shows the greed that is the root of all lust, as Stephen Levine said in the quote in an earlier chapter. In the sex book I wrote, I quoted Mao Tse-tung's widow as saying, "Sex is interesting in the early rounds, but for the long run, give me power." I see now how that statement shows how power and sex are so often hooked together. And that's why there's so much sex around powerful people in music, government, business, etc.

Another difference between developing an increasing competence versus a compulsive activity is that in competence the real focus is not on external results. In the ideal situation, what I am doing is part of a dance and it's the dance that's important. Only when I'm aware of the dance of life do I see that I have the complete awareness of all of life that tells me I'm as much in harmony as it's possible for humans to be. Sure, the results are great, but, oddly enough, that is secondary.

Bill Russell tells about the dance of life in his book, *Second Wind*. He tells about the times with the Celtics where he and the rest of the team and the opponents were all a part of a total flow, a dance, that was so beautiful to be a part of. And even though Bill Russell was as competitive a person as anyone, at those times he was so aware of the flow that the score didn't matter. It was all the dance. Russell never dared tell his teammates about his feelings because many of them didn't have that awareness at that time. We can learn about this "dance" in many different ways. Another thing to call the awareness of the dance of life is Zen, and there have been many books written telling about using what you are doing in order to get in touch with the total flow of life. Learning Zen through the art of archery or flower arranging or meditation are good examples.

That's what I'm working on with my golf. In this case my "Zen master" is the golf pro at Camelback golf course, a wonderful man named Arch Watkins. What I came to see through golf is that I was never where I was. I had all kinds of strange voices in my head. I would be starting to drive off the tee but my mind would be back at the last putt I missed. Or I would draw the club back telling myself that this time I would hit the good shot I hit on the driving range the day before. Then I would hear that other voice saying, "No, you're not, dummy. You're going to screw up this shot just like you always do." So I'm in the process of learning Zen through the art of golf. Arch doesn't know about that, but he doesn't have to. The only one who has to know about that is me. He obviously has his own awareness. I'm still working on mine.

I do have evidence that I'm getting a little closer to the dance, and my handicap is coming down, but then I have days like the day that I was driving home from a lesson and had the thought, "There's got to be more to life than learning to hit a seven iron." I then started to think about a business I could start, but nothing came of that, partly because God was watching over me very carefully and partly because I don't act on crazy thoughts as casually as I used to.

A while back I had made a series of good strides in my golf swing. Things were all coming together and I was so excited about how well I was going to do in our regular Monday morning golf game. I was really going to tear the course apart, beat my partner in our friendly game, dazzle the onlookers, and drastically lower my handicap. On the long first hole, I was right up beside the green, something I had never been able to do before. I parred the hole, which is the hardest hole on the course. I birdied the next hole. When I got to the green on the third hole, all of a sudden what I was doing hit me. I started to shake like a leaf. I could hardly hold my putter I was so weak. My greed for a good game was so strong that a few fine holes filled me with fear that I would lose this thing I had. And sure enough I did lose it. The wheels fell off the wagon and the golf went to pieces. And I was humbled again by golf, which is one of the reasons I need it.

I started skiing when I was young but skied poorly for thirty years. I decided I wanted to learn to ski powder, took lessons, and with the help of a fine teacher and my sons was finally able to ski the deep powder and make the nice curves down the mountain. But I grew tired of it and gave it up. I had skied so much and most of the challenge was gone. Golf is different. There is so much challenge there that there is no end to it. And it catches my fancy. So that looks like the way I'm going to be learning my Zen.

Where I'm at now with my golf is seeing my greed as my biggest swing problem. I want the kind of game I want, when I want it, so I can score and look good. That's all greed and little respect. I don't have much physical coordination or much muscle memory. The young son of a friend of ours shot an 85 on his second time out. But he is a gifted athlete and I'm not. The point of learning Zen through the art of archery is to learn the dance of life. The fact that the Zen master can shoot out the light of a candle is beside the point. To him, that's not the big thing. The big thing is that he is one with the bow and the arrow. To me, my big thing is still too much the score and how I look. That's my greed. As my greed goes away, the big thing will be the dance with the golf club, the ball, the beauty of the course and the beauty of my friends. So I'll keep learning more about the dance and someday I may be able to dance with my golf club, too. And my greed may have diminished so it spoils less of my life. I'm entirely ready to be freed of that defect of character and I humbly ask God to remove that short-coming.

A year ago last summer in Bozeman, as I was teaching the School of Life, I was telling my students how much energy I had because of just recently being freed of another of my addictions, so I was going to put that energy into starting a new business. I found out later that one of the women in the class turned to her husband and said, "Here's where we came in." She was referring to the fact that what I was saying sounded a lot like the guy who had the heart attack.

There's a book that's been real helpful to me for understanding myself. It's called *Please Understand Me* by David Keirsey and Marilyn Bates. It's published by Prometheus Nemesis, P.O. Box 2082, Del Mar, CA 92014. It has a brief test in it on the things we prefer. Our preferences, when combined, give a very clear idea of our personality and temperament. The test is based on Carl Jung's theories, and one of the dimensions of temperament is the extravert-introvert dimension. On the questions relating to social situations, my preferences are for small groups or solitary activities. That reveals that one aspect of my temperament is introverted. I found from the book a very different understanding of what being an introvert means. It doesn't mean I don't like people. It means that although I enjoy being with people, socializing gradually depletes my energy and I need to seek solitude to restore my energy. An extravert enjoys solitude, but it depletes him. He needs to seek out people to restore his energy.

Another part of my basic personality and temperament that I was born with is to seek to be highly competent. That is a deep and valuable strength in me. But where my sickness comes in is in the way I twisted and distorted my desire for competence into a compulsion to do things well, to show that I was somebody. I think that a lot of us will do this. We take one of our strengths and distort it in the service of the ego, and end up having our strengths our weaknesses. And this distortion brings us into separation from our fellow men and, more important, from God.

But to me, the reasons I give for choosing separation are unimportant. The reasons are just the rationalizations I give myself. I believe the root of it is that the part of us that was born separate and alone wants to stay that way and will find any reason it can to justify that decision. At the same time, there is the hunger in us for what we haven't yet experienced, the hunger for oneness, for union with our brothers and sisters and with God.

There is another aspect of my personality revealed by my temperament test. I have the ability to visualize a clear course of action that will lead us out of the chaotic present. My ability to do that lets me make an important contribution to a business or some other organization. But my ability can easily be distorted into arrogance and coldness. It's easy for me to have the attitude of "I'm right, get out of my way." I'm learning that I need to go to the back of the room, shut up, and be a little guy. There are plenty of people who will see a good way to go. Right now I've got some more work to do that's more important than being a big, visionary leader for every outfit I come in contact with.

I see that my temperament is just fine. I like it. But when I take that temperament to extremes, I distort the gift that God has given me as an escape from the pain of my sense of inadequacy, and that keeps me away from my brothers and sisters, who are love.

There are lots of revolutions going on in our society and in other societies around the world in the name of liberation. I don't believe there can be any liberation for any of us until we see our union with one another, our oneness. Any liberation that teaches separation can succeed only temporarily. Because Gandhi saw that he and the British were one and joined in a deep common love for justice and truth, his campaign could succeed. Malcolm X visited India and came to see that preaching hatred for the whites, no matter how justified, was killing the cause. He saw the oneness of everyone. Eldridge Cleaver in *Soul on Ice* talked anger. A while back the spirit of love swept through his life and in a day he became a new man and began to live from love instead of anger. Anyone who saw the picture of Pope John Paul II in the prison with the man who had tried to kill him can tell the power of love and forgiveness by the look on the terrorist's face.

That's why my sense of separation doesn't mislead me anymore. It may frighten me and put me off for a bit but I can now usually come back quickly to the truth that love is all there is. Though I am following Jackie's advice and not working actively on a new book, I already have the title ready if and when I decide to write one. It will be called *Loving 'Em All—It Ain't Easy But It Must Be Done.* The knowledge that love is all there is is why separation isn't frightening in the long run. It cannot sustain itself. Eventually the advocates of separation reap the fruits of their choices and in an instant can switch and go the other way. That ability to have a spiritual awakening so we can switch and change immediately is not the sole right of us and our friends. Transformations of this type can take place in the ones we think are our enemies too. And these transformations have taken place throughout the world since the beginning of time.

Another area where I need the transforming power of the spirit is in my attitude toward women. I have come to see that from my earliest days I have had a deep fear of women. That fear often shows itself as a veiled or sometimes not so veiled anger. My relationship with Jackie is hurt by that fear. It wasn't Jackie, personally, I was afraid of. I would have been afraid of any woman I would have married. But it is natural Jackie would take my fear of her personally and wonder what she had done. She has now come to see that she didn't do anything. My fear of her was my problem and I have to solve it, which, I'm happy to report, I'm gradually doing. But I see, in the flashes of anger I feel at women I don't even know, doing things I don't like, that there's fear under the surface and I'd better keep on dealing with that. Anger I feel at some woman stranger isn't going to hurt her much, but it will sure hurt me. I don't want that fear and separation anymore and I'm looking forward to its going away. (In the past six months since that was written most of that fear has been taken away.)

In society at large, the transforming power of the spirit has been the constant bright spot in all ages. Out of ages of inconceivable darkness and corruption and pain has come light. It cannot be explained in any logical way, it just happens. That's why there's no degree of darkness that's too big to be handled because, to me, the back side of that seeming darkness is our hunger for each other and for God and for our spiritual quest.

10.

~

The Higher Mind
That Most Western Psychology
Won't Admit To

HOW DO WE GO FROM THE CRAZY MIND TO THE HIGHER MIND? How do we use what seems to be a crazy enemy bent on telling us only bad things about ourselves to lead us to peace? Even more, how do we use our crazy mind to find the God within? And, even more tellingly, how do we encourage the crazy mind to find the Higher Mind, the God within, that the crazy mind will then have to put itself under the discipline of? Putting it another way, how does the spoiled puppy come to see that it needs a master so the puppy can then live under his discipline and not run the whole show? Obviously, this is not a simple problem, but it is a very accurate example of the problem we are faced with in our lives and in our marriages and former marriages and in our multiple marriages to all the things in life.

In the course of my life I have opened my heart to many people. I have put down my ego as much as I could and shared the joy, the pain, the fear that was there. A lot of these people have shared in this way with me, too. Because of this, I have an emotional support system. This support system keeps me from dying from the most awful malady there is, which is a broken heart. A broken heart is the medical consequences of loneliness. Just the sheer fact of being married gives us up to seven times the protection from certain types of cancer as being unmarried! It doesn't matter how good the marriage is, there is some protection even in a bad marriage. Even pet owners have some protection from dying that non-pet owners don't have. Why is this? It's because being in relationships forces us out of our crazy mind and toward what we might call Higher Mind.

We all wear many hats in the course of our lives. For instance, I'm a psychologist. As a part of being a psychologist I read many journals and books that give wonderful theories about life. They may help me with understanding *your* life, but I can't seem to find any help for me in my own life. They give me theory but they can't give me the formula for connecting theory with practice.

I have a deep religious background. I've been a student of religions and the Bible and of the writings of the great people of all religious beliefs. I follow the more traditional beliefs, although I've read far and wide and have studied some of the wildest, most far-out practices. You come to a place, finally, where you realize that you can be so open-minded your brains can fall out. Here, once again, all of this study is theory. It's education for the intellect. There is no way even the most learned can tell me how to make the connection for myself between what I hear and see and read and what I must do for myself on my own personal spiritual quest. That is where Higher Mind comes in.

It took me most of a lifetime to see and understand a belief that is common to all religions, though the words used for this belief are different. Some of the words for this belief are: going within, the inner room, centering, the God within, and meditation. These words are found in all religions, Jewish, Christian, Buddhist, Muslim, and so on. I thought for years that those words were describing prayer. Not so. They are describing a way to bypass the intellect in order to get in touch with the Higher Mind. Doing this is not a substitute for prayer or a replacement for prayer. It is a totally different thing.

I also confused the simple word meditation with reading and thinking about something spiritual because in the Western world this is the most common understanding of the word meditation. But if you read the lives of the saints of all the great religions, meditation was something else to many of them. It was the path, oftentimes, to deep spiritual or mystical experiences, and not one of them wrote anything about reading or studying something in order to have this experience. They all speak about getting in touch with their inner self, the God within.

As I have come to experience more and more that God lives within me as me, I'm finding I'm better and better able to go within and get in touch with the love and strength I need to live life. I used to think I needed a lot of guidance from God. I see now that most of the time I have all the guidance I need for right now. My problem was that I wanted guidance for next week or next month. For today and especially for right now, what I need to do is very clear. Usually my only problem is my lack of willingness to admit what I need to do, or my lack of willingness to do what I need to do, or my lack of strength to do it even when I am willing to do it.

In the twelve-step programs the eleventh step says, "Sought through prayer and meditation to improve our conscious contact with God as we understood him . . ." As this word meditation was explained within this context I saw that they were talking about something different; they kept talking about quieting the mind. My wife tried Transcendental Meditation. She was bowled over by it. She loved the deep relaxation this made available to her, and although no mention of spiritual experiences was made in her initial meditation lessons, she immediately experienced the connection.

In meditation we go within ourselves. We use a word or a repetitious prayer to still our minds in order to come to the nothingness that is the spiritual place within each of us. The word I use is "hahm" on the incoming breath and "so" on the outgoing breath. But tests on people in deep meditation have shown a dominant alpha wave pattern, a primarily right brain function. For people with heart problems the doctors are giving a medication called "beta blockers" because they block the beta waves of the brain which are the waves that are our stress reactors. We also know that people who meditate show greater ability for right brain access than those who don't.

The simple conclusions that have meaning for most people is that meditation can reduce stress and can enhance creativity. This is the first step toward Higher Mind. It is a place that most people start. I also took TM after Jackie recommended it and experienced a sense of inner peace. But it was Baba Muktananda who put me on the path to finding God within. Because Baba, in his Siddha path, was so open to all beliefs I did not feel that I was a Christian doing a non-Christian thing. Muktananda says, "I do not tell people to follow me. I tell them to wake up and realize that they are God and then go home. What religion is being asleep a part of?" In his ashram in New York, there is a very beautiful statue of St. Francis.

When we get in touch with the God within, when we see that we are God and that everyone and everything is God, and that it is all love, then we can come into our birthright. No human power can relieve us of the deep compulsions such as alcoholism or drugs. No human power can relieve us from a traumatic childhood. No human power can bring us to acceptance of the loss of a child. But God has that kind of power. And where has God hidden that power? Within each of us. The last place we would think to look.

That healing power, that love, is what I call Higher Mind. It is the God within each of us which is the observer of all that we believe to be us. It is the witness that is witnessing our mind, the thing beyond that which we think we are. The Higher Mind is the voice of our spirit, or soul. We all know that when we die our bodies are absent of life. If life is gone and our brain, from where our thoughts come, is dead, then what is that thing that we believe has left?

We have many reports of people who were clinically dead for a period of time and they tell us of what they experienced. What is that part that leaves the body in these people who clinically are declared dead and then return to life? What part of them is experiencing what they experience? Their eyes are closed on the table and yet they see and describe what is being done to their bodies from a vantage point impossible to explain. Their bodies are on that table, they are clinically dead. Yet they think and move into other realms.

What is this thing? Is it expressed by that old religious word "soul"? This part of us that is Higher Mind or God within is not dormant. We have all experienced flashes of the spirit guiding us and helping us many times in our lives. Meditation is a way to get in tune with this and to be able to live in the spirit more and more of the time with more and more awareness. Meditation is a way of giving consciousness to the God within each of us, a giving of life to our spirit.

Anyone who has meditated for any length of time becomes aware that they can no longer continue to do a lot of things they took for granted. For instance, our physical self becomes aware of our excesses. We suddenly see that we eat too much or that we smoke too much or that we don't get enough exercise. Our mind becomes aware of our anger or our self-pity or our lust and so on. And the thing we have called our spirit suddenly becomes aware that it is just our thoughts about spirit that we are calling the spirit. We come to the place where we are aware that we have limited who we are by using a tool called *our mind* in such a way that it has become our master instead of our servant. We see that our work is to stop the excesses of the mind which have imprisoned us physically, mentally, emotionally, and spiritually.

In the physical realm we begin to discover that what we call *hunger* is just our mind thinking about a hot fudge sundae, and that we have spent our lives believing that we *are* those thoughts. We think of food and the thought becomes us and we believe we become hungry. We think of something or someone who has done something we perceive as hurtful to us and we believe we become angry. We have a sexual thought and we think that it possesses us, that we have to do something. Do you see? It all begins with our thinking.

A lot of people in the world today believe that heart disease and cancer begin in the mind, too, because they are such stress-related diseases. Scientists have found that the death rate from heart attacks of young people working at Cape Canaveral was fifty percent higher than for a matched control group. Autopsies showed no heart disease but lots of little muscle tears. They believe those heart attacks came from a feeling of helplessness at all the work that needed to be done, yet the work force was being cut in half. A "pink slip" telling you that you were out of a job could make your heart clench so fiercely that it would literally tear itself to pieces. This is the same kind of death some test pilots experienced as their planes spun out of control toward the ground. Autopsies on these pilots showed that their hearts had stopped before their planes hit the ground.

Another reaction to their helplessness was an impairment in their immune system which lets cancers start growing. So if their hearts hadn't killed them, cancer might have. All of that happened because those young people listened to their minds telling them things were hopeless and they believed their minds. The ones who didn't believe their minds had a better chance of living, I'm sure.

And, of course, all wars begin first in the minds of men.

It is in meditation that we can come to see why alcohol and drug abuse is a number one problem worldwide. Behind all compulsive behavior there has to be obsessive thought. The basic obsession is the belief that *something outside ourselves can make us well.* It is this basic belief that sets up the obsession, the thought. It is our mind telling us that this drink or this pill or this person or this sex or this move to a new place or this job is going to fill our lack. And this is the root of it all—giving our power away to our thoughts of something outside of ourselves. The reason why it is all so terrible now is because we all have so much power, and instead of using it to satisfy our thirst for the spirit, we are using it to destroy ourselves and all of our values. It is the power we all have to go against our own value system that sets our behavior so compulsively. It is the pain of continuously doing something we don't believe in to gain something of no real value to us that is destroying us and our marriages and our families.

All people of all times have had their gods. My wife puts it succinctly, "God is whatever we bend our knee to." Most of us go to church, but few of us take a look at what we really bend our knee to. For me, a lot of times a jar of peanut butter is what I bend my knee to. The young people of the 1960s and early '70s sang about the age of Aquarius. The age of Aquarius traditionally has been designated as the age of the spirit. This age is being expressed by a yearning and an ache which is mistakenly being filled by abuses, but, as this new age has begun to settle down, more and more people are beginning to seek God within instead of the false idols without.

My wife has often listed some of her false gods to newfound friends. One was alcohol and pills. Another was other people's opinions of her. Another was her crazy mind. Another was doctors. A big false god for her was her dependency on me and our children for love. By listing these false gods, she came to see how needy those false gods left her. Since that time quite a few years ago, she has watched daily to see what her knee is bending to.

There is a simple way you can find what your false gods are, if you are so inclined. Watch your mind when you get in a painful situation. What does your mind turn to? Many people's first reaction is to reach for a cigarette, a drink, something to eat, work, or someplace to go. By watching ourselves in these times of pain, we find the preoccupations and obsessions that serve our needs and we can begin the process of freeing ourselves from those preoccupations. But the necessary first step is being really willing to live without the preoccupation and the escape it provides. I would never have believed how hard it would be for me to face life straight on.

This morning, we had a problem. The final editing of this chapter was waiting for me out in my little shed behind the trailer. I knew I needed to stay with Jackie and talk with her about the situation involving another person she and I were faced with. And I did sit down and talk, but all the time I could feel my preoccupation with the book pulling on me like a magnet, saying, "If you will work on the book, you will find relief." So relief was just twenty paces away.

Many people do as I used to do and justify their preoccupations as being important. It's easy for me to say this book is important. I'll get a check for my advance when it gets to New York. I'll be helping the people who write me telling how the books helped them wake up to the God within them. But I don't buy that line of thinking anymore.

I've had the beautiful experience of having an activity that used to be an obsession that has turned into a pleasant activity that I do with balance, so I know the difference. I used to be an obsessive trout fisherman. When we went on vacations, I would have to go fishing in the late morning and again in the early evening, religiously. No matter what was happening, I had to go. It was very hard for me to take a day to make a side trip or something like that. My fishing was an obsession that I had to have, both for the time it took me away from things directly, and for all the other time I spent preoccupied with it. But something happened. My obsession with trout fishing was removed about fifteen years ago. I still go trout fishing. Now I even have a trout stream in my backyard, though I didn't have when the obsession was removed. Now I go fishing only when that is the lovely next thing to do in my life. I don't go to escape pain.

There isn't a single time I've gone fishing that I should have been doing something else. Fishing is still in my life as a fairly frequent activity but there is no compulsive component to it anymore. I don't think about fishing, play out fantasies of old trips, or spend much time planning the next trip. Sometimes I need to call ahead to reserve a day with my friend Ray Champlain on the Madison, but I don't give the trip any more thought until we go. There are no reveries. I may have a thought of the trip, but it is only a fleeting one, not a compulsive one. So I know what it means to have an important activity that used to be an obsession now fitting in completely naturally in my life.

I see that all my activities will fit in my life that smoothly when everything I do is done out of love and the need for an escape is gone. Then my book writing, my work, some of my hobbies and other activities will have no compulsive component and I will be living with God all day long in the direct experience of his reality for me. Perfection at that is heaven. But there is a lot of progress we can make toward that through the careful and diligent practice of our spiritual programs with God's grace.

One of the biggest obstacles people are faced with today in getting out of their crazy minds and into higher minds are all the philosophical and psychological concepts they are involved with. One of the most troubling problems facing many people today is the idea they are a minority. There are some problems in the fact of being a minority, but they are a small problem alongside the big problems coming out of the *idea* of being a minority. As a Catholic, I'm a minority. As a Catholic, my chances of promotion in the big corporations were much lower than for Protestants. Sure, I was better off than the Jews and the blacks. But I was a minority. When I had problems in business, I had a choice. I could see my problems as coming to me because I was a persecuted minority, or I could see my problems as coming because of my deficiencies as a human being. My crazy mind doesn't want to accept responsibility for my behavior. It wants to believe that I'm a fine human being who is just having trouble because people are picking on me. The deeper my minority status, the more reasons I can come up with why this is so. For this reason, blacks today have an enemy worse than their extreme minority status. That enemy is their own minds.

Prejudice against blacks is wrong and harmful to blacks and to the people who hold the prejudices. And prejudice needs to be resisted as each person feels necessary. But in a given situation, a Catholic, or a black, or a Jew, or a Chicano, or a woman, or an old person, or a young person needs to be careful. We need to take the problem we are experiencing and ask ourselves what part of this problem would we have no matter what our religion, color, age, or sex. So I've seen that it is important to each of us that we don't put the handicap of a lot of excuses fed to a sick mind on top of a handicap we already have.

In the people I've met I've been amazed at the changes in personality they had after they started taking responsibility for their own behavior, stopped blaming others, and started practicing the program. When you see that a fellow who was sleeping under bridges a few years ago has a house and a family and a job he goes to daily, you are able to grasp what can happen when a person turns to a society of people dedicated to a spiritual way of life. You see what happens when slowly, one day at a time, a person works a program of prayer and meditation and other disciplines. From watching this miracle over and over I saw that my mind, like theirs, was a crazy mind. I saw that it didn't matter if my mind had never taken me to a skid row in actuality; a spiritual program could change me too. I'm not a man who went to excess in mood-altering chemicals, but I am a man who went to excess in everything else.

I slowly came to see that we can all leave our skid rows of the mind, whatever they are, but that most of us won't do anything about our problems because we think that we are not *that bad*.

A lot of us want to work on little areas of our lives. It might be weight or workaholism or anger and the like. In my experience, working on these little areas doesn't work to bring about lasting change. The reason, as I see it, is that all of our compulsive behavior, our pettiness, or whatever, is simply symptomatic. And when we clean up one area of our lives we simply switch compulsions. We will slide sideways, replacing one addiction with another. The new compulsion may seem to be less harmful to us but it isn't. I see this so clearly now. A person lost in fantasy is just as lost from God in their compulsion as the most dangerous sex criminal. Sure, there is more danger to society from the sex criminal, but on the inside of the two people, one is fully as lost as the other.

We quit smoking, we turn to food. We go on a diet and we start to smoke like crazy, or we start to buy clothes or run around. Some people go on a diet and turn compulsively to sex. Others give up sex and gain a hundred pounds. We—all of us—have to face that it is the last compulsion that is the hardest. My wife found this out when she met a heroin addict one day. His arms still bore deep scars from his addiction. He was sitting there saying, "Getting off the heroin, that's nothing. It's getting off the beer that's the hard thing. There's something about beer that makes it harder to give up than heroin." No! We all know that this is not true. What this young man was so upset about was having to give up the last of his mood-altering chemicals.

We can't get any of the spiritual programs at a deep level if we are still addicted to a single mood-altering chemical. Some of those chemicals we produce in our own bodies. A workaholic is addicted to his own adrenalin. People in the exciting sports or in dangerous activities are often addicted to that adrenalin rush. My addiction to my sexual compulsion produced the drugs inside that kept me far enough out of it that I couldn't get the spiritual program I was writing about at a deep level. Now that I've been off that drug of mine for two years, I'm having many new awakenings. I am experiencing many things I had been taught about and could write about but hadn't experienced as fully before.

For most of us, a diet, quitting drinking, stopping the pills, paying more attention to the wife and kids and less attention to work just isn't going to do it by itself. All we'll do is get a little bit crazier each day and then we'll go back to doing our own thing once again because it's worked for us in the past. The only solution there is for us, in my opinion, is finding a spiritual program that can help us to experience God of our own understanding at a deep-enough level so that we can have a spiritual awakening.

Part of doing this also is that we commit ourselves to being with a group of our peers, and being under their discipline. We have to get involved with a group of some kind. "Me and Jesus on the mountaintop" won't do it. So whether your spiritual path to your higher power leads you to commit to a church, a twelve-step program, to a guru, whatever—do it. Become involved, and relate to the people there. Share what you find with others. Then you'll begin to know that God lives within you as you and within me as me, and you'll begin to grow.

A long time ago I heard a very moving story but I didn't fully see its application until recently. A woman told me her father was a particularly inquiring person. He thought about how one rotten apple will soon spoil all the other apples around it. He got some rotten apples and tied them to apples on a tree. He was amazed to find that the rotten apples didn't hurt the apples that were still on the tree.

I recently saw what that story means. It says: As long as we're connected to life in fellowship with our fellow human beings, we live; as soon as we separate ourselves from them, we start to die. Now I see so clearly how the people in my spiritual program are the tree of life to me. As long as I keep in contact with them I live. When I think I'm okay now, that I don't need them anymore, I start to die. I'm the apple, and God's people and God are the tree, and I must never forget that and never believe the lies my crazy mind tells me. I need to use my Higher Mind to go to the God within.

I believe, as Emmet Fox said so movingly in his daily reader:

"There exists a mystic Power that is able to transform your life so thoroughly, so radically, so completely, that when the process is completed your own friends would hardly recognize you, and, in fact, you would scarcely be able to recognize yourself.

"It can lift you out of an invalid's bed, and free you to go out into the world to shape your life as you will. It can throw open the prison door and liberate the captive.

"This Power can do for you that which is probably the most important thing of all in your present stage: it can find your true place in life for you, and put you into it.

"This Power is really no less than the primal Power of Being, and to discover that Power is the divine birthright of all men."

Over and over, I see that the spiritual teachers are all talking about the same thing. One of the obstacles I had a hard time getting over was my lack of training in the nature of the mind and how to discipline it with a spiritual program. When I sent a copy of my first book to a favorite priest, he wrote back saying I'd written a fine manual of spiritual development. I see now that's what these seven books I've written with Jackie's help are. They are the manuals for, and of, my spiritual development written as I was experiencing that development. I feel good about the fact it is all put down on paper for me and you to see and think about. People ask me if it's fun to write. I say, "No, that's not the word for it. Satisfying is closer." But, more to the point, I wrote these books because I had to. While there was some compulsion operating in doing the books, I believe most of the writing came as a bird's song. It just comes from the birds because that's just part of being a bird.

The Schools of Life that I teach in Bozeman in July and Phoenix in January are schools of spiritual development. Someone was asking me what I taught in a School of Life. I said, "I tell the students that what's happening to them is all their own fault and to quit it. Put it all down and walk away a free man or woman." Most of my students are able to see this simple idea when they are finally in the company of a group of people as desperate and as receptive as are the students who go to the trouble of coming to my schools. So my students put it down, quit blaming others, join some kind of spiritual program, and make contact with God as they understand him.

In all this work, I see my students fighting the same resistances I fought. Many of those resistances are in the climate of Western psychology. That's the old ideas we have. They are the ideas we need to stop distorting and twisting in our own service.

Jackie said Taylor Caldwell has a character in one of her novels say that in the twentieth century the devil appeared in the form of Sigmund Freud. That's funny, but I think it is unfair to Freud. Sure, he had some ideas we cite as we head toward our own destruction, but I don't think he would recognize many of his ideas as espoused by us. But I do think we need to look at our present psychology and we need to consider some ways out of our predicament. Later, I'll quote a letter from Carl Jung that has been crucial to me in finding my way out of the rat's nest of Western psychology.

Western psychology, by and large, in my opinion, is very limited because it is so limited in its conception of the mind. By and large, Western psychology considers that the conscious, the subconscious, and the unconscious mind is all there is. To understand this, you have to understand how psychology in the United States came about. Up until the late 1800s and early 1900s psychology as it was beginning to develop was part of the philosophy departments of all the universities around the country. Then psychology, feeling its oats as a fledgling science, began to try to wrest its sovereign rights from the philosophy departments.

Psychology started proving it was a science by measuring, predicting, and controlling different behavior in different ways. There was Pavlov and his dogs, and making them salivate to the bells. Psychologists measured the time it took for a person to respond to a light signal, trying to figure out what it was in the mind to cause people to react to stimuli, some of the basic things in psychology. There was the stimulus-response theory that developed and Watson tried to build a psychology on that. Most recently people like Skinner, working off the learning that we do and our behavior, sought to take the idea of the scientific prediction and control of behavior as far as possible.

Then we've had another group in psychology which has tried to be broader, which has embraced a more holistic psychology, and these are the humanists. By and large they are holistic only up to a point. Most of them fall short of anything called metapsychology, anything beyond psychology—a God or some kind of higher power. You see, when psychology broke away from philosophy, to get its identity as a science it had to restrict itself to things that were measurable. Thus, what is a very inexact science had to become a very exact science in the minds of its practitioners.

When it comes to the thinking part of our brain, the mind, that is where all the knowledge to date is constantly up for grabs. The mind can't be restricted to what we feel and see and do, no matter how much we would like it to in order for it to be an exact science. So, just like an angry adolescent child leaving home, psychology threw out a lot of stuff philosophy had to offer, and I think psychology is coming to regret this increasingly more.

In the present field of psychology there is one overwhelming prejudice. You are not allowed to look at God. You cannot consider any concept of a higher power in any psychology department in any major university in the United States that I know of. There are maybe a few exceptions. There are a couple of transpersonal psychology sections within some psychology departments in a couple of universities in California. And there are a couple of psychology departments that, by their nature, are transpersonal in California. I don't know of any others.

With few exceptions here and there, the spiritual aspect of man as manifested in his psychological makeup is a forbidden subject, except in relationship to "man and his myths." God as myth is acceptable to most. Carl Jung is the notable exception among the great names in psychology. But even he, after he split from Sigmund Freud, did not publicly dare speak of his beliefs until he was older. He worked underground with his patients and in his private letters, as we know now, in order to keep his credibility in the field. If you read the Freud-Jung letters, you'll understand. Here was Sigmund Freud chastising Carl Jung like he was a little boy because of some of his views that differed from Freud's. It was only much later in his life that Carl Jung felt he could publicly speak out and felt that he didn't need to worry anymore.

Carl Jung, in the early 1930s, had an alcoholic patient named Roland H. who kept getting drunk. Jung told Roland H. that, in his opinion, Roland was hopeless unless he could have a spiritual experience that could change his personality. Carl Jung told Roland that he had seen such things happen to a few drunks, and that it was Roland's only hope. After that statement Roland sought out a spiritual group—the Oxford Movement. He had a spiritual awakening as Jung had hoped and he got sober. He helped a friend of his named Ebby get sober. Ebby then came to a friend of his named Bill W., and from Ebby's story to Bill, and Bill's need for a way to stay sober, Alcoholics Anonymous evolved.

Some six months before Carl Jung died, Bill W. told him this story. From Carl Jung's letter, you can clearly see that it wasn't until then that his particular view, that a spiritual awakening could do what psychology couldn't do, was known, except to a few people. I would like you to be able to see Jung's letter, which was so vital to my being able to put aside so much of what I had been taught and believed about the mind.

30 January 1961

Dear Mr. Wilson,

Your letter was very welcome indeed. I had no news from Roland H. any more and often wondered what has been his fate. Our conversation which he has adequately reported to you had an aspect of which he did not know. The reason was that I could not tell him everything. In those days I had to be exceedingly careful of what I said. I had found out that I was misunderstood in every possible way. Thus I was very careful when I talked to Roland H. But what I really thought about was the result of many experiences with men of his kind.

His craving for alcohol was the equivalent on a low level of the spiritual thirst of our being for wholeness, expressed in medieval language: the union with God.*

How could one formulate such an insight in a language that is not misunderstood in our days?

The only right and legitimate way to such an experience is that it happens to you in reality, and it can only happen to you when you walk on a path which leads you to higher understanding. You might be led to that goal by an act of grace or through a personal and honest contact with friends or through a high education of the mind beyond the confines of mere rationalism. I see from your letter that Roland H. has chosen the second way, which was, under the circumstances, obviously the best one.

I am strongly convinced that the evil principle prevailing in

* "As the hart panteth after the water brooks, so panteth my soul after thee, O God" (Psalm 42:1).

this world leads the unrecognized spiritual need into perdition, if it is not counteracted either by a real religious insight or by the protective wall of human community. An ordinary man, not protected by an action from above and isolated in society, cannot resist the power of evil, which is called very aptly the Devil. But the use of such words arouses so many mistakes that one can only keep aloof from them as much as possible.

These are the reasons why I could not give a full and sufficient explanation to Roland H. But I am risking it with you because I conclude from your very decent and honest letter that you have acquired a point of view about the misleading platitudes one usually hears about alcoholism.

You see, alcohol in Latin is *spiritus* and you use the same word for the highest religious experience as well as for the most depraving poison. The helpful formula therefore is: *spiritus contra spiritum*. Thanking you again for your kind letter, I remain,

Yours sincerely,
C. G. Jung

Jung's point that we need to go beyond "mere rationalism" was such a help to me. I had the belief that psychology was a dead end for me by then but doubted myself. To see that Carl Jung believed this way helped give me confidence in my own belief, and seeing the resistance he had faced, gave me courage. Earlier, when I developed the ideas in my book about mutual need therapy *(I Ain't Well—But I Sure Am Better)*, I presented them to the state psychological society. Many of the people there were outraged. A few refused to read the paper as soon as they saw the drift of it and they turned it over on the table in front of them. All that mutual need therapy is, is a report of the evidence about how over a million people got well using the program of Alcoholics Anonymous. I guess there are a few psychologists around the country who use my books, but it's no mass movement, I'll tell you. There are the transpersonal psychology people, but the pervasive feeling in psychology is that God is a myth and that any kind of a higher power has to go. Later, I found the Jung letter and it helped me feel less alone in my experience.

My practical experience, of course, comes from AA. I soon saw that this was a whole new society, a subculture, which was bringing about what psychology wants to bring about: a change in personality. This is a society that took men and women who were the dregs of society and turned them into productive, integrated human beings. This is the first understanding I had of a suprapower within the mind which could integrate the personality.

The clearest understanding that I've ever seen expressed of this suprapower within the mind I found in India and its people. They have a teaching that's about five thousand years old and their psychology is totally different from ours. The essence of their psychology is that the mind is an excellent servant but a terrible master. Sounds familiar, doesn't it? What is their master? They believe that the master is the witness of the mind. It is that part of us hidden within that is watching us think, and they believe a whole man is one who has awakened the witness and is then freed of the reactions brought about by his thinking. I then realized from this that the higher power that can bring about a change of personality and *the witness* are one and the same thing.

In the Western world, when psychology separated from philosophy and called itself a science, our intellect, our thinker, became our master. Intellect is what we are talking about when we say the word *mind.* And we did this not realizing that intellect lies on the surface of our personality. We made the surface the whole thing and are paying the price today.

Gandhi was a man who caught the interest of the whole world. We asked ourselves, how could this skinny little man have brought the British empire to its knees? He did it by using a force which he called *satyagraha.* In writing about his struggles in South Africa, Gandhi, as quoted by Eknath Easwaran in his book *Gandhi the Man* described *satyagraha* this way: "Truth *(satya)* implies love, and firmness *(agraha)* engenders and therefore serves as a synonym for force. I thus began to call the Indian movement *satyagraha;* that is to say, the force which is born of truth and love of nonviolence." Gandhi said that this force is the force of man's soul.

It is interesting, for the purposes of this book to see where Gandhi says he learned nonviolence. "I learnt the lesson of nonviolence from my wife, when I tried to bend her to my will. Her determined resistance to my will, on the one hand, and her quiet submission to the suffering my stupidity involved, on the other, ultimately made me ashamed of myself and cured me of my stupidity . . . in the end, she became my teacher in nonviolence."

In Gandhi, and in the disciplines he followed in order to live in *satyagraha,* we see that it is possible to find integration of the personality. In my opinion, the first thing we have to do is to recognize that there is something greater than the crazy mind.

In all of the eastern religions, in all of their holy books is the concept of I AM. This is the witness, this is God who dwells within you as you. Western religions have chosen not to develop this concept, although it is to be found in the Bible and in the writings of most of the great saints and the early desert mystics of our religions. In Christianity we say, "the kingdom of God is within," but so often we live the opposite.

What is so beautiful about all of this is that there are so many paths to God. It is foolish to argue about the path as long as it leads to the temple. But once we have been carried to the temple it is foolish to argue about the path. So no one is ever restricted to only one path to God; the path we each must find for ourselves is the path that is just right for us. It is so kind that God provided so many paths since we, his children, are so different.

In Christianity we have a saying from Christ: "by their fruits ye shall know them." And this is our indicator of the true path for us —the fruits. When we are on our true path we radiate love, we radiate God.

The understanding I have is that the mind is the servant and the Higher Mind, the God within, is the master. And without that master directing the servant, and without the servant being under subordination to the master, there is utter chaos.

How we reach the God within is through sitting down and meditating with a blank mind concentrating on the word that stills our mind. We talked some about this in our last book and I won't go into more detail here. We also meditate when we live life lightly and delicately in a meditative way. So all our life is a meditation.

A while back, in meditation, I saw that the meditative state was an intimation of immortality. You sit down in meditation and all the external stuff falls away. There are no fears, no cares. Everything is all right. It's like an out-of-body experience. It's just pure consciousness, the God-stuff that makes up Jess and has that essence, that sees and knows and is everywhere, and can pervade another person or chair or horse with no consequence to the other person except maybe touching their consciousness. You then see what death is, where you are free (but not in some relief sense). It's just that the hold of the mind and the body and the world falls away.

A long time ago I heard it said the point of all this spiritual training is to unite the conscious and subconscious mind so that you become single-pointed. You aren't divided anymore. I see what that means better now. Our mind and our energies become more concentrated, not so scattered, and we are more and more able to realize who we are and to act on that knowledge.

Over the years I tore my body down by constant self-isolating behavior and living in fear. I managed to need two heart surgeries and two pacemakers and have a highly developed spastic colon where my guts start rumbling and I get sick to my stomach when there is a lot of stress in my life. I'm thankful for those obvious indicators of what I was like and what happened. As I learn to live in love, my heart and my colon will give me quick feedback on how well my spiritual program is really progressing. I have lived twenty-three years since my heart attack through God's grace. That same grace will heal the spastic colon I developed as I live more and more in the Higher Mind with God.

11.

―――――∽―――――

Jackie's Chapter—
Getting into Action

THERE'S ONE THING I'VE SEEN in this field of spiritual development. We all want to *know*, but we aren't too strong on the *doing*
part of it. One of the most devastating things I ever heard said
about a person was a statement made by a son about his mother.
He said, "Mom has read every self-help book and religious tract
that has ever been written and I've never seen her practice a
single idea from any of them."

For a lot of us, being a knowledgeable bystander to life is the
way we have chosen for ourselves. We seem to be convinced that
knowing is enough. When one of our children was in treatment for
drugs and alcoholism, another of our children said to this one,
"Mom has told you over and over the reasons why you feel like
this, and you've taken the reasons and made them your excuses." I
think this is true of a lot of us. When we choose education over
action, when we want to learn instead of to do, our accumulation
of knowledge becomes our excuse, our reason for staying the way
we are and for not doing anything positive for ourselves. Most
often we tell ourselves that we don't want to do anything until we
have all the facts, or until we fully understand. The truth is that,
for most of us, we don't want to walk the walk. We want that easier,
softer way. And there is no such thing!

How do I know this? Because I'm just like you. I'm dominated by my mind. I think that this screwed-up mind sitting on my shoulders is going to *think* me into right action. I continually fall into the trap of believing that my mind will do it for me. Why do I fall into this trap? Because my mind tells me this is so—and I believe my mind over all the wisdom of the ages beginning with the Bible, which told me that the mind is a perfect servant but a terrible master.

I believed for years that my thoughts were me! And, furthermore, I believed that I had the power, through enough education, to change those thoughts and then I would feel better. Well, I changed those thoughts. I became a vast storehouse of knowledge and labels and psychological knowledge and understandings and not a lot happened except I kept getting crazier and crazier.

Finally I heard an old alcoholic say, "When we're trying to solve a problem, it helps to know what the problem is." I thought about that and my mind told me that I had thoroughly identified what I thought was the problem. I not only had educated myself and identified my own problems, but also could label and identify you.

My friend Horst Esslinger, the psychiatrist in West Germany, once said to me, "Jackie, I felt terrible one day when I realized that a lot of the alcoholics and neurotics I dealt with in the clinic were coming back to see me a year or two later, and they were 'weller' than I was. I thought about this and realized that I had too much knowledge. I was so smart that I knew what they were going to do before they did, when they were my clients—and this was dangerous for me. I saw that I was smart but that I didn't know so much about living. Too much knowledge can be dangerous. It keeps me from doing my own work."

Some of the most confused people I know are the psychologists who recognized they had a problem at an early age, learned about their problem, got a degree in psychology, and then escaped from their own problem into dealing with other people's problems. They sidestepped walking their own walk and moved into solving it vicariously. These types are voyeurs in the field of mental health. They love to label and categorize and pass judgments on other people's lives, while their own lives stay just as screwed up as ever. Father Martin, a priest I know, says it this way: "Just because you've had brain surgery, this doesn't make you a brain surgeon."

A lot of us, through reading and studying and going to psychiatrists and attending any one of the thousands of educational week-ends offered in this country in any given month, have enough intellectual knowledge to supposedly make ourselves, our families, and our whole town well—right now, today. The simple fact is that this isn't the problem. The problem is putting *down* our problem, now that we've identified it, and beginning to live our lives in a healthy, loving, outgoing way. Most of us choose not to do this. We like our problem. We like having our problem. That's because our *problem* is really our *answer;* it's all we know right now. Until we see this we can't put it down. We can't put down an answer until we've found another answer.

Alcohol and tranquilizers were never my problem. They were my answer. They became my excuse, they became my reason for not being responsible for my own life. Education became my answer, and I proceeded to learn all that I possibly could about my disease. This part of my growth was my "education will set you free" syndrome. Then I turned to the spiritual and called this part of my growth, my "Me and Jesus on the mountaintop" syndrome. I then saw myself immersed in helping Jess and the children with *their problems* and here was another answer for me. I called this phase my "Super Mom makes amends" syndrome. And all this time I saw that there was a part of me that knew that I was doing what Horst Esslinger had talked about. I was using my knowledge and my intellect to avoid doing my own work, to avoid casting myself completely free of all that my mind told me to help me learn who I was and what I needed for myself. The craziest I get nowadays is when I get into theorizing and having to have reasons. I can't stand this.

I saw Betty Friedan on television a few months ago. She's a grandma now. And I looked at her and I remembered how confused I had been, years ago, when Betty first appeared on the scene. I was confused by what she was saying, even though she was saying a lot of things that I had thought myself. And I remembered how frightening it was to be raising kids in the 1960s and early '70s and to try to put together how to do it with how I had been taught. One of the biggest things that I had been taught as a young girl was to be careful of a man's ego. I was told that the ego is the only thing that a man has that gives him the courage and determination to go out and make a good living to support his family, so I must never say or do anything that might damage my husband's ego. And I heard that statement made by the wisest woman I knew at the time, and I believed! I tried my best not to be a destructive wife. I never wanted to be a "bitch," that epitaph to validity for women, and I tried. I tried so damned hard that I have asked my children to put on my tombstone:

JACQUELINE CAREY LAIR
MAMA TRIED

One of the most heartwrenching things that ever happened to me was once when I was giving a short talk to a lot of people on what it was like in our family. In a moment of complete candor—an affliction of mine—candor—I told these people that, as each of my children was born, sometime in the first week or two of their lives I secretly held them up to God, when I was alone, and told God that I dedicated my child to him. I did this at least four times that I know of. I didn't do this with Janet, our first, as she was hospitalized for the first month of her life.

As I told this little story on myself, I half-laughed and half-cried at the walk that "God's children" and I had taken in the past thirty years. I looked out in the audience and saw to my amazement countless women with tears in their eyes nodding their heads also. They knew what I was saying about how it was back then. To my amazement, about six or eight of them had made the same offering of their children to God that I had. Amazing! I thought I had been alone in that.

Life was simple when I was a young mother. We baked tollhouse cookies and made Halloween costumes, went to the PTA, gave birth to countless babies and dedicated them to God! If we were sick we went to the doctor and he told us what was wrong and we took his pills. If we felt screwed up we went to a psychiatrist and talked about ourselves and tried to change ourselves so that we would feel better. Our husbands went to work and to PTA sometimes, and played poker and went fishing, and took the family camping, and got promoted and demoted and moved a lot, usually into a bigger house for the wife and the kids. Our children would grow up to be teachers or priests or nuns or advertising men or soldiers or mothers just like me, of course! The oldest one was just a teenager when Kennedy got killed, and in the next ten years we raised four teenagers in the Vietnam war and the beginnings of the drug culture.

God—how many of you can remember telling your children that they could talk to you about anything? If their friends were using drugs, all that your kids had to do was come home to Mom and tell her and she would help. We didn't know then that no *human* power could relieve anyone of an addiction and that some-day we would be sitting in treatment centers grieving that what we thought was helping was instead enabling them to stay imma-ture and childish, and that there really is no "right" way to raise a kid. How many of you remember not knowing what to do, but thinking, "For God's sake, do *something*"? How many of you are aware of working so damn hard to be a "good" mother? How many of you tried to do it right, tried to raise them in such a way that they would never have to know the pain that you had when you grew up—only to find out that this was childish and immature on your part—you had spoiled them?

How many of you remember finally realizing that God and country and the Republican Party weren't all that they were cracked up to be, because they wanted to take your boys and put them into Vietnam, and you *knew* that this was wrong, wrong, wrong? Going back even further, how many of you remember finally figuring out that to have another child was going to destroy you, your sanity, and your marriage, and knowing that there wasn't a safe method of birth control around?

I remember the relief that I felt when my doctor told me I was a candidate for a hysterectomy. Then I remember my horror when I realized that my church forbade it unless I was going to die if I didn't have it, and that the state of Minnesota in 1960 would not allow a woman to have a hysterectomy unless she had five living children and her husband signed his permission.

Do you remember the mothers who were against the Vietnam War and started a group that used a slogan that said, "War is not healthy for children and other living things"? Do you remember back then we thought twice about joining a group like that, be-cause Richard Nixon was still around and he was always a re-minder of McCarthyism and we didn't want anyone thinking we were Communists or bugging our telephone? God, what a para-noid time we raised our children in. I thought twice and then I joined that group. That was the first time that I remember step-ping out of my tollhouse cookie mode. And the first time that I was aware that raising a family was a terrifying thing.

I promised my boys that they would never have to go to Viet-nam. The oldest son was nine years old when Kennedy sent some of the first boys to Vietnam. He was frightened and asked, "Mom, will I ever have to go to war?" I said, "No, Jess, you'll never have to go to war. Mom promises." I thought it an easy promise. Who had ever heard of a little skirmish that would last on and on and on? *Ha!* Before it was over, I sat and listened to the radio to hear what draft number that boy would get! And I looked at my husband and said, "If it's under fifty we're going to Canada." He said, "The hell we are!" And I felt like he was a complete stranger for one of the first times in our marriage. And I knew that the world, as it was at that time, would say that he was right and that I was wrong. And I knew that the idea of moving the whole family to Canada was crazy, and it was, but it symbolized something that was happening to me. I knew I wasn't naïve anymore, and I knew that a lot of the things that I had taken for granted and that I thought I believed, when my church and my school and my family told me that they were so, weren't valid for me anymore. My God, what do I do now?

I had to start thinking for myself and finding out what I believed in. I was a feisty one. I was a pain in the ass to my husband a lot of the time, but I was also a great pleasure to have around because of my feistiness and my ability to see life on the bias in a way that made a lot of things funny to him and to me.

I was hellishly neurotic for a long time and saw some psychiatrists over a period of many years, but in light of what I know now, I see that I was not so much neurotic as I was trying to do a lot of things that I didn't believe in. And while my head was saying that I had to do these things, my heart wouldn't follow along. The most wonderful thing that was ever said to me was said by a psychiatrist, Walther H. Lechler. "Jackie," he said, "thank God on your knees every day that your spirit would not die. Thank God that you stayed one of the noisy ones. I deal every day with people whose spirits die, and they are the truly sick ones. They don't know what is wrong anymore. They don't know their feelings, and these people are the hardest ones to help."

I wanted to argue with him that I would rather not be able to feel than to feel some of the pain that I have known. But he comes from Germany and he knows too graphically what it means to have a whole country not able to know or to express their true feelings. He recognizes the danger of this more than most of us ever will.

As I have gone through the growing-up process known as "marriage," I have been ready to chuck it countless times. But commitment is a belief of mine for me. I don't believe that my commitment can make another committed to me, but when I make a contract and it is binding, it is binding for me. It could mean that I would have to live alone in my marriage because my mate doesn't see commitment as I see it, but that would not mean the end of my life. I am committed, not dependent.

I had to learn the difference in these two things the same way I had to learn most everything of value in my life—through experience. And I don't believe anymore that commitment means that I can do things that are impossible for me. I don't believe that my marriage vows demand that I live in ways that are dangerous to my health and well-being. I was many years coming to the realization that there were two or three things that I was doing that I could no longer do. I had to take the risk of saying, "This way in which I am living I can no longer live. I can't control what you do, Jess, but if you want to join me in a new way of life, I want to be with you. Otherwise, I must go on alone. I will not divorce you, but if you choose divorce, then I must accept that too." For the toll-house cookie lady to come to the ability to say this and mean it with all the love in her heart is the result of a lot of hard work and a lot of change. I'm proud of that.

One of the wisest men I know said this: "In the end, we all must come home to the living God who made us—in the entire business of living." I heard what he said and I have been trying to do this.

Looking at television that day, I knew suddenly that I loved Betty Friedan. I knew that reading this magnificent lady so many years ago was the beginning of a new way of life for me. I knew that growing up for me was the most painful thing that has ever happened to me, and that the first step was taken when I recognized that I had the right to be a human being instead of somebody's daughter or wife or mother. Without Betty Friedan I would never have taken that first look at the fact that I was a totally male-dependent woman in an imperfect world and that I had to begin to learn exactly *who I was*.

So that's what seeing Betty Friedan again brought back to me.

Most of us have a difficult time coming home to the living God who made us because we have a hard time allowing our intellectual knowledge to bring us into conscious awareness. We consistently read and study to find out *why* instead of *how*. The simple question "Why?" sabotages our knowledge. There are two things that kill an awful lot of living for me and other people. The first is the question "Why?" and the second is constant agreement. Constantly agreeing kills more growth, it seems to me, than constantly disagreeing. Most people who disagree with everything get called on it after a while. Those who constantly agree never get called on it. I know a minister who is smothering his own growth, the growth of his family and his church, by constantly agreeing with everything everyone tells him about himself.

When we always look for reasons for why we are the way we are, when we are constantly studying for new understanding, what we are really doing is looking for something or someone to blame. I've never seen an alcoholic have a spiritual awakening as long as he or she had one thing left to blame for the way they are. Any alcoholic who reserves any blame for anyone or anything as any part of why they are alcoholic will get drunk again eventually—I don't care how long they've been sober.

This isn't true just for alcoholics. This is true for all of us. If we have to have a reason outside of ourselves for why we are miserable, we will always go back to misery. When we blame someone or something for our misery, we give that person or that thing or that circumstance complete power over our lives. When they "do something to us" or when "that thing" out of my childhood happens again, or when "that circumstance arises again" we are right back into being controlled by outside circumstances.

This is a hard concept to accept. We all want to scream, "But . . . !" But, but, but! I had to come to see that as long as I was into blaming, I had to find some way to control my life and those around me to keep the misery from happening. This never works. This makes me dependent and when I am dependent I am fearful and manipulative and I people-please. Or I am angry and aggressive or I flee into work or travel or any one of hundreds of maladaptive behaviors, including the sneakiest variation of the same theme: I'm independent and I don't need anybody, and I can do it myself, and who needs you?

All of these things lead right back to the mind. How we think is who we are. We believe we are our thoughts, and as long as we believe this, that is what we are and that is how we act and react. All of our behavior is determined by what our computer mind tells us. And as long as that is what we are, I can see no way to bring about change in our lives that will have any lasting effect or value.

If we are having pain in our marriage and we want the pain to go away, we all do the same things. We begin to "think" about our problem. We start to read. We begin to study. Then we start to analyze and diagnose and then we start to fight and then we seek help and then we begin to "think" we understand where the problem is, and then we begin to have hope, and then we make resolutions and resolve to try to do things differently, and then we wake up one morning miserable again and we start the process all over. And all of it is in our minds. It is our thinkers that have all the power, and our thinkers are into analyzing and comparing and judging and selfishness and power and greed and control. Our thinkers are the "I" part of us. "I want, I need, I believe, I see, I know, I will, I think."

When we spend our life seeking knowledge about the business of living the way we do, we are using a tool that God gave us to use in the outward circumstances of our life to deal with that which it knows nothing about. Our intellect cannot know who we really are, it can only study the data we feed it and make judgments based on that data. As they say in computer language, "Garbage in, garbage out."

Someday, if we mean what we say, the day has to arrive when we begin to acknowledge that our intellect is the biggest single limitation we have in the business of living on the physical, emotional, and spiritual level. Then and only then can we begin to see what "will" is, what self-discipline is, what wholeness is all about. The day comes when we see that they have to do with *doing* something, not thinking about it, or understanding it, or studying it. Just doing it!

Every alcoholic and overeater alive is aware that willpower is to no avail against their compulsions. At the same time, these people know that they have willpower beyond measure when it comes to finding the alcohol they need or the food they want. What is the difference? Who among us has never gone on a diet only to find ourselves standing helplessly at the refrigerator in the middle of the night dishing up some ice cream or making a sandwich? Not many of us can say, "I never did that." Almost all of us have.

What is going on when this happens? It is us allowing our minds to tell us what to do. Why do we do this? Because we think our minds are us, and we permit our minds to think anything they want to think. We have never learned the discipline of controlling our thoughts. At first, none of us is able to be very responsible for the first thought that comes into our minds on any given subject. There we do not have much choice. Where the choice comes for us is in the entertaining of those thoughts.

The first step any of us can take toward controlling the master and bringing him back into being a servant is to meditate, of course. The second step is to become aware of our thoughts during the day. We will soon see a pattern there. We will begin to see what thoughts are charged with meaning and what thoughts just pass easily through and are gone.

When we become aware of a pattern in our thinking that is causing us to be some way we would rather not be or to do something we would rather not do, then we are ready to take a course of action. We want to break up our thought habits, because that is all they are—habits. Suppose I have the habit of thinking negatively about my work. The minute I am aware that I am having a negative thought, I let it pass through my mind and choose to find something else to think about. If that doesn't work, I have to get up and do something. Say a prayer, ask for God's help, go for a walk, call someone on the phone, anything that works for me in the business of changing that destructive thought pattern.

The thing many of us will come to see is that it is the "entertaining" of those thoughts that causes us so much grief. That word entertaining is a very apt word because by entertaining a thought pattern we are soon into fantasizing and our thoughts have become our world and we are defeated.

When we meditate we come in touch with what Stephen Levine calls "wisdom mind." This is what Christ called going within. This is the process many of us use to find out who we really are. And this inward seeking, rather than being narcissistic, is the true way to find out who we are and thus free ourselves to come out into the world in healthy ways instead of selfish ways. This is the only true road to the spiritual goal of selflessness and the only way to achieve some measure of peace in this world that I have been able to find.

If we truly want to find a new way to live, a way to gain some measure of control over our minds, then we have to recognize that reading, studying, thinking, analyzing, and judging have cast us upon a rocky shore. We have to be willing to give up a lot of our old ideas, a lot of our old ways. We have to begin once again, and we should first begin with elementary things. We begin with our physical lives. We have to take a look at what we eat. We have to take a look at the amount of exercise we get. Do we overindulge, or do we underindulge? Balance is what we are seeking. It is not good to be overweight, but it is just as wrong to be too thin. We start to do something about it. Do we smoke? Do we drink? We have to bring that into balance. How do we dress? How do we take care of our hair, our fingernails, how often do we bathe? We have to take time with our physical self. We have to take care of our bodies, and our appearance, but always with balance. We must begin to pay attention to how we are dressing our bodies. What messages are we sending with our clothes, our makeup, our jewelry? What about our voices? What tone of voice do we use with others? How often do we listen? How much sleep are we getting? Is it too much, or too little? What do we think about when we go to bed at night? Do we rehash the day, or do we thank God for the day? What is our first thought in the morning? Is it negative or positive? Our thoughts before we sleep affect our sleep, our dreams, and can affect the way we feel when we get up the next morning.

All too often we don't pay any attention to our emotional life. For the vast majority of us, our emotions are things we either stuff or deny. Emotionality is like a fat, ugly relative—we want to hide it or wish it would go away. Emotions need to be recognized. As Carl Jung said, and it bears repeating: ". . . emotion is the moment when steel meets flint and a spark is struck forth, for emotion is the chief source of consciousness. There is no change from darkness to light or from inertia to movement without emotion."

If you don't feel emotion about doing something for yourself, in order to change what is happening in your life or in your marriage, believe me, you won't do it. Without emotion, there is very little energy. And yet we all are embarrassed by emotion. I am a very emotional woman. At any given moment I know exactly what I am feeling, and most of the time it shows. Jess and most of the kids go nuts at this a lot of the time. They hate to see my emotions so plainly in my face or voice because a lot of times I am right on and it's hard for them to deny something when they have such a barometer around. Of course, as Jess says, "I only hate to see your emotionality when I feel it's negative. I love the way you laugh so much and dance around the house and revel in a sunset or sweep a baby up in your arms. I love the way you sing silly songs to me or talk crazy to me to make me laugh."

I point out to Jess that he cannot have one without the other. The way I feel about it is, "I'm like Miss Piggy. What you see is what you get."

For many of us the expression of emotion is almost an impossibility. Society and our own fears have brought us to the place where "being cool" is not an act but a fact. There is nothing wrong with an emotion truly expressed in the moment of feeling it. Where emotions get into trouble is when we "think" them instead of feeling them. Our minds have taken over here too. And unfortunately our minds can only do one of two things with our emotions, deny them or exaggerate them.

When we were told to control our emotions as very young children, that is all we were told. None of us learned that the control and use of emotionality is an art. So for us, what controlling the emotions means is stuffing them, and training our minds to deny our feelings. If this art is not learned, the emotions lie there boiling and then come back into our minds over and over again and we refeel these in our minds until they are exaggerated out of all proportion. And then the feelings come out sideways in angry demeanor, where we kick the dog, or in crying inappropriately, or even in hyperhilarity or aggressive hale-and-heartiness, all of which are false expressions of the truth about ourselves.

What happens when we learn to stuff our feelings is that we begin to feel guilty about emotionality and to find its expression by other people an embarrassment to us. We tend to flee our own emotions and the emotions of others at this point. It's all rather bizarre, but that's just because we, as an essentially puritan nation, never understood that feelings are all right and that there are safe ways to express them and that this is all right to do.

The emotion that gives us the most difficulty, of course, is anger. The inability to express anger becomes the stumbling block for all of the other emotions, and because anger is so powerful, not being able to deal with it gives many of us an angry demeanor a lot of the time. Anger has so much power. It give us energy at a faster rate than any other emotion. The problem is not the anger, but what to do with all of that energy. If the energy is not expended and we swallow the energy, it can tear up our insides with ulcers and heart attacks and strokes and many other physical manifestations that can do violent harm to us.

Expending the energy in harmless ways is the key to dealing with anger. First, we admit we're angry, then we admit that screaming and yelling and hitting and throwing things isn't the answer, then we should go for a walk or jog or go swimming or involve ourselves immediately in some form of exercise that will require the expending of that energy. It's the energy level that needs to be brought back into balance; it's not the anger that needs to be expressed outwardly. Once we have expended that energy and feel the energy drained, we can then take a look at the situation and attitudes that were the source of our anger and deal with those things realistically and rationally.

If you have a health problem that constricts your ability to exercise, talk to your doctor about ways to use up that extra energy. The energy of anger is just like a hurricane or a tornado, they are energy too, and they have to spend themselves in order to dissipate. It's essential that we come to understand this. Without dissipation of the energy that comes with emotion, especially a powerful energy-giver like anger, that energy will turn inward and hurt us or go outward and hurt others. When the energy of anger gets bottled up inside of us and is not spent, we become depressed. Depression is nothing but frozen rage—anger turned inward. Emotions are energy sources and we must pay attention to our emotions and treat them with respect. They are a part of our humanness and will not be denied, no matter how much we may try.

Spiritually we have to come into balance, too. When people are having a lot of trouble in life, they either try to escape from the God idea or escape into God. The first way causes us to deny all belief in a higher power and the second way causes us to feel we know God personally, "Me and Jesus on the mountaintop," you know. There are problems with both of these ideas and the problem is the same: they both give us the feeling that we're unique. When I see people who think they're unique I know they've got a God problem. When trouble comes, we need to humble ourselves, find a God of our own understanding, and submit ourselves to a jury of our peers. We need to find a group of like-minded people who can show us God through their lives and who will accept us and love us and discipline us. This can be in a church, a synagogue, a mosque, a twelve-step program, a Bible study group, whatever you can find that will help you with your spiritual growth.

I emphasize finding a group of people to go on our spiritual journey with because we are social animals and without the ability to commit ourselves to a group we are out there alone and lonely and we are bound to come into error, and then nothing's going to happen for us except more pain and suffering.

I know of a few ministers who have been brilliant orators and God-like men. Without the discipline of anyone, these men, almost without fail, all took their idea of God and built a monument to themselves and eventually ended up outcasts. Even people who have dedicated themselves to doing God's work are not exempt from being under the discipline of a group, either a church hierarchy or a church board or a jury of their peers. I have learned that it doesn't matter anymore how beautiful the words that one of these people speaks seems to me. If they are not members of a group, they cannot last.

There's a famous surgeon in this country who has gifted hands and technique. He has set up his own institute and has become his own God. He answers to none of his peers for the surgeries he performs and his reputation is going downhill fast. Such a man is just like the itinerant preachers. Without a disciplining group to answer to it is soon all ego and he too will crash. It is a simple law of life—a spiritual law if you will.

It is in balance that we slowly come into peace of mind and acceptance and love. And through taking the steps necessary to come into balance, our mind slowly becomes our servant instead of our master, and we can begin to look at our mate and our family with understanding, compassion, tolerance, and a growing love.

With a balanced life and more peace of mind we will come to see that we have more control over the things we do and say to others. We will begin to convey our true selves instead of being at the mercy of outside circumstances. The inner person and the outer person will slowly become one and the same.

12.

~~~~~~~~~~~~~~~~~~~~~~

To Be Continued
in Our Marriage

JACKIE AND I CELEBRATED thirty-five years of being married on July 7, 1984. As you can see from the book, we earned it. As I look back on our quiet celebration, I want to say how glad I am that she was to be my spiritual partner, my soul mate. I'm sure there couldn't have been a better one for me.

I've told you how marriage looks for me. I just realized this past week, as the book was being finished, that here is a marriage book without a chapter on love, or on sex or on communication or children. Those were all the things that, a long time ago, I would have expected to be in a marriage book. But they aren't talked about separately. Yet, as you see so well by now, the whole book is on love, and sex, and communicating, and children because the whole book is on God as I understand him and that's what's at the center of all those things.

I was thinking this morning, as I was ready to write this last chapter, that we have a choice of living in two realities. We aren't just stuck in one reality like we think we are. The major theme that runs through the letters I get from people is the fear and anger and despair they have about the reality they live in. They want to know how they can possibly be expected to live in their reality and they don't even consider that so many of those things around them can be changed. Yet, there is a way out for them. All those things around them *will* be changed the minute they do one thing: change their thinking, their understanding.

In this book, I've told you how coming to a new understanding of marriage changed my marriage. Those are the same ideas that we can use to change our understanding of the world. The marriage we are in is not a cold, hostile, and threatening marriage. The world we face out there is not a cold, hostile, and threatening world. When we come to have the understanding that God lives in everyone and that everyone is working out their own spiritual quest, then we can relax and do our own work. We don't need to understand the exact way everyone is working out their spiritual quest, we just need to accept that fact. I know how frightening it all is at first. I know how hard it is to find like-minded people at first. But out there waiting for us are people we can open our hearts to, and they will open their hearts back to us.

Once we are sufficiently broken by life that we are forced to open our hearts even though we still don't want to, we don't think so much about how hard that is. When we finally see we are drowning, it is easy to yell for a life preserver and come out of our foolish idea of self-sufficiency. Once we are broken enough by our excesses and the prices we paid for them, then we become transparent and vulnerable. As we get the new rewards for living in a new way, we become more willing to live out in the open more of the time until finally we are firmly established in a new way of life.

Our fear, coming out of our crazy mind, is the problem. But on that point, too, we finally get fed up with our crazy mind and say to it, "Why don't you shut up!" We finally get tired of all the excuses our mind has given us for its failures. We finally get desperate enough to look some other place than our crazy mind for help. Eventually we find what we are seeking hidden in the last place we would ever think to look, deep below the craziness, in the still, quiet voice of the God within.

Once we've made that contact in a solid-enough way to be able to hold on to it for a while and to get back to it reliably, we begin to see a new reality. When you go down on skid row, you see the bums lying there. You're overwhelmed by the hopelessness of their wretched condition. But that's not the reality. The reality is that some of those hopeless drunks are just a short time away from a spiritual awakening that will lift them out of skid row and put them right in the center of a loving family.

Your mind balks at that as a possibility but it happens every day. I can give you the names of people who used to be there and are now running the mission for drunks or are carpenters or attorneys. Still your mind balks and you say, "But that's not all of them." That's right, but it doesn't have to be all of them in that way. They've all got a date with the God who made them. It's just that the way they meet God isn't as clear to us as it is in the case of the ones who get up and walk away into a new life, right in front of our very eyes.

There's another kind of skid row here in Phoenix, on Van Buren Street. Van Buren is a main route downtown, so everyone has a chance to see what's going on. Here's where the women stroll in front of the cheap motels and massage parlors so they will be handy to the guys from all walks of life who are looking. Not all these women and men will stay on Van Buren all their lives, either. Some of them are just days away from a spiritual awakening that will finally open up for them the new way of life a deep part of them hungers for. When that happens, most of us will never know about it because one of those women or men will be a co-worker or friend. Their secret past will go to the grave with them, except for the few like-minded friends who are trusted enough to know about each other's secret past.

Many of the people who write me letters see what they think are the realities of skid row, Van Buren Street, and their marriage. They don't see the other reality. That reality is that the specific people who are on skid row change over time because some of the people have gotten up and walked away and now work out of an attorney's office or an electrician's truck. There's the same number of people there but that's because new people have made the choice to go there and have that experience. The same with the women and men on Van Buren Street.

So there is another reality. That's the reality my spiritual partner, my true companion, has been absolutely vital to me in helping me find. I spent my early, egghead life subscribing to special magazines like *New Republic* so I would be sure to know of every problem every place in the world. You couldn't bring up a problem I didn't know about and wasn't already worrying about. If you ever did come up with a problem I didn't know about, that was a sign I needed a new magazine to add to the ones I had to protect me from the embarrassment of having missed a problem. I spent a long time living in that reality. I don't want to live there anymore.

The reality I spend so much of my time in now is the reality I've found using the principles and practices in this book and earlier ones. I guess the best way to describe that old reality is the reality of fear. The name for this reality is the reality of love. Love is the absence of fear. Fear and love are incompatible. The more fear, the less love. The more love the less fear.

To me, what it means to be a man is to live without fear. I'd guess that's what it means to be a woman, too. If the absence of fear is love, then that means that for both of us, for Jackie and me, living fearlessly is living with love. And, by the same principle, when I'm living in fear, I'm living away from love.

As I have mentioned, there were two crucial choice points in my life that stand out for me. One was when I said I would never again do anything I didn't believe in. The other was when I determined to go back into my marriage and stop being a baby. So many experiences that I'm now having in these days make me more and more grateful for those two awakenings and the fruits they have produced. I know I've got plenty of learning to do yet. But I'm now so much happier with some of the things I see myself doing with the grace of God and the help of my spiritual partner.

I now find myself going through experiences that have great pain for me, yet I see a quiet part inside that's calm about what's happening to me. I went through a tough deal in Chicago some time ago where I reaped some awful consequences of my earlier arrogance and greed. I was able to call Jackie and say, "I'm getting the hell kicked out of me up here and I deserve every bit of it. It's good." Because it was good. I grant you that I haven't yet digested the whole experience, but I've already found the good in most parts of it.

Another example of the strength I've seen in myself is in relation to a man who had formerly brought out the absolute worst in me. Because of my compulsion and greed, I was in a power struggle with him. Now, in my dealings with this man, I can sit quietly and wait for God to work in the situation. I used to take him into my head and obsess on him, but with the help of my program and my friends, I got him out of my head.

The most important place I'm seeing strength and lack of fear is in our marriage on both our parts. Jackie has had to face life-and-death issues with me for twenty-two years, so that's nothing new. What is new is the quiet and peace and gentleness in her now as she faces those issues with so much love. I've lived twenty-three years after a heart attack. The average is way lower than that even for guys who are young when they had them. I've lived through two heart surgeries, even though the one four years ago was very close. The doctors couldn't get the internal bleeding stopped and finally had to sew me back up and get me off the heart-lung machine and just hope the bleeding would stop on its own. It did stop.

But heart surgeries can have some unfortunate side effects that aren't talked about much that do physical damage to the body and the brain. Some of my emotional storms were quite likely aftereffects of the surgery, but we can never know which ones. Talking to my fellow heart-surgery patients has helped make this clearer to me because they had so many of the same emotional side effects and were surprised at them because they had no idea what they were coming from.

The way I've handled all of my emotional storms in the past is to pretend to be King Kong and get on my horse and go elk hunting or go out and work long hours at a time. Jackie and my doctor let me do that, because it seemed the best way for me to live, because I didn't seem able to accept any other solutions to the problems. It has given me lots of living in some ways, but at the price of the diminished awareness that denial costs. I'm prepared to find a more aware way to live my remaining years. This has meant that recently, Jackie has often had to raise or be a part of fearful discussions between us, on how best to keep me alive. She's done this with love and little fear. That's beautiful to be a part of, and to watch and be a recipient of. It makes the work I have to do for me in the area of watching my physical health so much easier for me.

I can still get on my horse and go on an expedition. But I have to have awareness of what I'm doing, what's going on, and when not to do that anymore. That's something that's really hard for me and my friends. My friend Ralph, whom I hunt with, is prepared for the fact that I might make a mistake or die up in those hills. He well might have to throw me over a horse and carry me out. Some people want to scream at me, "Don't go! You shouldn't go! You shouldn't hunt elk anyway, that's too hard for you." They may be right, but so far I haven't seen it that way. It has seemed to me that in the fall I am drawn to the hills. I put my gun down for a year and sold off all my guns, but that wasn't comfortable to me. So I'm back carrying a gun. Up to this point, God as I understand him, hasn't communicated to me that I should stop. That might happen to-morrow, but so far it hasn't happened.

The place where it means the most to me to see fear leave me is in the hard times in the marriage. They aren't the hard times that they used to be back in the Ice Age. The hard times now aren't like that, but they are still hard enough. Now, in hard times, I see myself facing what happens with an inner calm I'm so grateful for. That calm doesn't come from the fact we've been married thirty-five years. Plenty of thirty-five-year marriages aren't calm and are hitting the divorce courts. Plenty of other people with long marriages are frightened when a thirty-five-year marriage hits the divorce court, which tells me they aren't quite sure about their own long marriage.

What I'm seeing is my strength and lack of fear. Jackie can be talking to me about some problem, or about her feelings, and this used to be hard for me. Now, she can express any kind of feeling she has and I can be fairly calm and not run from her like a dog. I'm not calm in a controlled way, but a peaceful way. I can be quietly asking myself what part of what is going on has something to do with me. I can admit to the parts of it that have something to do with me without being defensive and threatened. And, I can wait peacefully for the hard time to end. When it's over, I haven't confused things by a lot of reactions that used to muddy the waters. I haven't contributed to the problem, whatever it is. So the problem can be resolved some way, much more quickly and smoothly. I guess the feeling I most have at times like this is steadiness or integrity. That feeling is so precious to me.

As I mentioned earlier, Jackie has this same quiet with me. My troubles are different and the ways I express them are different, but the peace and strength we both bring to the working out of those problems is the same. The big learning I've had in this area is how fear on my part created problems in the past. I used to always be running away from Jackie and the kids into my compulsions, and they could never find a way to express what they needed to say to me. Now, they can, a little better, because I'm not always showing fear and anger.

I saw this so clearly with a friend of mine in the early days. I took him out to go riding one afternoon. I had Whiskey, a lively horse, which is the only kind I like. Since I had the use of another, more lively horse on this occasion, I had my friend get on Whiskey in the corral so we could adjust the stirrups for him. As soon as my friend got on, Whiskey started rearing and jumping around. I had hold of his bridle and held him. I couldn't figure out what was wrong. I had my friend get off and checked the saddle to see if there was something under it. There was no bur under his saddle or problem of any kind I could see. So I had my friend hold Whiskey's bridle while I got on. Nothing happened. Whiskey was as quiet as could be. Then I saw the problem. I knew my friend had some fear of horses, but I didn't know he had so much fear it would create a problem like that.

We solved it by putting him back on Whiskey and walking him around the corral until he and Whiskey got over their fear and its consequences. That experience helped me see what my fear does to the people around me as well as to me. I saw how much my fear stirred people up and brought out fear and then anger in them. I saw that in my life I was actually creating many of the reactions I was afraid of facing.

I went to a number of horsemanship clinics put on by Ray Hunt, who is really good at teaching a gentle way to work with horses. The more I worked with horses, the more gently I could go among them. I can go up to strange horses now without stirring them up. Sometimes, I find I even have something to offer, because a few of them will come up to me for the pleasure of my company.

There is a story about Tom Dorrance, the man who taught Ray Hunt, that has guided me like a star. Ray tells how you can send old Tom out in a thousand-acre pasture with thirty colts in it and tell him to bring in the buckskin colt. Old Tom can walk out in that pasture without a rope or halter and walk up to those colts. He will talk to those wild colts for a while and then turn and walk in. The buckskin colt will follow him in and the rest will stay. "But," as Ray says, "old Tom has a lot more to offer a horse than I do." Sure he has. Old Tom has a deep love for those colts, a love so deep any horse can feel it, and they respond because there is nothing any of us wants more.

Through my books I have seen that I've gradually come to have a little more to offer people. People wrote me and wanted to come to school to me so I finally started the Schools of Life. People bought tapes from me and listened to them over and over again.* They were able to find a new way of life partly through the way

* Jess Lair tapes and School of Life, Bozeman and Phoenix, P.O. Box 249, Bozeman, MT 59715.

God had spoken through me. But for a long time I had to admit to those people that I could do for them what I couldn't for my own family. I had so little to offer my own wife and my own children.

What is so especially touching to me now is that I have a lot more to offer my wife and sons and daughters and son-in-law. What I have to offer is a clearer sight of the me, the Jess, that God lives within. I see now that going to all those Ray Hunt clinics was one of the many things I was doing to see this principle more clearly. I thought it was so I had more to offer everybody. I'm seeing now it was so I had more to offer to the most important people God put in my life, the ones closest to me.

I do a lot of the things people around me suggest to me as a help to my spiritual quest. Sometimes I still get impatient with others when I see them refuse what is offered to them and in the next breath ask me what is it they should do. People will tell me that one of my books saved their life and that they need the next one desperately. Once in a while, I'll make the mistake of telling them that another book is out that is more recent than the one they read. Almost invariably they will say, "Oh, I know that. I'm waiting until it comes out in paperback." They're waiting for the $3.95 version of the book that will save their life because they don't want to spend $10.95 to save their life. I would really shake my head. But those experiences were good for me. They helped me see that being a little laid back and lackadaisical like that makes a lot more sense than the overdriven striving that has been so deep in me. So rather than tell you a bunch of things to do that I do, I'll just let you read between the lines so you will do whatever you're moved to do for you.

There isn't anything we can't take to excess, including using spiritual programs as a way of running away from ourselves. But it is our nature to take things to excess. We find a beautiful spiritual program but are frightened by the self-knowledge and responsibility it presents us with. So we turn it into a set of rules and follow them religiously and become a new kind of hypocrite.

Most people don't think of it that way, but an exercise program is a spiritual program. Body and mind are hooked to spirit. We can't improve one without helping the other two. In exercise programs we see this same excess. Dr. Kenneth Cooper recently made the statement that "if you are running more than three miles, five times a week, you are running for something other than cardiovascular fitness." In other words, he said that if something is good, it doesn't follow that a lot more of it is better. He mentioned the Ancel Keys study reported in the September 1980 *Lancet* where a twenty-five-year follow-up of men on a low cholesterol diet showed less risk of dying from heart disease but showed more risk of dying from cancer.

The way I see a study like that and a lot of the running and other things being done today is a fear of death and aging and a desire to live forever. The part of me that's afraid of death and wants to live forever is the part I would prefer to leave behind. All I need to do is live today in as much awareness of God's will for me as I can manage. If I do that, tomorrow will take care of itself.

It's like an old guy I heard. He finally came to the place where all his "I wants" were burned up. When he got something from God, he was grateful and thanked God. When he did something stupid, he admitted it as soon as he recognized it and told God he was sorry. As he continued along in his life, he came to see that if God's idea of a salmon included everything it needed for its complete fulfillment, would God's idea for us include anything less? This helped me see that I didn't need to learn to love. I had that already in me. All I had to do was stop doing the things that made it impossible to be in touch with the love that was in me. That was a reassuring thought and, as I've found it works for me, a reassuring experience.

In the final stages of writing this book, all of a sudden I was sick at some of what I saw myself doing. I was so full of the marriage book that I had fast, ready answers to all questions on marriage. I was so smart, I couldn't stand myself. I thought, "If you're so smart, how come your marriage is like it is right now and how come you are like you are? Tell these people the truth. You're no big shot like you sound. You're just a very little shot or no shot at all. You're a little guy who is fifty-seven years old, has just had his pay cut way back, isn't in the shape to go out and move mountains anymore to dazzle some new employer, works in a little ten-by-ten-foot shed out behind the trailer in Phoenix, and is sitting there writing away to a whole bunch of people you've never met. And here you've got this elaborate castle in the air built about marriage and how you understand all the ins and outs of it. It's a deeply spiritual process and all the ins and outs are known only to the one who figured this whole thing out and that sure isn't you."

That's where I was the evening of December 31, 1983. And that was just fine. A few days later I told Jackie about it. She said I was depressed. Maybe I was. But I told her I didn't think so. I think my view had a great deal of reality to it. The reality, as I see it, lies between the two extremes of knowing and not knowing. I had gone too far over into the knowing. I had to go there as I was seeking the synthesis of this book. I can't finish a book until I see it pretty clearly, and that was where I had been for a good part of November and December of 1983. I had come to the understanding of the book I needed, so I could put all the pieces together so they were internally consistent. What that means is that every part is consistent with every other part. Even though there are statements that seem to contradict each other, the parts of the book all fit together. The contradictions are only those that are necessary because of the subject matter. We are describing the indescribable, so there are necessarily contradictions and paradoxes. But the statements that can be reconciled with each other are, as much as possible.

As my old friend Gerry Sullivan said, in a book every word must know every other word. That means the same thing has an internal consistency. I can't say that two plus two equals four one place and then say two plus two equals five in another place. I can't say that pain is helpful to us in showing us where we need to change or get in harmony and then someplace else talk about how to avoid pain.

So, for some time I had been caught up in figuring things out and coming up with answers that satisfied me as to why things were the way they were. All that work served its purpose. But now that that purpose had been served, it was time to go over to the other end of the world. That was the place of "not knowing."

What helped to free me from my four days of doubt about what I was writing was Zen. One expression of the central goal of Zen is that it is to "burst the bubble of rational thought." When you are given the *koan* of "What is the sound of one hand clapping?" your rational mind is finally overwhelmed by the dilemma and your mind caves in. I don't presume to understand that Zen *koan*, but I have experienced my rational mind being overwhelmed so that I could finally give up trying to figure something out. When that happened, I was finally ready to learn. I was then ready for a piece of Zen that has been of great help to me: "Only go straight, don't know." Most of the time, this is the way I seek to live my life.

But there are times I must do something differently. I must shift gears and be a writer because, for the moment, that seems to be part of my nature. While I'm writing, I can fall over into the trap of "knowing." There is the story of the great Zen master who was revered in his city in China for his good life. A representative of the Emperor came to the city and was honored at a banquet. The old Zen master was asked to introduce the honored person. The next morning, the Zen master told the people that he was renouncing his Zen mastership to go back and become a student of Zen again. He said, "The reason I am doing this is because when the time came for me to introduce the Emperor's representative, my tone of voice was different than it was when I was introducing the other guests of honor."

No matter what I write, I can't forget that I don't know. But I can't hide in that idea of not knowing and use it as an excuse not to write. What got me out of the soup was the realization that it is only through the use of words and accepting all the limitations of those words that Zen teachers are able to teach Zen. Rational thought and the rational mind were used by the two great Suzukis in the process by which they showed us how the power of the rational mind can lose its hold on us.

I can write all I want for anyone who wants to read what I say with no harm to myself as long as I keep a clear eye on the dangers on either side. I have had a lot of experiences with marriage through my marriage and all the people who have shared their marriages with me. I have studied the process of marriage for a long time with the advantage of some special perspectives. One of these special perspectives is the one given me as a student of the twelve steps. Another special perspective is that of an experimental psychologist and the help that discipline gives me to become a more careful observer of behavior and of that behavior's accompanying conversation, which often is the exact opposite of the behavior. And a third perspective is that of a lifelong student of life married to a wife who has always shared the same interest.

I can know all I want about marriage and its spiritual aspects as long as I keep a firm grip on my "not knowing." I don't mean that as some little word game. It's a serious matter to me. The first story in the book *Zen Flesh, Zen Bones* is in that first position for a purpose. The story is of the Japanese philosophy professor who told the Zen master he wanted to learn about Zen. The Zen master invited the philosopher to tea. As the Zen master was pouring tea, he filled the philosopher's cup and kept on pouring. The philosopher finally yelled, "Stop, stop, the cup is overful." The

Zen master stopped pouring and said to the philosopher, "This cup, like your mind, is overful with ideas and speculations. Until you empty it, there is no room for Zen." My head, too, must not be so overful with ideas and speculations of marriage that there is no room for Zen. I must not have things so well figured out that there is no room for mystery. I must be ready, at a moment's notice, to throw away anything I've said and believed in so I can go some new way shown me by God's grace.

In this book I have created a learning experience for you. Again, as my old friend Gerry Sullivan says, "A learning experience is when you are put in a situation you cannot get out of without coming to some new ideas you didn't have before." Then you are truly a richer person because you still have your old idea and you have a new idea. You can try out the new idea on life. When it helps you do some things the old idea didn't help you do, then you are the richer for it. It is not a matter of the old idea being right or wrong, simply how useful it is to you. That way, you're not wrong when you take on a new idea. You just look at it from the standpoint of being useful and use it or not depending on how promising it looks to you. Then, when you put it to the test in your own life, you're able to see how useful the idea really is to you.

If this has happened for you in this book, then in that small way I am your teacher. Always, when the student is ready, the teacher appears. I have recognized many people as my teachers and have gone to some considerable lengths to get their teaching into my life more fully.

A part of me doesn't want to let you go. I'm just like the host at a lovely party where everybody is having a good time. As the people start to leave, the host tries to prolong the party. It's real close to the time for me to close. This is the end of the book. I have told you a nice, neat, well-worked-out story about what marriage is and how it works. I've also talked a lot about God and how God works. But the most important thing of all for me is what I have to close with and that is this: When I have everything all neatly worked out, there is no room for God as I understand him. So while everything I have said is something I believe in and trust my life to each day, what we are talking about is something so big and so huge, it is obviously beyond any human understanding and any human description. That is the power of God and the ways of God.

There is only one thing I am certain of and that is that my need is to be as broken, transparent, and vulnerable as is humanly possible for me right now and I need to stay that way and not get carried away with myself. As you've seen, I've gotten carried away with myself a lot and I don't like what I see about myself and what I see myself doing when that happens. Fortunately, I've got my lovely spiritual partner, my true companion, to help keep me on the path. I'm a child of God and an inheritor of the kingdom of heaven. For me, that's all I seek: to be God's man.

I say good-bye to you with love and respect.

Love, Jess.